Indigenous
Confluences

Charlotte Coté and Coll Thrush
Series Editors

POWER IN THE TELLING

Grand Ronde, Warm Springs, and Intertribal Relations in the Casino Era

BROOK COLLEY

Foreword by David G. Lewis

UNIVERSITY OF WASHINGTON PRESS

Seattle

Copyright © 2018 by the University of Washington Press
Printed and bound in the United States of America
Maps by Pease Press Cartography
Composed in Charter, typeface designed by Matthew Carter
22 21 20 19 18   5 4 3 2 1

University of Washington Press
www.washington.edu/uwpress

Library of Congress Cataloging-in-Publication Data on file

ISBN 978-0-295-74335-6 (hardcover), ISBN 978-0-295-74336-3 (pbk),
ISBN 978-0-295-74337-0 (ebook)

To my mother, Carol Younghird-Holt, and my daughter,
Wren Youngbird Siino, who are my past, present, and future

CONTENTS

FOREWORD

Brook Colley came to me some years ago and began asking questions about the casino conflict between the Grand Ronde and Warm Springs tribes, a conflict that lasted from 1998 to 2013, when Warm Springs proposed building a casino near Cascade Locks, Oregon, alongside the Columbia River. At first I was hesitant to talk with her. At the time, there was little communication between Grand Ronde and Warm Springs that was not extremely negative. Colley is also a descendant of the Warm Springs tribe and, as a Grand Ronde member and part of the tribal staff, I was wary. Staff are discouraged from making potentially political statements, and I worried that speaking with her might affect my position. At the same time, I felt a responsibility as a member of one of the tribes involved—I wanted to help all of us better understand what was happening. So as an exercise in intertribal relations and applied anthropology—being a professional anthropologist—I chose to take part and give Colley my unfiltered opinions.

Now, years later, I have come to see Colley's work as extremely important in helping untangle the issues at play, leaving behind contentious political rhetoric. Colley's research and writing have inspired me to think deeply about the casino disagreement specifically and, more broadly, about the historical factors that fed into it. Tribes face many problems, and to me those problems are embedded in the histories of how we got here, to a place of intertribal opposition, contention, lawsuits, and bad feelings. I assign significant responsibility for this divisiveness to the manner in which the federal government has controlled and erected barriers in front of tribes for generations.

Elders tell the story that all of us Natives are living in a "crab basket," and whenever one of the crabs tries to crawl out, those below grab them and pull them back in. I have always wondered what this meant. Are we destined to remain at our status? Is there no real opportunity for any of us, because we are simply living the human condition? I have come to see that the problem lies not with the crabs but with the basket they all live in. This is an artificially woven environment, a political structure that the crabs did not construct but was made by others with the intent of keeping all the crabs in the basket. Tribes remain under the control of the federal government, fighting among themselves for the limited remainder of the resources they are allowed to have.

Tribal nations in the United States were removed from their lands, dissociated from their cultures, and reprogrammed to be Americans by the federal government. For more than two hundred years, each new generation of federal politicians has constructed new and malignant tactics to reduce and eliminate tribal nations. In the early nineteenth century, the strategy was warfare, and tribal lands were taken by conquest. In the 1850s and after, the strategy was treaties, as it proved cheaper to buy land and remove tribes to smaller parcels than go to war. In 1887, the Dawes Act codified the strategy of eroding tribal holdings by reducing the acreage of reservations. The Dawes Act included the Trojan Horse of using blood quantum as a measure of Indian-ness for the sake of federal policies. Unless Native people had one-half or more Indian blood quantum, they could not gain an on-reservation allotment. This US government notion of blood quantum also found its way into tribal citizenship policies, which today operate to eliminate enrollment—and Native status—for the future generations of many tribes. Further, by the 1910s, many of those who had received reservation allotments had passed away, and their allotments were sold and thus removed from reservations.

In the 1950s, the federal government sought to simply designate some tribes as "assimilated" and therefore not deserving of the benefits of treaty rights or reservations. This policy was ostensibly intended to give tribal members the freedoms and rights of every other American citizen, including the "right" to not live on an impoverished reservation. But many tribes saw termination as cultural death, and some tribes succumbed. One hundred and nine tribes were terminated and all their lands liquidated. Many tribes successfully fought against termination and advocated that status be restored, and in the 1970s and 1980s many tribes regained federal recognition. Grand Ronde was one of the tribes so restored, in 1983, while Warm Springs was able to stop their termination bill.

Throughout this history, tribes lost political and economic power as they went from owning all their lands to owning little or nothing. Most tribes were very poor and appeared to be doing nothing to better their situations, when in fact federal policies have impoverished tribes. The Trade and Intercourse Act, for example, first passed in 1790 and renewed through the 1830s, managed tribal economic development with the aim of "civilizing" Native people, prohibiting tribes from selling products outside their reservations unless Congress passed a special bill.

It is in this context, and within this history, that gaming became an avenue of tribal economic development. In the 1980s, the US government sought ways to help tribes become economically self-sufficient and thus not dependent on federal funding, which some considered welfare. Gaming was attractive because it seemed to offer the same opportunity to all tribes regardless of their land or resource base. However, the resulting legislation did not take into account the messiness of tribal removal to reservations. It did not acknowledge the arbitrary nature of what tribes had been relegated to what reservations. In truth, tribal boundaries were not always firm borders: many tribes were heavily interrelated, and cultures and traditional resource areas overlapped.

Warm Springs and Grand Ronde are related peoples. All the Chinookan (Kiksht) tribes on the Columbia River were related to one another. Chief Kiesno of Sauvie Island, in the mid-nineteenth century, was related to the people of the Cascades (Watlala) as well as to Clatsop chief Concomly at the Columbia River estuary. Kiesno also had relations with the Clackamas at Willamette Falls and within the Tualatin Kalapuya tribes. In a sense, all the tribes of western Oregon are interrelated, regardless of language groups. But this did not mesh with the federal treaty structure, which imposed strict divisions between tribes. The subsequent decades of living apart on separate reservations has caused further social and political divisions between tribes. Where traditionally tribes in the region had highly developed protocols for visiting with and using the resources controlled by other autonomous villages, these structures were broken down by federally imposed bureaucracies and oversight. Tribes were left with the legal structures of the United States for solving political conflicts, which has meant lawsuits and political strife.

At the same time, there is a history of cooperation among tribes. In the 1940s, when the liquidation of reservations was first being discussed, the larger tribes began gathering together to devise strategies to defend themselves from termination and from other federal policies that worked against tribal interests. In this decade, the National Congress of American Indians (NCAI) and the Affiliated Tribes of Northwest Indians (ATNI) were born. These organizations became powerful alliances that countered, in many cases successfully, the proposed termination bills. But western Oregon tribes, which had few resources and small reservations, were often terminated without their explicit agreement.

Individually tribes are weaker and more at risk from federal policies that can degrade and eliminate them. Those that join together are stronger and can withstand such assaults on their tribal structures. I firmly believe that tribes need to identify and rid ourselves of the colonial structures that make us vulnerable and find ways to return to our traditional relationships with one another. Our current tribal governments were created by the US government, with all manner of policies and laws to disempower tribes, and we need to deconstruct, decolonize, and reinvigorate our communities to again work together in mutual support for our future survival.

In *Power in the Telling*, Colley listens to our people's experiences of the casino conflict and shows that both Grand Ronde and Warm Springs have the best intentions for their peoples. Both tribes feel they are preparing for the future of their people and defending their rights to traditional territories. Both tribes share a history of colonization, treaties, and removal to reservations. Warm Springs happened to reserve a much more permanent and larger reservation than Grand Ronde. Later, Grand Ronde happened to be located such that their gaming operations could take advantage of the most populous areas of Oregon, the Portland region and the Willamette Valley. Both tribes have found that they cannot grow their economies with the original limited resources and trade rights allowed by the federal government: logging has become unprofitable for both tribes as timber sales have dramatically decreased in recent years; and both tribes have a limited capacity for profitable agriculture, given poor soils and restricted water rights.

Federal policies have historically restricted tribes' abilities to control their own livelihoods. Tribes were segregated according to treaties regardless of previous cultural practices and claims to traditional lands. Colley documents the now-historic conflict between the Warm Springs and Grand Ronde over one such treaty boundary, at Cascade Locks. These federally established boundaries and policies form a significant "basket" that manages and controls tribes. Tribal leaders and members, however, have the power to work beyond such imposed boundaries and find commonality, to decolonize and restore traditional relationships. Tribal peoples know that as long as we live within the federal administrative structure, we are not truly sovereign, and we desire more than anything to restore and heal the hearts of our brethren and to live in peace in our territory.

DAVID G. LEWIS
Takelma, Santiam, Chinook, Molalla (Grand Ronde)
Salem, Oregon, July 2017

PREFACE

They Tell Their Own Stories

Shiyo! Brook Colley, daquadoa. Hello! My name is Brook Colley, and I am a citizen of the Eastern Band of the Cherokee Nation with Wasco, Japanese, and Irish ancestry. I want to begin by recognizing the many tribes and bands that call Oregon their ancestral territory and highlight the continued sovereignty of nine tribes of Oregon. As a Native person and an educator I have been taught that when I introduce myself, naming my tribal and ethnic relations is a way I honor my ancestors, and naming the tribes that have ties to the land is a way I recognize the historical and continued presence of Indigenous peoples.

One of this book's goals is to bring into focus Indigenous peoples' perspectives and interpretations of their own tribal histories in order to better understand intertribal relations and political decisions in the tribal casino era (1988–present). A significant portion of my research was an oral history project in which I conducted thirty-three oral interviews from 2007 through 2014 with citizens and employees of two Oregon tribes, the Confederated Tribes of Grand Ronde and the Confederated Tribes of Warm Springs. Interview questions focused on such key subjects as the casino economy, Grand Ronde and Warm Springs history, intertribal relations and conflict in Oregon, and the Warm Springs proposal to build a casino in Cascade Locks, Oregon, which led to discord between the two Native nations.

Through these interviews I explore how parallel and intersecting histories have shaped the views of these communities on the casino issue. Interviewees consisted primarily of past and present Grand Ronde and Warm Springs leaders working in public relations, cultural resources, and other tribally funded programs and departments. Of the thirty interviewees, fifteen were Grand Ronde tribal members, two were nonmember Grand Ronde employees, eleven were Warm Springs tribal members, and two were nonmember Warm Springs employees. I interviewed thirteen men and four women from Grand Ronde and ten men and three women from Warm Springs. In addition, ten were elders at the time of their interviews, six from Grand Ronde and four from Warm

Springs.[1] I interviewed people one on one in all but one case, that of a father and daughter who had both served on the Grand Ronde Tribal Council.

To grow my list of sources I asked each person whom they thought I should interview next, but not everyone recommended to me was available to participate. I would sometimes find it difficult to schedule interviews in advance of my visits to Grand Ronde and Warm Springs, although people generously gave their time to talk with me once I arrived in person. In several cases key players had "walked on"—were no longer living. A few recommended people were not interested in being interviewed, and in two instances I lacked an appropriate introduction to individuals that protocol required.[2] The most challenging constraint was the limited time I could spend in the communities of Grand Ronde and Warm Springs, which made it impossible for me to interview everyone I would have liked to interview.

I have tried to provide a balance of the voices and viewpoints of the people I interviewed. Quotations represent the views and perspective of each narrator and not the official position of a Native nation or community as a whole, but most echo the wider community and repeat or rephrase things said to me by many tribal members and nonmember tribal employees. Throughout my research, I met with each interlocutor more than once after the initial interview in order to review quotations, verify that they were phrased in a way that fully captured their meaning and intention, and ensure that intended meanings would be clearly conveyed. When quotations from transcripts did not exactly reflect what people wanted to express, I would ask for rewording, and I continued this process until arriving at words that unequivocally reflected what they meant and wanted to say.

This relational approach to research methodology, alongside my dual commitment to both the academy and Native American communities, builds on the theoretical perspective of "Radical Indigenism" first articulated by Eva Marie Garroutte (Cherokee) in her 2003 book *Real Indians: Identity and the Survival of Native America*.[3] When working with Indigenous narrators, Garroutte proposes that researchers take Indigenous knowledge seriously and work with Native people to tell their stories from their perspectives. Expanding on this methodology, Garroutte and Kathleen Delores Westcott write that "a strategy guided by Radical Indigenism does not make narratives the object of analytic scrutiny in order to reveal something beyond themselves—the genres they embody, the underlying power structures they presuppose, the mechanisms by which they persuade, or the like. Although professional academics value such questions, ordinary Native American people seldom (in our experience) view them as especially relevant to daily concerns. They tell their stories not to invite their dissection, classification and reconstruction within academic categories, but because they have something to say."[4]

Oral history narratives constructed in this manner acknowledge Native people as active agents in history creation and provide countering views to dominant narratives. Conversational knowledge shared by narrators often accounts for both individual and collective memories, helps us to better understand how the past informs contemporary issues, thoughts, and concerns, and can provide a more holistic picture of the relationships between peoples as well as relationships to land and place. As Charles E. Trimble (Oglala Lakota) explicates, "The information in the memories of community members, whether unchanging or adapted, first person or traditional, reflect how people understand and shape experiences, power, and identity."[5] Engaging in oral history brings Native knowledge and agendas to the center of discourse and can generate greater mutual understanding within and between tribal communities.

Central to my research is the conviction that people are the primary sources, archives, and experts on their own lives. In this person-centered approach, the stories told by any individual are meant to provide not a universal account but rather that person's interpretations of events.[6] Instead of claiming one universal "truth" about history and events, I highlight the multifaceted ways in which Native peoples construct truth: sometimes as a reflection of lived experiences and perspectives forged in conversations within a community, sometimes as tactically crafted positions that serve immediate community needs, and sometimes as long-term strategic plans that concern the survival and flourishing of Indigenous peoples more broadly. The recollections and stories of these narrators and their analyses of current events throughout this book demonstrate that Oregon Native communities are active participants in critical contemporary discussions that shape political, economic, and social outcomes.

When researching and writing about the tribal casino economy, actively seeking tribal voices is important because these voices are often left out, marginalized, or misrepresented in the mainstream public record. Central to my methodology as a Native American studies researcher is my belief that the most important contributions from this project originated from Native peoples and their allies, people who have significant and unique insights, represent complex perspectives, and offer astute analysis. Their contributions bring to light deeper and more challenging themes that extend well beyond the subject of tribal casinos.

Like all Native nations in Oregon and elsewhere in the United States, Grand Ronde and Warm Springs each have stories that tell of their existence, survival, and continuance. As a result of both parallel and divergent experiences, each nation responds in a unique way to economic opportunities, which significantly influences how they perceive, participate in, and interact within the tribal casino economy. As communities, Grand Ronde and Warm Springs interpret the stories of the past and the dreams of the future in distinct and revealing ways. It is my hope that this research will open up space for an honest and productive assessment of intertribal tensions and conflicts in the casino era.

TERMINOLOGY

As I was reflecting on the issue of terminology and naming, I came across a letter to the editor in the intertribal news source *Indian Country Today* (*ICT*). The letter, written by Jerre Conder of Wills Point, Texas, reads as follows:

> I have recently discovered your website, and plan to return often. I have one question, however, that troubles me. I am wondering why you sometimes resort to the "Politically Correct?" misnomer "Native Americans" to describe yourselves, rather than what seems to be preferred—"American Indians"; "First Peoples"; or even "indigenous tribes" . . . as well as, of course, specific tribal names. As far as I know, there is not an American Indian bone in my body, but having been born in the United States, I am properly called a "native American." Must you exacerbate this confusion?

The *ICT* editors responded,

> Ah words. As a publication we use Native, Native Peoples, Native American, American Indian interchangeably because—as you rightly surmise regarding Native America—there is no term that aptly describes the collective groups of people who existed on Turtle Island prior to Columbus (First Peoples is most commonly used in reference to the nations of Canada). Most individuals today would refer to themselves by nation (Kiowa, Mohawk, etc.), and shrug when it came to "choosing" what name to be called. Whatever gets the point across will have to do.[7]

In order to get my point across, I use the term "Native peoples" if I am discussing Native Americans in the broader social context of the United States.

Linda Tuhiwai Smith (Ngāti Awa, Ngāti Porou) writes that the use of *Indigenous peoples* as an umbrella term emerged from the 1970s American Indian Movement and that Indigenous peoples, despite their diversity, constitute a "network of peoples who have been subjected to the colonization of their lands and cultures, and the denial of their sovereignty, by a colonizing society that has come to dominate and determine the shape and quality of their lives, even after it has formally pulled out."[8]

Drawing from Smith's explanation, I also use the terms "Indigenous" and "Indigenous peoples" in order to situate distinct and varied communities in a wider national and international context of colonialism. When referring to federally recognized tribes involved in the tribal casino economy (as well as state-recognized tribes), I will refer to them as *Native nations* to underscore their claim to political and cultural sovereignty and their government-to-government relationship with the United States. When referring to a distinct tribal group, I will always use the term preferred by that tribe.

ALPHABETICAL ORDER

Whether I write about the Grand Ronde and Warm Springs tribes in the same sentence, paragraph, section, or chapter, in every case I mention Grand Ronde first and Warm Springs second. This has nothing to do with a desire to privilege one Native nation's voice over the other (I believe there are potential benefits and drawbacks from being named either first or second). I made the arbitrary choice to list the tribes alphabetically.

METHODOLOGIES

As Smith argues in her foundational text on Indigenous methodologies, conducting research about and with Indigenous communities is "a humble and humbling activity."[9] In part this is because this research is always personal and political, and researchers must constantly think about whether and how their research benefits and promotes self-determination for Indigenous peoples. Further, Indigenous research requires sustained community interaction and involvement (for example, my study took place over ten years, while my engagement and commitment to Native communities is lifelong), in which research goals are developed with the legal, ethical, and cultural concerns of Native nations in mind. In addition, my training in the interdisciplinary field of Native American studies profoundly shaped my approach to this research, as does my positionality. At times I am a community insider—I am a federally recognized Native person with ancestry connected to Native nations of Oregon—and at other times I am a community outsider (because I am not a citizen of either the Grand Ronde or Warm Springs tribes). Ultimately *how* we do what we do in our scholarship matters: how we work with the communities we study, how we think about problem-solving, and how we frame the research questions we ask. All of this informs the ways that I, as a Native person and as a scholar, have approached understanding intertribal relations in the casino era.

ACKNOWLEDGMENTS

It is with immense gratitude that I write these acknowledgments. While any flaws in this research are my own, this book would not have been possible without the many individuals who gave generously of their skills, knowledge, and friendship. First I want to thank the citizens and employees of the Confederated Tribes of Grand Ronde and the Confederated Tribes of Warm Springs who shared their stories and insights with me. Their perspectives are the heart of this project. Thank you, Angela Blackwell, Charles "Jody" Calica, Gerald J. Danzuka Jr., Brent Florendo, Jefferson Greene, Rob Greene, Kathryn M. Harrison, Chief Delvis Heath Sr., Wendell Jim, Tony Johnson, Dennis C. Karnopp, Reynold L. Leno, Greg Leo, David G. Lewis, Justin Martin, Stacia Martin, Bryan Mercier, Chris Mercier, John Mercier, Lewis "Louie" E. Pitt Jr., Will Robbins, Eric Sabin, Charles Scott, William "Wink" J. Soderberg, Aurelia Stacona, Aurolyn Stwyer, Delson Suppah Sr., Ronald Suppah Sr., Valerie Switzler, Siobhán Taylor, Eirik Thorsgard, Robert P. Tom, Leon "Chips" Tom, Kathleen Tom, Faye C. Wahenika, and Wesley "Buddy" West. My gratitude extends to the great storyteller Ed Edmo, who allowed me to record his version of the Bridge of the Gods story and to whom I owe a steak dinner. Se-ah-dom Edmo, thank you for reminding me to look again at the Bridge of the Gods legend and incorporate it into my work. Randy Scott, thank you for your steadfast support of my scholarship and for your positive attitude, enthusiasm for collaboration, and friendship.

My successes are a community effort, and I want to acknowledge teachers, mentors, and colleagues who have given generously of their time, expertise, and friendship while providing me with supportive and healthy intellectual communities. Thank you, Roni Adams, Jade Aguilar, Alma Rosa Alvarez, Thomas Biolsi, Doug Clark, Anna Cox, Steven J. Crum, Kylan de Vries, Rebecca Dobkins, Echo Fields, Valerie Feldman, Linda Heuser, Sarah Hopkins-Powell, Funie Hsu, Bill Hughes, Jonneke Koomen, Wesley Leonard, Martha Macri, Stella Mancillas, Jean Maxwell, Sean McEnroe, Beth Mechlin, Beth Rose Middleton, Erik Noftle, Roy Pérez, Mark Shibley, Carey Sojka, Dee Southard, Peg Swain, Hulleah J. Tsinhnahjinnie, Marjorie Trueblood-Gamble, David West, Edward Valandra, Stefano Varese, Joanna Wong, Rachelle Yankelevitz, and Megan

Ybarra. You all challenged me to think critically, offered me opportunities, and encouraged me in my intellectual pursuits. Other individuals who supported this project with their skills and time include David Abel, Kristina Casper-Denman, Enrique Chacón, Teresa Cisneros, Melissa Duclos, Justin Harmon, Alexander Mayer, Faith Russell, Francesca Sapien, and Jasmin Marie Yaeger. Jack D. Forbes (you are missed), thank you for teaching me that Native American studies practices a pedagogy of love and respect. I also want to acknowledge my dear friend and mentor, the late (and great) Kermit Rhode, who encouraged me to find my voice and speak out against injustice. Finally, there is not a sufficient word to describe the love and gratitude in my heart for Cutcha Risling Baldy and Gina Caison, who teach me every day about the joys of friendship and who deeply enrich my scholarship and life. Our bond extends beyond borders.

My family is the center of my world. I would not be the human being I am today without the influence of the Blucher family, the Bruce family, Grandma Agnes Colley, Grandpa Ken Colley, Uncle Rich Colley, Kara Colley, Sage Colley, Rye Colley, Orville Danzuka, Chava Florendo, Spencer Godard, the Godard family, Misty Holt, Bill Hunt, Katie Johnson, Travis James Johnson-Knight, Jonathan Miles, Aunt Myrtle LaShomb, the Polley family, the Roth family, Dominic Siino, Jo Ann Smith, Tommie Smith, Aunt Ruth Taylor, Sharon Wilson, and Grandma Carol Youngbird. The time I spent with Aunt Ruthie Smith and Uncle Russell Smith in Warm Springs is so precious to me, and I will forever be grateful for their stories and generosity. I'm especially thankful for my father, Relan Colley, and siblings Sky Colley and Jade Colley, who easily share their laughter, beautiful complexity, good nature, ethical values, and quick intellect. And with gratitude, I remember my beautiful, difficult, and fierce mother who lives on in my beautiful, difficult, and fierce daughter, Wren Youngbird Siino. Sgi! Thank you.

POWER IN THE TELLING

CHAPTER 1

At the Place Where
the Cascades Fall

THIS STORY BEGINS WITH A PLACE. THE CASCADE FALLS IS A GEO-graphic location in the Columbia River where it flows westward between present-day Oregon and Washington states, in an area known as the Columbia River Gorge. It was identified in two treaties negotiated in the 1850s between the United States and Native peoples who would afterward become the Confederated Tribes of Grand Ronde and the Confederated Tribes of Warm Springs. The section of the river that contains the Cascade Falls, sometimes called the Cascade Rapids, runs alongside the present-day city of Cascade Locks, Oregon, located approximately halfway between Portland and the city of The Dalles, Oregon, accessible from Interstate 84. It was here, in Cascade Locks, that the Warm Springs tribe proposed to build a casino, the Bridge of the Gods Columbia River Resort Casino, in a bid that would extend for fifteen years (1998–2013).

The place where the cascades fall is a site of tremendous change. Though accounts vary, Native peoples from along both sides of the Columbia River have stories in their oral traditions about the Bridge of the Gods, an ancient land bridge that resulted from a massive landslide in this location. One of these stories speaks to an ongoing conflict between two brothers, Wy'east and Klickitat, who had everything they needed to be satisfied but still fought over land, resources, and power, much to the displeasure of Great Spirit. This story offers a history of place while also embodying lessons about how people from the river should and should not behave according to their distinct cultural tradition. The legend, which ultimately ends when the two brothers are turned into mountains, conveys a warning against conflict and jealousy.[1]

In time, the force of the Columbia River eroded the famed Bridge of the Gods, and the rapids that resulted became prime fishing sites for Native nations

MAP I.I. Grand Ronde, Warm Springs, and Cascade Locks in relation to Portland

that lived along the river. Chinook peoples residing along the river orchestrated an extensive trade network, had highly developed fisheries, and managed vast resources. In addition, they formed economic, social, artistic, and political relationships with other Native nations over generations. Shortly after American settlement violently displaced many Native nations from the region, the US Congress sought to make the river more navigable to increase travel and trade opportunities, and in 1896 it commissioned the Cascade Locks and Canal in order to make it possible for ships to travel up and down the river without having to portage around the falls. In the late 1930s, construction of the Bonneville Dam to generate electricity resulted in the total submersion of Cascade Falls, much to the distress of Native peoples who had steadfastly continued to practice a way of life that depended on fishing along the river and maintaining intertribal relations formed around this economy.[2]

In 1998, the Warm Springs tribe sought to expand their gaming operations from their Indian Head Casino, opened in Warm Springs, Oregon, in 1995, to meet the economic needs of tribal members. After vetting several locations on their reservation in central Oregon as well as tribally owned trust lands in nearby Hood River, Warm Springs tribal leaders set their sights on an industrial park within the city of Cascade Locks. Though this land was neither part of the tribe's historic reservation nor held in trust for the tribe, the location is culturally and historically significant to the Warm Springs people, and it is part of their recognized ceded lands where they have reserved treaty rights.[3]

Having chosen the location at Cascade Locks, Warm Springs leaders worked to secure trust land and a state-tribal compact so that they could build a new casino there.[4] They hoped that a casino located closer to the Portland metropolitan area would generate more income than their modest Indian Head Casino, located on their reservation in an isolated and minimally populated region of central Oregon. Though Warm Springs had exhibited tremendous tenacity over many generations, the tribe was experiencing desperate economic conditions that many feared threatened their stability. The proposed Columbia River Gorge Casino represented possible long-term economic stability and much-needed employment opportunities for tribal members.

After Warm Springs proposed to build the casino in Cascade Locks, Grand Ronde, a Native nation located about sixty miles southwest of Portland, raised objections. By 2001, Grand Ronde tribal leaders had begun to lobby actively against it, arguing that gaming policy in the state allowed only one casino per tribe, and that the casino must be on reservation lands. Grand Ronde was just beginning to build infrastructure and was striving to heal from social and cultural ruptures resulting from multiple generations of disastrous federal law and policies, particularly termination legislation enacted in the 1950s, which ended the government-to-government relationship between some tribes and the federal government and was aimed at getting Native Americans to assimilate into the dominant society. Grand Ronde leaders felt that a Warm Springs casino in the Columbia River Gorge would draw customers away from Grand Ronde's Spirit Mountain Casino and thus significantly and negatively impact Grand Ronde's economy. They foresaw dire consequences for their people, as large revenue loss would require major cuts to programs and services for tribal members. Complicating matters, Grand Ronde leaders pointed out that their people too had historical and cultural ties to the land at Cascade Locks because one of their treaties also names the Cascade Falls as geographic boundary. They argued that they should have a seat at the table to discuss tribal economic development in that region.

These types of conflicts remain important to understanding the complex landscape that Native nations involved in the tribal casino economy must

negotiate. Over the years, I have heard a number of tribal leaders wryly comment that for every ten problems solved by the income earned from this economy, nine new problems arise. While statements like these are anecdotal and
hard to quantify, they do speak to the fact that tribal people sometimes feel
that there are new, occasionally unexpected, and not always positive consequences of the casino economy on tribal communities. One such troubling
consequence appears (at least on the surface) to be an increase in intertribal
conflict that stems from intense debates about tribal casino policies and competition for limited state gaming markets.

While Native nations might prefer that their differences of opinion about
casino politics in the casino era remain private, intertribal conflict has been
covered regularly by regional and national media, and Native people and non-
Natives alike have been quick to criticize. When Native nations in the gaming
business become involved in actions such as opposing competing tribal casinos,
disenrolling tribal members, and blocking unrecognized tribes' applications to
gain federal recognition they are often charged with being solely motivated by
greed and self-interests.

Consistent with national trends, Native nations in Oregon have experienced
intertribal disagreements that appear to stem from the tribal casino economy.
For instance, Grand Ronde and the Cowlitz Indian Tribe of Washington State
have been involved in a multiyear debate over Cowlitz's plan to build a Class
III casino in La Center, Washington, and the Cow Creek and Coquille Indian
Tribe have disagreed over the latter's plans to open a Class II casino in Medford,
Oregon.[5] Though Native nations have often worked together to protect and
expand their sovereign rights, increasingly Native nations in the casino era are
employing new tactics to protect their investments, including litigation, alliances with federal and state government officials, and partnerships with nongovernmental organizations and citizen groups.

After Warm Springs proposed to build their casino in the Columbia River
Gorge, particularly after setting sights on the Cascade Locks location,
reporting on this topic in Portland's *Oregonian*, the state's most widely read
newspaper, focused on the relationship between Grand Ronde and Warm
Springs. This coverage progressively became framed in terms of conflict and
competition.[6] The newspaper harshly criticized Grand Ronde for opposing
Warm Springs and portrayed Grand Ronde as a greedy competitor, hungry for
the Portland metro area market. The dispute between Grand Ronde and Warm
Springs was framed as another instance of Native nations fighting over casino

markets. The discourse on tribal casinos as exemplified in the *Oregonian* has, for the most part, insufficiently contextualized tribal motivations and historical events that led to the creation of the casino economy.

A fair and accurate analysis of the tribal casino economy must take into account how ongoing projects of colonization continue to be manifest in contemporary forms. These new projects and power relationships maintain what semiotician and literary theorist Walter Mignolo calls "coloniality" or systems of "knowledge, beliefs, expectations, dreams, and fantasies upon which the modern/colonial world was built."[7] Projects of coloniality are visible in the media discourse around tribal casinos and in imagery generated about this economy, articulated in public forums, and manifested in policy that regulates it. The recognition of ongoing projects of coloniality provides an analytical tool that can help expose and deconstruct ideologies that racialize and marginalize Native people, forward false perceptions of tribal histories, work to limit economic opportunities, and reproduce legal fictions that undermine tribal sovereignty. As environmental scientist Elisabeth Middleton argues, "This is not a disempowering, victimized perspective, focused simply on colonialism and its ongoing manifestations. Rather, it is a stance of liberation: recognizing coloniality *acknowledges* the entrenched subtleties of colonialism that linger in both formerly colonized and colonizer societies, and this acknowledgement offers a pathway toward the conscious development of decolonial institutions and ideas."[8]

As Middleton suggests, explicit recognition of the continued presence of coloniality entrenched in systemic manifestations of violence, marginalization, and oppression is not the final goal. Once projects of coloniality are named, the task must turn to both internal and external forms of decolonizing, or "countering the devaluation of indigenous identity, knowledge, and lifeways that came with colonialism."[9] Notably, decolonization as a social and cultural process asks Native peoples to rethink and reframe their perceptions of themselves through a decolonized lens. An approach of this sort would encourage tribal leaders to examine holistically the events and experiences of coloniality that shape and affect their contemporary lives, understand how these forces have in some cases reordered intertribal relations, and forward decolonized policies (economic and otherwise) that align with Native peoples' values, identities, knowledge, and ways of life.

Using a decolonizing framework, this book explores the colonial logics entrenched in the tribal casino discourse as well as the ever-present, complex, and sometimes even contradictory ways in which Native nations have engaged in struggles for sovereignty and self-determination. Examining the histories leading up to the events that followed the Warm Springs Bridge of the Gods Casino proposal, the book illuminates ruptures in tribal life caused by federal and state laws and policies, explores the impact of the non-Native public and mainstream media in framing tribal relationships, and accentuates powerful histories of survival embodied in modern Native nations. On this basis the examination of intertribal conflict also reveals possibilities for intertribal cooperation in the casino era.

Ultimately I argue that, while the tribal gaming economy has reframed tribal-federal and tribal-state relationships, it has also reframed tribe-to-tribe relationships. Critically examining intertribal tensions in the casino era brings into sharp focus deeply normalized systems of inequality (colonial-settler logics) that continue to permeate both Native and non-Native thinking on the topics of Indian gaming and intertribal conflict. As such, I argue that the circumstances that lead to intertribal conflict are directly influenced by complex social events and structural systems that are sustained by external governments, public opinion, and the media. I maintain that the assertion of the rights and interests of any single Native nation by opposing another Native nation's assertion of their rights and interests, though seemingly effective in the short-term protection of economic resources, actually works against long-term goals of decolonization, which requires the return of land, resources, power, and rights to Indigenous peoples.

Using a case study approach focused on the relations of two Native nations in Oregon, my research offers a decolonizing and critical intervention into the tribal casino discourse by placing Indigenous peoples' knowledge at the center of this inquiry. As such, this book's central argument is that while intertribal conflict in the casino era is often framed as a consequence of tribal corruption and greed, even framed this way at times by Native people, it cannot be understood without a deeper analysis of Indigenous peoples' perspectives on and interpretations of the historical, social, and political conditions that produced contemporary tribal communities, the tribal casino economy, and the intense politics on and off the reservation over tribal gaming. Contemporary tribal concerns (including intertribal conflicts over casinos) cannot be separated from the complex legal structures and historic events that underlie the lived experiences of tribes in Oregon. Through the years, Warm Springs and Grand Ronde have responded to the same federal laws and policies, intermingled with the larger non-Native public, and adapted strategies to survive as separate peoples.[10] Though all tribes across the country have had to react and respond to shifting policy eras, Grand Ronde and Warm Springs have shared more closely a regional outgrowth of colonialism, one unique to Oregon.

While there exist many parallels and shared experiences between Grand Ronde and Warm Springs, they also have distinct and divergent histories. For example, over twenty seven distinct tribes and bands would become Grand Ronde, including the Chasta, Kalapuya, Molalla, Rogue River, and Umpqua.[11] Several distinct tribes negotiated treaties in the mid-nineteenth century, though many of these were not ratified due to intense pressure from Congress to have the lands in western Oregon cleared for settlement.[12] Treaties that *were* finally ratified did not include reserved rights language or, in most cases, the exact details of where a tribe's reservation would be located. Comparatively, Warm Springs consists of three tribes, the Wasco, Warm Springs, and Northern Paiute peoples. In 1855, the Warm Springs and Wascoes negotiated one treaty with the federal government that clearly defined the tribes' reserved rights and reservation boundaries, and this treaty was ratified by Congress. Once the tribes relocated to the reservation in central Oregon, Warm Springs was fairly isolated from the broader settler society. Grand Ronde, however, experienced continuous pressure from nearby settlers who coveted the community's lands and resources in densely populated western Oregon. In the 1950s, tribal experiences again differed as Grand Ronde's government-to-government relationship was terminated by an act of Congress, and Grand Ronde tribal members were no longer eligible to participate in federal Indian programs, no longer had a recognized tribal government, and were denied federal protection of their lands and resources. Meanwhile, Warm Springs successfully defended against termination legislation.[13] As a result of both parallel and divergent tribal experiences, the tribes are unique in their responses to economic opportunities, and this contributes to how each perceives the tribal casino economy and participates in it. Though both eventually entered the tribal casino economy in 1995, they did so from very different historical, economic, and political standpoints.

These convergences and divergences recall the main themes from the story about the Bridge of the Gods. In light of this story and its multifaceted teachings, it is perhaps poignantly fitting that a conflict between Native nations over land, power, and resources would take place near the site of the ancient Bridge of the Gods and that a disputed casino would bear its name. However, unlike the two brothers fighting over an overabundance to their eventual undoing,

Grand Ronde and Warm Springs were compelled into competition over scarce resources and opportunity, perhaps also to their mutual detriment. This analysis of tribal perspectives on tribal histories as they affect intertribal relations will help readers, and perhaps Native nations themselves, better understand and even empathize with Native nations' varied political decisions in the casino era.

TRIBAL ECONOMIC DEVELOPMENT

Conditions are difficult, at best, for Native nations that seek routes to autonomous self-sufficiency.[14] As historian Richard White articulates, "The collapse of [Native peoples'] subsistence systems and their integration into world markets brought increasing reliance on the capitalist core, lack of economic choice, and profound political and social changes within their societies."[15] While tribal economies have always been subject to change and adaptation over time, European capitalist exchanges with Native peoples (as well as the colonial settlement of the United States) led to a diminishment of tribal economies. Capitalism became the prevailing economic paradigm during an era of European expansion beginning as early as the fifteenth century, begun by competing European colonizing nations and followed by the fledgling United States—much to the tremendous detriment of Native American peoples, their resources, and their land.

From the late sixteenth century to the late eighteenth century, rival colonial nations such as England, France, and Spain fought primarily over land and extractable resources. In many cases, economic relationships between Native peoples and non-Natives were inequitable and disruptive to precontact economic systems while also engendering violence within and between Indigenous communities. The US government—and its citizens, who sought permanent settlement on Native lands—continued and magnified the practice of land acquisition and resource exploitation, driven by a seemingly insatiable desire for land and wealth. Though the presence of European capitalist markets was central to the economic, political, and cultural chaos Native nations experienced from contact onward, White points out that the near-complete diminishment of Native peoples' subsistence systems took place over several generations and involved a "complex interchange of environmental, economic, political, and cultural influences."[16] Largely through treaties made in the nineteenth century, the vast majority of the land in the United States was transferred from Native communities to the settler society. Simultaneously, small areas of Native nations' land were retained, primarily as reservations, and remained under Native governance.

The assault on tribal economies in the United States did not end after the establishment of reservations. Native-controlled land and resources have been and continue to be exploited—for gold, timber, coal, oil, and uranium—in ways that disadvantage Native people and harm their relationships to specific geographies. Some traditional economies continue in contemporary tribal communities.[17] Frequently, however, these economies require clean, undammed rivers and sufficient unused and unpolluted lands as well as agreements with the dominant society not to limit tribal access to fishing, hunting, and harvesting sites or to otherwise harass Native peoples participating in these economies.[18] According to sociologist Duane Champagne (Turtle Mountain Band of Chippewa), when a nation-state continuously limits the economic possibilities of tribal communities, either by settling lands, exploiting resources, or polluting ecological systems, it is an abrogation of human rights.[19]

Native peoples have had to find ways to adapt and transform according to their circumstances. As historian, theologian, and activist Vine Deloria Jr. (Standing Rock Sioux) and political scientist Clifford Lytle argue, "Like other Americans [Native peoples] have to adjust to economic trends, respond to changes in political climate and thought, and act responsibly in relation to others. Indians have survived and that means that they have successfully and consistently adapted themselves and their institutions to new situations."[20]

At times the strategy for survival involves adapting to, and even adopting, the economic principles and practices of the dominant capitalist culture. In this vein, historian Donald L. Fixico (Shawnee, Sac and Fox, Creek, and Seminole) contends that "American capitalism, deriving from a tradition of Eurocentrism, has continued through the twentieth century to exploit tribal nations for their natural resources, thus forcing Indian leadership to adopt modern corporate strategies to ensure the survival of their nations and people."[21]

While modern development theories that value growth and profit continue to be applied to tribal economic development strategies, economist Dean Howard Smith (Mohawk) provides a critique of such theories as they have been applied to tribal nations. Smith argues that fundamentally Western theories of development have not worked for tribal nations, in part because theorists do not engage with Indigenous knowledge or goals. Instead Native nations themselves must develop a social compatibility paradigm that balances economic needs with cultural integrity.[22] Historian Colleen O'Neil discusses the problems attendant on an either/or, traditional/modern economic dichotomy, arguing that development needs to be situated in a new frame-work, unique to each distinct nation's specific set of circumstances.[23] Despite a complex and contentious history of economic development in Indian Coun-try, Native nations respond creatively to meet the needs of their members, defend their sovereign rights, and develop tribally specific businesses. For generations, Native nations have been adaptive, incorporating and trans-forming capitalistic economic models, making them into distinctly Native American endeavors. A major example of this is the emergence of gaming in the 1970s.

THE INDIAN GAMING REGULATORY ACT
AND THE CASINO ERA (1988–PRESENT)

The year 2018 marks the thirtieth anniversary of the Indian Gaming Regula-tory Act (IGRA), a federal law that in 1988 created a statutory framework for the regulation of gaming operations owned by federally recognized Native nations and an outline of their legal authority to sponsor casinos on their res-ervations, thereby ushering in the casino era. The history of this era must be understood within the context of the history of development discourse and the economic needs of sovereign Native nations. As tribal chair Anthony R. Pico (Viejas Band of Kumeyaay Indians) notes, "The courts have long held that Indians have the right under the Constitution to govern ourselves. But hav-ing that right without adequate economic resources is a hollow dream."[24] We might reframe the discussion of the casino economy by thinking through the attendant issues of Native health—physical, economic, and cultural. Researcher Eric C. Henson (Chickasaw) of the Harvard Project on American Indian Economic Development explains, "Building a casino is not so much about money from gaming as it is about Native nations striving for economic self-sufficiency and deciding for themselves what kind of economic activity they will pursue."[25] Therefore, when analyzing how tribes have participated in the casino economy, it is paramount to remember the particular vectors of tribal history that inform the decisions that have led them into this era.

The tribal casino economy represents a substantial sector of the economy for Native nations in Oregon. According to a report by the economic consulting firm ECONorthwest, in 2011 "casinos and tribal government supported by gam-ing collectively had an economic impact totaling $1,506 billion in output, 13,153 jobs, and $506.9 million in wages and benefits in Oregon."[26] The first Native nation in Oregon to open a casino was the Cow Creek Band of Umpqua Tribe of

Indians in 1994. By 1995 Grand Ronde had opened their successful Spirit Mountain Casino located along Oregon Route 18 between Portland and the coast, and Warm Springs opened the Indian Head Casino that year on their remotely located reservation, placing it adjacent to the Kah-Nee-Ta Resort, fourteen miles from US 26.

There are nine federally recognized Native nations in Oregon, eight of which operated Class III casinos in 2017.[27] Class III casinos feature high-stakes games such as blackjack, roulette, craps, and slot machines. The casinos of Native nations such as Grand Ronde, which are located closer to metropolitan areas, have had the greatest economic success, while the gaming operations of Warm Springs, located off the Interstate 5 corridor and away from large cities, have been less lucrative. In 2009, Jeff Mapes of the *Oregonian* highlighted this discrepancy, reporting that Grand Ronde's casino received annual profits of about $62 million, while the Warm Springs casino generated about $2–4 million a year in profits.[28]

In the late 1970s, a few Native nations tried to generate revenue for their communities by opening small, on-reservation bingo operations, and two subsequent court cases confirmed Native nations' rights to operate gaming establishments. In 1979, the Seminole Tribe of Florida opened a high-stakes bingo parlor, but this operation was closed down by Broward County sheriff Robert Butterworth. Relying on a civil/regulatory, criminal/prohibitory test developed for Public Law 280 in *Bryan v. Itasca County* (1976), the US Court of Appeals reasoned in *Seminole Tribe of Florida v. Butterworth* (1981) that if a state only regulates rather than prohibits gambling or particular forms of gambling, then Native nations may run gambling operations on their reservations.[29] In other words, if particular forms of gambling are not considered criminal in a state, then Native nations are allowed to engage in them free of state interference. The court found that Florida prohibited some forms of gambling and that overall its public gaming policy was regulatory. As a result, the Seminoles could keep their gambling operation open. This was the first formal recognition by a federal court of Native nations' right to conduct gaming operations on their lands.

The second important case was *California v. Cabazon Band of Mission Indians* (1987). The Cabazon Band was running high-stakes card games on their reservation that State of California authorities tried repeatedly to shut down. The US Supreme Court held that states do not have jurisdiction over tribal lands unless Congress explicitly articulates transference of jurisdiction from the reservation to the states. California argued that Public Law 280 (1953) and the Organized Crime Control Act (1970) gave the state jurisdiction over tribal lands.[30] Here again a court used the civil/regulatory, criminal/prohibitory test to determine that neither of these laws gave California regulatory powers over Indian gaming operations on tribal lands. The decision turned on whether federal and tribal interest in the gaming operations preempted the authority of state interests. As the federal government sought to strengthen tribal governments and economies, the Court ruled that this goal preempted state interests.

Unhappy states then lobbied vigorously for the IGRA and for provisions in it that would make it mandatory for Native nations to negotiate with states for terms and conditions. The states argued that they should be the ones to regulate Indian gaming, for four reasons:

- The need to control criminal activity associated with gambling, and the tribes' supposed inability to control such activity
- The loss of state revenue if the tribes or the federal government regulated Indian gaming instead of states
- The inexperience of tribal governments in regulating gaming
- The lack of faith in the federal government's ability to regulate Indian gaming.

Native nations lobbied staunchly against state regulation, favoring exclusively tribal regulation or a combination of tribal and federal regulation.[31]

In response to these various lobbying efforts, Congress added a state-tribal compact requirement in the IGRA that stipulated that states and Native nations were required to negotiate a regulatory structure for Class III gaming on tribal land. Since the passing of the IGRA, a revenue-sharing component has become a common feature of state-tribal compacts for Class III gaming operations.[32] The IGRA also outlines how Native nations must use gaming revenue, such as for strengthening tribal governments and communities or providing social and cultural services to members. In order to regulate gaming under the IGRA, Congress established the National Indian Gaming Commission (NIGC), a new federal agency. According to Kathryn R. L. Rand and Steven A. Light, founders of the Institute for the Study of Tribal Gaming, the IGRA continues to be an uneasy and often unequal political and legal compromise between Native nations and state governments, one that narrowly affirms tribal sovereignty while simultaneously developing systems of state control over tribal economies and lives.[33] Furthermore, the IGRA raises controversial issues concerning the definition and scope of tribal sovereignty, the rights of Native nations to self-determination and autonomy, the public perception of Indian gaming, and the extent of federal power over Native nations.[34]

In order to understand the tribal casino phenomenon, one must attempt to comprehend the impact of more than five hundred years of colonialism on Native American cultures and the dynamic present reality of those cultures. As Native nations assessed their economic circumstances in the casino era, games and gambling were transformed from an institution of social cohesion into an instrument of revenue generation for cash-poor or land-poor communities.[35] The casino industry has thereby played a significant role in modern tribal development—and, in turn, the industry has been shaped by the participation of Native people.

For example, as an enrolled member of the Eastern Band of Cherokee Indians and recipient of yearly dividends from my nation's casino in Cherokee, North Carolina, I have a direct interest in the tribal casino economy and the ways in which Native peoples participate in this industry.[36] Each year my siblings and I are aided by the money we receive from the Eastern Band; this money has helped pay for rent and college tuition and has put food on the table. For this we have been grateful. The year that I turned twenty-five, I traveled with my siblings to Cherokee, North Carolina. My great-aunt Myrtle hosted our visit. Myrtle was tiny but filled with pluck, and she took us to visit the Harrah's Cherokee Casino Resort, where we had lunch and she gambled a little at the slot machines. Built in 1997, Harrah's was the first major casino (Native or otherwise) to open in North Carolina. Since that time it has both literally and metaphorically changed the landscape of the reservation.[37] The funds from the casino have provided many social and cultural services to a once deeply impoverished community as well as an annual per capita payment to its members. While I would not claim that the success of the tribal casino industry is solely responsible for the contemporaneous changes in Native communities, it is interesting to note the ways in which the growth of this economy parallels other important developments in Indian Country. On a personal and a collective level, the casino economy has affected tribal members in numerous ways, and these changes must be understood within a larger trajectory of Native activism.

During the civil rights movement era of the 1960s and 1970s, Native peoples in the United States struggled to have their inherent and treaty-defined rights as well as their cultural distinctiveness recognized and respected by the dominant society and the federal government. Becoming broadly known as Red Power, intertribal coalitions of Native political and cultural leaders began to articulate the language of this pan-Indian movement. For example, Native American intellectuals and activists such as Vine Deloria Jr. (Standing Rock Sioux), Billy Frank Jr. (Nisqually), and Hank Adams (Assiniboine-Sioux) argued for the recognition of tribal sovereignty (Native nations' inherent right to govern themselves) and Indigenous self-determination (Indigenous peoples' right to determine their own futures free from colonial paternalism). Drawing on the rhetoric generated by the Red Power movement, self-determination for Native Americans was articulated in a number of congressional acts—including the Indian Civil Rights Act (1968), the Indian Self-Determination and Education Assistance Act (1975), the Indian Child Welfare Act (1978), and the American Indian Religious Freedom Act (1978)—that at least ostensibly were intended to defend Indian children, religion, and self-governance. For many Native people, this period was given over to learning or relearning how to feel good about being an Indian. It was a time to reclaim, revive, and share what had previously been removed or stolen and a time to revel in the parts of ourselves that had never been taken, that had been successfully defended.[38]

The introduction of the tribal casino economy dovetails with this momentous period. After the Seminole Tribe and the Cabazon Band of Mission Indians made important inroads into this economy in the 1980s, it became a real possibility for other Native nations in the United States. Though the numbers of participating Native nations and gaming operations fluctuate, in 2017 the National Indian Gaming Commission (NIGC) identified 243 Native nations operating 540 gaming facilities in twenty-eight states.[39] Although these numbers indicate that fewer than half of the 567 federally recognized tribal entities (nations, tribes, bands, communities, Pueblos, and villages) have entered into this economy, they nevertheless illustrate the pervasiveness of the casino industry in Native America. In addition, as legal scholar Walter R. Echo-Hawk (Pawnee) notes, the wealth produced by the tribal gaming industry can be an "equalizer" that puts "dollars for social justice into the hands of savvy tribal leaders."[40]

Much of this history can be observed one way or another in Oregon. To see the potential success of Native nations who participate in the tribal casino economy, one need only to look at Grand Ronde. Supporting the largest membership of any Oregon tribe, Grand Ronde's casino in the present is one of the top tourist destinations in Oregon and a multimillion-dollar annual industry.

However, the casino's success relies on its ability to draw customers from Portland and the state capital of Salem, thirty-two miles east of Grand Ronde. Though casino operation can be a risky business to engage in, Grand Ronde has enjoyed some economic success for the first time in several generations, and capital from the casino pays for government infrastructure, cultural programs, health care, elder services, and many other programs and services. Casino profits have afforded Grand Ronde tribal members access to higher education, opened doors politically at state and national levels, and given the tribe opportunities to reconnect with culturally significant lands and resources.

Warm Springs did not experience similar success after they opened the small Indian Head Casino at their Kah-Nee-Ta Resort. Responding to community concern about the casino economy on the reservation, Warm Springs members had voted to try operating a tribal casino on a short-term basis. This was done in order to gauge the social impact of a casino on the reservation community and assess its fiscal benefit. While the Indian Head Casino was successful, it did not generate what were seen as substantial profits, largely due to its isolated location several hours away from Portland and other urban centers. It was for this reason that in 1997 Warm Springs began to explore other options in the gaming industry, including a casino in the Columbia River Gorge at Cascade Locks, which came to be called the Bridge of the Gods Casino.

Though Grand Ronde's opposition was not the only barrier to the Bridge of the Gods Casino, intertribal relations were severely tested during this period. Leaders from both communities stated that they felt that they were doing what they had to do in order to support the needs of their own tribal members. While at times they also acknowledged that the other tribe was doing the same to protect their community, the resulting commentary illuminated that conflict stemmed from more than competition over business. The sentiments also revealed underlying tensions and concerns about kinship, identity, and political alliances, as well as shared and divergent histories.

INTERTRIBAL RELATIONS IN THE CASINO ERA

For me, the process of understanding the specific history of the casino era has proven to be as much a personal journey as an academic project. As such, one core methodological approach of this book is to not efface my presence in my research. As I explain above, my own life has been affected by the tribal casino economy, and in my attempt to reframe the discourse about the casino economy I choose to highlight my own involvement in the constructions of truth that this project illuminates. The topic of intertribal relations, conflict, and cooperation in the casino era first piqued my interest during a research trip to Warm Springs in 2006, several years after debates between Grand Ronde and Warm Springs over the Bridge of the Gods Casino began. During this visit I met with tribal members to discuss the subject of tribally owned casinos, and I spent time with Secretary-Treasurer Charles "Jody" Calica (Warm Springs), who, because of his position, had substantial power with the Warm Springs Tribal Council. I was especially interested in how the proposed casino in Cascade Locks had affected the relationship between Grand Ronde and Warm Springs. Calica told me that communication over this matter had become difficult and that there was little hope of fixing it.

I asked him what he thought needed to happen to bring the people involved back to the table and to find a solution that would respect the hopes, fears, and needs of both sides. He responded that he thought someone needed to help reframe the discussion and inspire new ways to promote understanding. "Maybe it will take someone like you," he said. The breath was knocked out of me for a moment, and I felt afraid. When I left his office, I meditated on the kinds of responsibilities I had as a Native person and as a scholar. I breathed in the hot desert air full of the aromas of juniper and sage. The words of Secretary-Treasurer Calica helped me to give meaning to the role I wanted to fill within the discipline of Native American studies and to define my orientation and approach to my research.

The academic community has approached the tribal casino economy in a number of ways. Some legal scholars have focused on the legislative history and contemporary politics of Indian gaming,[41] while others have taken anthropological approaches, developing case studies that typically emphasize individual tribal experiences with the gaming economy.[42] Some scholars have explored the ways in which the tribal gaming industry has affected aspects of tribal life, such as complicating the process for Native nations seeking federal recognition or creating new popular stereotypes of Native people based on notions of Indian wealth.[43] These studies of the gaming economy often investigate changes to Native nations' relations with states or the federal government and explore disputes between Native and non-Native communities. While I also explore these themes, after my conversation with Secretary-Treasurer Calica I decided additionally to examine the little-studied topic of how this economy has affected intertribal relations and to engage a humanizing and problem-solving approach to intertribal conflict in the casino era.

Intertribal debates and conflicts that occur in the tribal casino era can be contentious, painful, and complicated. They also bring into sharp focus the differences, both real and imagined, between Native nations: how they came into existence in their contemporary forms; the legal status and rights that have been reserved, retained, or restored; whether they have lands or resources; whether they are close to or remotely located from settler societies; what kind of cultural ruptures they have experienced; and what revitalization projects they have initiated. These differences in tribal experiences are often blamed for conflicts between tribes. I argue, however, that the inequitable contemporary conditions might be better understood as symptoms of the ruptures of Native life caused by colonization and injustice perpetuated by Eurocentric domination and colonial violence.

It should not be surprising that conflicts and internalized acts of oppression are pervasive within and between Native communities—particularly when it comes to the casino economy. Author Deborah A. Miranda (Chumash/Esselen) reminds us in *Bad Indians: A Tribal Memoir* to be mindful that self-harming behaviors in contemporary Indigenous communities (as evidenced in high rates of suicide, domestic violence, and poverty) stem from a genealogy of colonial violence, including forced removals, genocide, and countless assaults on culture.[44] There is still a great deal of unresolved grief within Native communities. Like other Indigenous peoples internationally, Native Americans have suffered tremendous wounds as a result of devastating epidemics, traumas, and ongoing attempts to assimilate Native people and dispossess us of our cultural identity and relationships with each other and the land. These wounds and this grief have led to myriad social, cultural, and economic problems that persist across generations. When Native people talk about the problems and possibilities of the tribal casino economy, their responses and reflections are often interwoven with anger, frustration, and pain that stem from distress that is passed from generation to generation and is visible in manifest dysfunction in their cultural world. The persistence of this trauma— a result of historical violence—becomes most obvious when conversation turns to topics of cultural identity, rights, and relationships to land and place.

Race and ethnic studies scholar Lawrence W. Gross (Anishinaabe) has reasoned that Native peoples suffer from "post apocalyptic stress disorder," meaning that they have seen the end of their world but not the end of their worldview.[45] While survivors of this apocalypse worked to rebuild their cultural world and recover from multifaceted upheavals, almost simultaneously new wounds were inflicted throughout the process of colonization. Like other communities around the world who have resisted forces of colonization, Native peoples have at times rejected and at other times internalized the oppressive systems and racist orientations of their colonizers.[46] When power (albeit limited), opportunity, and economic security seem to be at stake, Native people are capable of using these oppressive systems against one another, despite the fact that they might hurt themselves and their own interests in the process.

While referencing a comment made by Vine Deloria Jr., Echo-Hawk notes that one of the most pressing questions facing Native peoples in the twenty-first century is "will we survive?"[47] From the beginning of the colonial period onward, from 1492, this was a pressing question for Native communities that were forced to realize that their continued existence as a people and culture were no longer assured. In *Radical Hope: Ethics in the Face of Cultural Devastation*, philosopher Jonathan Leer discusses the experience of Crow leader Plenty Coups, who witnessed the US attempts to obliterate the Crow nation in the late 1800s and early 1900s. In the face of what must have appeared to Crow people as the end of their world, Leer argues, they appear to have exhibited a "radical hope" that Crow culture would continue in some form and imagined cultural revival as a possibility in future generations. This radical hope for the regenerative potential of Native nations may have influenced Plenty Coups when he let biographer Frank B. Linderman record his story so that generations in the future might "bring 'it' back to life."[48] This question of survival and the anxiety that surrounds it is certainly a factor in what motivates twenty-first century Native nations to consider economies such as the tribal casino economy. For some Native nations the tribal casino economy can represent just this sort of radical hope for future generations of Native people and cultural revival.

INTERTRIBAL CONFLICT

It is important to note that intertribal conflict, in general, is not new. There are numerous examples of historical occasions when Native nations fought, intensely debated, or fundamentally disagreed with one another. Well before settler societies colonized the Americas and the United States was founded, oral histories and archaeological evidence shows, Native peoples engaged at times in prolonged and bloody conflicts. For example, oral histories of the Haudenosaunee Confederacy (also known as the Iroquois Confederacy) tell of a time before contact with European colonial powers when the five nations (the Onondaga, Mohawk, Seneca, Oneida, and Cayuga) were engaged in a horrific civil war. The war is said to have taken a severe toll on all five nations until a prophet known as the Peacemaker brought the Great Law of Peace to the people. This outlined a new form of governance that allowed the nations to unite in peace under a confederacy. While this case provides an example of an intertribal conflict predating colonial contact, it also offers a brilliant and still quite applicable model of conflict resolution between Native nations.

The impact of colonizing activities by nations such as Spain, France, England, Russia, and eventually Mexico and the United States on intertribal relations has been well documented. In the Southwest, for example, Jennifer Nez Denetdale (Diné) explains, "Tension, conflict, and peace marked the colonial period as Navajo relations with Pueblo peoples, the Spaniards, the Mexicans, and then the Americans, shifted along a continuum of kinship and peace to conflict and war," and these "cycles of peace and conflict . . . were directly related to the slave trade, of which Navajo women and children were the primary targets."[49] From the introduction of new economic alliances forged to support the European fur trade of the seventeenth and eighteenth centuries, intertribal conflict in the colonial era was often both directly and indirectly connected to an ongoing colonial invasion of Indigenous land and usurpation of resources as well as the effects of Eurocentric hierarchical and coercive models of social organization on tribal communities.

Native American people share a unique connection to one another, unified to a large degree through the experience of colonialism and the political and social dominance of the US settler society. However, Native nations continue today to be diverse in their size, legal status, politics, languages, and cultural practices, and they sometimes profoundly disagree over a wide assortment of issues. It becomes clear that almost all contemporary examples of intertribal conflict, once analyzed, have in some significant way been shaped and nurtured by the activities, laws, and policies of the US government and settler society, often with a multigenerational effect on Native nations.

One example is the Hopi-Navajo land dispute, in which two Native nations that were known historically to have coexisted and cooperated found themselves in a struggle over land and scarce resources. Though the history of this dispute is quite complex and layered, its apex occurred in 1974 when the US government signed into law the Navajo-Hopi Land Settlement Act, which redrew the boundaries of both nations' reservations and required the forced relocation of an estimated 12,500 Diné (Navajo) families from the disputed territory.[50] Authors of a report by the Navajo Nation Human Rights Commission note that "the partition of lands between Navajos and Hopis was shaped by the imperative of the United States government to determine legal ownership of surface lands. And in the process, determine who had authority to grant leases to coal companies."[51] From land disputes in the Southwest to efforts of the Eastern Band of Cherokee Indians to block Lumbee recognition in the Southeast, examples abound of the intertribal conflicts across the United States.

While Native nations have at times chosen to engage in intertribal conflicts and at other times been compelled into them, there are also numerous examples of Native nations organizing together and collaborating to defend, protect, and revive Indigenous ways of life. Intertribal coalitions forged in the Red Power movement of the 1960s through the 1980s articulated sound cases for tribal sovereignty and Native rights. These coalitions drew their strength from a political organizational model in which Native nations shared power, responsibilities, and successes. For example, national intertribal organizations like the National Congress of American Indians (NCAI), regionally based intertribal organizations such as the Affiliated Tribes of Northwest Indians (ATNI), and intertribal organizations that serve Native nations within state boundaries were founded to support the shared objectives and goals of Native nations.[52]

THE TRUTH OF THE PUMPKIN

In 2013 the Warm Springs Tribal Council voted to end their efforts to establish the Bridge of the Gods Casino in Cascade Locks or Hood River, adjacent to the Columbia River.[53] The following year, I visited Grand Ronde and Warm Springs and talked with people I had earlier interviewed there in order to ensure that I correctly represented their perspectives. When the topic of the casino came up, a few individuals sighed deeply, clearly tired of having to talk yet again about their experiences with this. It seemed that there was continued wariness and hurt between Grand Ronde and Warm Springs people, particularly felt by those most involved in the intertribal debates about the Bridge of the Gods Casino. A number of people felt that the rift between the two nations had spilled over into other conflicts over political and cultural space, including the question of which of the two nations should have recognized rights and responsibilities along the Columbia River at Willamette Falls and at Multnomah Falls.

Given the often-polarized context of the intertribal casino discourse, I wondered how my book would be received upon its completion. At several critical junctures I asked myself what its purpose was. Would community members and employees of the two Native nations central to the story—Grand Ronde and Warm Springs—view it as a mere rehashing of a dispute that many would like to put behind them? As I finalized my writing, I had a number of conversations with individuals from Grand Ronde and Warm Springs who told me that they were glad I was conducting the research. They felt that it was important for Native nations in the casino era to examine intertribal conflicts in order to discover new strategies to promote and strengthen intertribal relations in Oregon for the benefit of all Native nations.

From the conceptualization of my research to the writing of my findings, I have reflected on how this research might benefit the participants and their Native nations and promote these communities' goals of self-determination and sovereignty. I struggled to frame the issues illuminated by the proposed Bridge of the Gods Casino in a way that was accountable to the individuals who had given generously of their time and knowledge. At first it appeared that I was in a troubling predicament, as the two communities were articulating conflicting goals (on the surface, at least), and writing that promoted the goals of self-determination of one nation seemed to mean working against the goals of self-determination of the other.

When I brought up this concern with my father, he asked if I remembered the movie *Fiddler on the Roof*, set in 1905 tsarist Russia and featuring a protagonist named Tevye. My father reminded me of a scene that exemplified the trouble I was having in representing the findings of my project. In this scene Tevye listens to two men arguing over a topic, holding what seem to be diametrically opposed viewpoints. Tevye is asked to determine which man's viewpoint is right, which viewpoint is true. Tevye replies that the first man is right but that the second man is also right. A third man, watching this exchange, asks Tevye how it is possible that these two men who hold contradictory views can both be right, to which Tevye replies, "and you are also right."[54] Though the positions that two Native nations take concerning the casino economy may appear fundamentally at odds, once the issue is contextualized, it becomes easier to understand how they possess distinct and opposing perspectives. As a result of the conversation with my father, I began to look beyond the political positioning that places Native nations directly at odds, and I started to think about the production of perspectives, the ways that people derive their current viewpoints on intertribal conflicts, and the deeper meanings that underlie the articulations of these positions.

While writing this book, I often thought back to the Columbus quincentennial commemoration in 1992 and celebrations of Columbus's so-called discovery of the Americas. That year my mother taught a course at Oregon State

University entitled "Columbus's Legacy." To begin the class, she quoted Onon-daga chief Oren Lyons: "The Chief of the Onondaga Turtle Clan placed a pump-kin in the center of the circle and said, 'From where I sit, I can't see the other side of the pumpkin. All of us in this circle see it with different eyes. We must put our good minds together to know the truth of the pumpkin.'"[55]

Using the pumpkin metaphor, my mother challenged her students to reexamine the idea of truth and to reflect on their own position in relation to one another. By themselves, people around the circle could only know their own individual truths, seen from their own perspectives and inter-preted through their personal archive of lived experiences. But when gath-ered together to use their "good minds" and "different eyes" to better "know the truth," they could form a more complex, complete, and accurate under-standing of truth.

OVERVIEW OF CHAPTERS

The complexity of the issues illuminated by an examination of the Oregon tribal casino economy and the Warm Springs proposed Bridge of the Gods Casino reflects tribal experiences across the United States while also embody-ing distinct regional conditions. In Oregon and elsewhere in the nation inter-tribal conflict should not be and cannot be separated from a discussion of the complex legal realities and the ongoing effects of colonialism that Native nations must negotiate. Native nations that find themselves compelled to struggle with one another over limited gaming revenues often have parallel and interconnected experiences and histories. At the same time, they might have divergent legal, economic, political, and tribal experiences. Like Grand Ronde and Warm Springs, Native nations in the United States form unique perspectives on economic development opportunities available through the casino economy, and thus they respond differently to these opportunities.

In the text that follows, chapter 2 explores the parallel and divergent legal, economic, political, and tribal histories of Grand Ronde and Warm Springs that shaped each tribe's unique positions regarding the proposed Bridge of the Gods Casino. Chapter 3 considers national debates about the tribal casino economy, the early history of tribal casinos in Oregon, and Grand Ronde and Warm Springs members' complex response to the tribal casino economy. From there, chapter 4 examines discourse produced about tribal casinos, images and narratives of Indians shaped within this discourse, and the emergence of a tribal casino discourse in the *Oregonian* newspaper, particularly focusing on journalistic coverage of the Bridge of the Gods Casino proposal. Chapter 5 offers a survey of the fifteen years during which Warm Springs worked to gain approval to build the Bridge of the Gods Casino in Cascade Locks. This includes examination of the difficulties inherent in the process required to take off-reservation lands into trust for gaming purposes and a look at the federal, state, and regional obstacles that Warm Springs encountered in this process. Through a series of interviews conducted with members and employees of Grand Ronde and Warm Springs in the years 2007–14, chapter 6 investigates intertribal relations and intertribal conflict in the casino era and the possibilities for intertribal cooperation and reconciliation. I consider the broad climate of federal and state politics that Native nations must negotiate strategically, and ultimately it is my hope to offer insights that Grand Ronde, Warm Springs, and by extension all Native nations can use to promote mutual understanding.

The most important contributions to this book come from Grand Ronde and Warm Springs people and their allies. They have provided unique and significant insights, astute analysis, and complex perspectives, and they have moved the conversation well beyond the subject of tribal casinos to deeper and more difficult themes, such as perceptions of intertribal difference, contested treaty boundaries, and continued colonial dismissal of tribal sovereignty. Perhaps Grand Ronde and Warm Springs together will be able to see the truth of their disagreement from new perspectives.

Though the Warm Springs Tribal Council officially ended efforts to open a casino at the Cascade Locks site, an examination of the Bridge of the Gods project and the events surrounding it provides valuable insights on intertribal relations, conflict, and cooperation in the tribal casino era. Close examination of the histories leading up to and following the proposed casino reveals the ruptures to tribal life caused by federal and state policies. But it also brings to light powerful stories of survival embodied in modern tribal communities and shows the connections between Grand Ronde and Warm Springs. This is a book about these two Native nations and their relationship to the tribal casino economy, to each other, and to the place where the cascades fall.

There Is Power in the Telling

Oregon Tribal Histories

Human beings have no way of knowing that we exist, or what we have survived, except through the vehicle of story.

Culture is ultimately lost when we stop telling the stories of who we are, where we have been, how we arrived here, what we once knew, what we wished we knew; when we stop our retelling of the past, our imagining the future, and the long, long task of inventing an identity every single second of our lives.

—Deborah A. Miranda, *Bad Indians: A Tribal Memoir*

NATIVE NATIONS' STORIES OF COMMUNITY RETELL THE PAST, INTER-pret the present, and are told and retold to remind citizens that they exist and what they have survived as Indian people. The stories include information about their Indigenous ancestors and how they lived; places and resources that were important to their ancestors (and are important to them); encounters with colonizers and settler societies; traumas that have caused deep intergenerational grief, stress, and cultural ruptures; the formation of contemporary Native nations; the struggle to resist and survive colonization (sometimes against all odds); and collective dreams for the future of their nation. Additionally, Native nations have stories about their relationships with regional politics, politicians, policies, and with other Native nations that share regional experiences. It is through these stories and relationships that the distinct culture and identity of each tribal community is forged and maintained.

In this chapter, I offer some sociohistorical context for the Confederated Tribes of Grand Ronde and the Confederated Tribes of Warm Springs that puts these two communities into perspective in order to better understand the Indian gaming economy in Oregon and the tribal viewpoints articulated during discussions about the proposed Bridge of the Gods Columbia River Resort Casino. The chapter explores the shared histories of Grand Ronde and Warm Springs as Indian peoples, as well as their divergent experiences as distinct Native nations.[1] Grand Ronde and Warm Springs have each had to react to rapid shifts in federal Indian laws and policies, and both have forged political and social relationships with surrounding non-Native communities while they have also developed distinct, unique identities as contemporary Native nations. As such, each of these Native nations carries stories that are embedded with emotions connected to both cultural pride and anxieties.

Although both Native nations have experienced oppression and marginalization at the hands of colonial and settler governments, they each in their own ways have resisted, adapted to, and in some cases accommodated projects of colonialism. Grand Ronde and Warm Springs may share many similarities with Native nations across the nation, but as Native nations located in Oregon, these two communities also share a specific regional experience of colonialism. The events, experiences, and stories of identity in turn shape each nation and how it reacts and responds to challenges and possibilities that arise in the casino era.

"IT'S MY TURN NOW":
REFRAMING THE NARRATIVE OF OREGON TRIBES

There is power in the telling of Native American regional histories, and Wasco elder George W. Aguilar Sr. recognized this in *When the River Ran Wild! Indian Traditions on the Mid-Columbia and the Warm Spring Reservation* (2005). In this history by a Wasco about Wascoes, Aguilar talks about "old-timers" who had their chance to tell history, referring to other Native elders of his tribe. He articulates this oral tradition and his responsibility within it: "Nearly 75 years of my lifetime have come and gone since hearing of the historical events from the old-timers. It is my turn now."[2] In contrast, Dorothy O. Johansen and and Charles M. Gates in *Empire of the Columbia: A History of the Pacific Northwest* (1957) speak for other kinds of old-timers: academics who have written histories in a manner that relegates Native people to marginal positions, as the "background" or "prelude" to the implicitly more important story of Euro-American expansion and nationhood. They assert, "The aboriginal cultures of the Pacific Northwest were background to the history of the region. They were also unique and of sufficient interest to deserve some attention as a prelude to our story."[3] Taken together, these varying perspectives help illustrate

MAP 2.1. Approximate locations of Native nations in Oregon, 1840–50

how Native nations in the region have had their histories framed both internally and externally.

In the Pacific Northwest, competing ideologies of the right of occupancy versus the right of discovery played out between nations such as Russia, England, Spain, and the United States. All advocated for what they considered their right of discovery, a doctrine by which land could be claimed by a national government as long as it was not already occupied by other Christian nations.[4] Conflicting claims put forward by competing European nations meant that Indigenous nations' claims to their lands and resources were often disregarded. Later, when the United States gave a nod of acknowledgment to the notion of Indigenous rights through occupancy, it failed to protect Native peoples from encroachment and coerced treaty signing, perpetuating land grabs by US citizens. This history of settler encroachment and coerced land cession in Oregon (as elsewhere in the United States) is often obscured from public view or rendered innocuous, as if colonization and settlement was inevitable, blameless, and even righteous.

In order to disrupt the narrative of the inevitability of colonization and the superiority of European civilization, I strive to reframe the years of infiltration and invasion of Oregon (and specifically along the Columbia River and in western Oregon) as prelude and background to the stories of Grand Ronde and Warm Springs survival and struggles for autonomy. Since time immemorial, Native peoples have lived throughout Oregon's diverse geography: from the Cascade Mountain Range to the Columbia River Gorge, and from the turbulent coastal shores to the high desert. Native peoples of Oregon are varied and complex, with many languages and dialects spoken.[5] Travel and cultural exchange was a way of life for Oregon Indians; communities interacted, learned from one another, traded, and intermarried.[6] It is important to understand that every part of Oregon was "owned" by Native peoples, though pre-invasion systems of landownership should not be mistaken as parallel to European concepts of private property. It may be more accurate to think of the land as having ownership of Native people, who were shaped by and responsible for the land that they tended.

On July 13, 1787, the US Continental Congress established the Northwest Ordinance, in which it declared its intentions to expand the United States westward. The ordinance laid out a policy for interacting with Native populations: "The utmost good faith shall always be observed towards the Indians; their land and property shall never be taken from them without their consent; and, in their property, rights, and liberty, they shall never be invaded or disturbed, unless in just and lawful wars authorized by Congress; but laws founded in justice and humanity shall from time to time be made, for preventing wrongs being done to them, and for preserving peace and friendship with them."[7] But US citizens repeatedly violated the ordinance. In 1818, the United States and Britain declared Oregon "free and open" to citizens from either of the two nations. In 1819 they withdrew their claims to Oregon, and Russia withdrew theirs in 1824. Both England and the United States assumed that the claims made by Spain and Russia to rights of discovery passed to them.[8]

In the 1840s, migrating American settlers began to overrun the lands of Native nations in Oregon, bringing with them preconceived attitudes toward Native peoples. Based on their prior interactions with Native peoples—for example during the forced removals of Native nations from the southeastern states to Indian Territory in Oklahoma, or with plains nations as they traveled the Oregon Trail—many settlers saw Native peoples as "savages" and "barbarians."[9] Deadly European diseases, such as smallpox, scarlet fever, and whooping cough, led to additional chaos and devastation in Native communities. Though it is impossible to know the exact impact of these diseases on Native populations in Oregon, it has been estimated that by the 1850s as many as 80–90 percent of Native people in the region had perished from European-introduced illnesses.[10]

The British withdrew their claim on Oregon in 1846 and agreed with the United States on the 49th Parallel as a northern boundary. President James Polk signed into law the Act to Establish the Territorial Government of Oregon (also known as the Organic Act) in 1848, which established Oregon as a territory under US jurisdiction. This act also reaffirmed Native nations' titles to their lands and extended the "utmost good faith" policy that was outlined in the Northwest Ordinance.[11] Congress passed the Donation Land Claim Act in 1850, in which white settlers were offered free "public" land. Historian William G. Robbins assesses that this land transfer was "arguably the most generous federal land sale to the public in American history."[12] A major problem with this legislation was that the land did not belong to the United States; Native land titles had not been extinguished. However, this fact did not appear to discourage American settlers from migrating to and claiming land in the region. After years of harassment by settlers, Wasco leader William Chinook wrote in 1853 to Joel Palmer, superintendent of Indian affairs in the Oregon Territory: "We are tormented almost every day by white people who desire to settle on our lands, and although we have built houses and opened gardens they wish in spite of us to take possession of the very spots we occupy. . . . If it is the land of the white man . . . when did he buy it? . . . [If] it is our land then whites must not trouble us."[13] According to historian Stephen Dow Beckham, 7,437 claims by non-Natives were filed under the Donation Land Claim Act, covering 2.5 million acres of land in western Oregon.[14]

As more settlers coveted lands in the West, pressure increased on the US government to clear the land of Native people. In order to obtain legal title to land in Oregon, the United States entered into treaty negotiations with Native nations. Native leaders argued strongly against being removed from their homes. In 1850, Congress formed a treaty commission and appointed Anson Dart to negotiate with Native nations. Dart oversaw the negotiation of the first six treaties with tribes living in western Oregon. These treaties are important examples of resistance to removal by the Clatsop, Tillamook, Chinook, and other Native nations that successfully negotiated to retain land in their own territories.[15] Before treaty negotiations were finalized, Congress dissolved the commission, and the treaties were never ratified. Dart negotiated another thirteen treaties in 1851, but again Congress did not ratify them because they failed to completely remove Native peoples east of the Cascades.[16]

The discovery of gold in 1852 by James Cluggage and John Pool at Jackson Creek in the Rogue River Valley increased the fever of settlers to move to southern Oregon, which in turn increased instances of violence between settlers and Native people.[17] For example, Beckham describes:

> In early August some of the starving Indians in the upper Rogue River Valley raided the cabins of the white settlers. They killed two men and wounded others. Fear swept through the white community. Men, women and children rushed to Jacksonville for protection. The men in the small town captured two Shasta Indians and, on August 6, hanged them. That afternoon other settlers rode into town. One family brought along an Indian boy about seven-years-old. Seeing this small boy, the miners ran through the town screaming: "hang him, hang him. . . . Exterminate! the whole Indian race. When he is old he will kill you." In spite of the pleas of some white people, the miners grabbed the boy. They threw a rope around his neck and within minutes had murdered him. His body was left hanging beside that of the two Shasta men killed earlier that day.[18]

While it is true that Native peoples of the Rogue River Valley engaged in battles to keep their land and to find food, the miners often framed their violence in genocidal terms and used genocidal tactics. Hungry Native people, driven to extreme lengths in order to survive, killed two settlers; in return, miners killed three Indians who had nothing to do with the crime, calling for the extermination of *all* Indian people, including, in this case, a young child. As the drive to annihilate Native people intensified, a volunteer group of coastal miners formed, calling themselves the Crescent City Guard. In at least one instance they were recorded entering Jacksonville, carrying a flag that read "EXTERMINATION."[19] Resistance to this violence came in many forms, and the bands commonly referred to collectively as the Rogue River Indians (including the Takelma) often fought against the encroachment and the increasing aggressiveness of settlers in the region.[20]

Dart's successor in 1853 was Joel Palmer, whose charge was to remove the remaining Native peoples from their lands through treaty negotiations. In this time of grief and destruction, facing a flood of migrating US settlers, colonial violence, and the onslaught of disabling illnesses, many tribal leaders saw negotiation as the only available option. From 1853 to 1855, Native nations in

MAP 2.2. The nine federally recognized Native nations in Oregon in 2018

Oregon negotiated numerous treaties with Palmer, many of which were never ratified by Congress. Native nations often did not learn that their treaties had not been ratified until after they had made their way to what they understood to be reservation lands. Shortly after this treaty-makingperiod, in 1859, Oregon became a state.[21]

Despite the tremendous ruptures to tribal life that followed colonization and settlement, Native peoples still live all over Oregon. Currently there are nine federally recognized Native nations in Oregon: the Confederated Tribes of Grand Ronde; Confederated Tribes of Siletz; Confederated Tribes of Warm Springs; Cow Creek Band of Umpqua Tribe of Indians; Confederated Tribes of Umatilla; Coquille Indian Tribe; Klamath Tribes; Confederated Tribes of Coos, Lower Umpqua and Siuslaw Indians; and Burns Paiute Tribe. Most Native nations are confederations of Native peoples that were forced to move together onto reservations. In many ways, the historical experiences of Native nations in Oregon reflect colonial encounters emblematic to other Native nations across the United States.

Bryan McKinley Jones Brayboy (Lumbee) argues that colonization is endemic to the United States.[22] I agree with Brayboy and make sure to tell the students in my Native American studies classes that colonization of Indigenous lands and lives in the United States is an *unfinished* process, one that has never been fully achieved and is not over. Executive director of the National Indian Child Welfare Association Terry Cross (Seneca Nation) asserts that in order for colonization to succeed, colonizers must take wholly (in every respect) the land, resources, governmental sovereignty, legitimacy of thought, and children (the future) from Indigenous peoples.[23] These colonial projects have, in general, never been completed: Native peoples have not been erased, and they have not vanished. In many ways the opposite has occurred. For example, in Oregon, Native nations work hard to revitalize and strengthen their communities, in many cases using revenues generated by tribal casinos. Contradicting the still-prevalent ideology of the "vanishing Indian," in which Native Americans are cast as a race of people inevitably disappearing to make room for more "civilized" colonial nations, both Grand Ronde and Warm Springs continue to have distinct tribal identities that are shaped and maintained by the stories told and retold in their communities, continue to assert their sovereignty as Native nations, and continue to recognize specific responsibilities to the land that "owns" them.[24]

GRAND RONDE: FROM RURAL
CONCENTRATION CAMP TO NATION

The Confederated Tribes of Grand Ronde incorporate many Native peoples who lived on lands that stretched over much of western Oregon between the Cascade Mountains and the Coast Range.[25] As tribal historian David G. Lewis (Grand Ronde) describes, "The Grand Ronde Reservation formed as a rural concentration camp where twenty-seven tribes eventually created a community identity."[26] The groups that were rounded up and relocated in the mid-nineteenth century represented distinct cultures, speaking five major languages with more than twenty dialects.[27] The only language that was shared in common was a trade language called Chinuk Wawa, sometimes referred to as Chinook Jargon.[28] As such, Chinuk Wawa "became the lingua franca to most of the people in the community."[29] It is still spoken and taught at Grand Ronde.[30]

MAP 2.3. Ceded lands claimed by the Confederated Tribes of Grand Ronde

The diverse Native nations that would form the Grand Ronde negotiated several treaties with the federal government in the mid-1800s under uncertain and chaotic conditions. Reflecting on the conditions suffered by Grand Ronde people during this period of removal and forced relocations, Eirik Thorsgard (Grand Ronde) explains, "The people didn't want to leave their ancestral lands, and they didn't want to leave the bones of our ancestors that were in the ground. They worried about food, education, and people mistreating us. All those things are mentioned during treaty negotiations. Some of this information was handed down through oral traditions. The treaty signers were concerned about making sure that the people who came to Grand Ronde, regardless of which tribe or band they came from, could live and be happy. And they had to do it under duress."[31]

Several treaties negotiated with Native nations that would later be a part of the Grand Ronde confederation were never ratified. Ultimately seven ratified treaties were made with Native nations in western Oregon that became Grand Ronde. These were the Treaty with the Umpqua–Cow Creek Band

(September 19, 1853), Treaty with the Rogue River (September 10, 1853, and November 15, 1854), Treaty with the Chasta (November 18, 1854), Treaty with the Umpqua and Kalapuya (November 29, 1854), Treaty with the Confederated Tribes of the Willamette Valley (January 22, 1855; also known as the Treaty with the Kalapuya), and Treaty with the Molalla (December 21, 1855).

Between 1854 to 1856, Native people from western Oregon, the Oregon coast, and along the Columbia River were coerced or forced to relocate to Yamhill Valley, which would later become the Grand Ronde Reservation.[32] Describing parts of a widely known story of the removal period told in the Grand Ronde community, Tribal Council member William J. "Wink" Soderberg (Grand Ronde) explains, "Our twenty-seven tribes and bands lived all the way from the California border to southern Washington, and that's where our tribes were gathered from."[33] During the process of removal and relocation, Lewis writes, "the U.S. Army resettled members of some tribes on different reservations in Oregon and Washington, including Grand Ronde, Siletz, Warm Springs, Umatilla, and Yakama."[34] Native nations were often split apart and resettled onto more than one reservation, which added to the disruption of Native communities and has contributed to intertribal contentions concerning claims to treaty retained rights in ceded territories.

Many of the people removed to Grand Ronde were subjected to long walks, often after long and bloody encounters with settler groups organized as volunteers—whose intention was to murder as many Native people as possible and take their lands. For example, Beckham describes a historical account in which Indian Agent George H. Ambrose walked a group of Rogue River and Takelma people from the temporary Table Rock Reservation in southern Oregon to the Grand Ronde and Coast reservations.[35] During this long and arduous march, the group was stalked and terrorized by a settler group led by "self-styled executioner of Indians" Timoleon Love, who shot at and killed at least one man when he was separated from the larger group and attempted to kill more on several other occasions. This forced march spanned thirty-three days, during which the Takelma and Rogues walked 263 miles. At the start of the march there were 325 people, the same as at the end; in the course of the journey "eight people died . . . and eight babies were born."[36]

The Grand Ronde Reservation along the South Yamhill River was established in 1857, pursuant to treaty arrangements and an executive order. Soderberg reflects on the experiences of his ancestors living on the reservation after removal: "You've got to remember, all those tribes, they're different. They've got different customs. They've got different languages. Therein lay the puzzling part of how we were going to get along. Because some of them didn't like each other, and none of us spoke the same language. So how do you communicate? We're all on the same reservation."[37]

In the early years of the reservation, Native nations often remained segregated in separate settlements, according to their tribal affiliation. Lewis asserts that Native people were not allowed to leave the reservation, were under constant threat from settlers, and lacked adequate supplies. Unscrupulous Indian agents were known to have redirected funds and resources, meant for the people imprisoned at Grand Ronde, into their own pockets.[38] These conditions, Lewis argues, kept the Grand Ronde people "in a constant state of stress over their safety and security."[39] Despite the conditions, Native nations at Grand Ronde began to form a collective identity and make use of the land base they still retained.

Grand Ronde people were again subjected to settler encroachment after 1887, when the Dawes Act (or General Allotment Act) was passed. Because of this act, throughout several subsequent decades the collective reservation landholdings of the community were significantly diminished. One rationale for the Dawes Act was that Native people needed to become farmers and own private property like their white neighbors. Allotments scattered the tribal members onto various parcels of land while simultaneously making un-allotted lands available to non-Natives. While not a perfect solution to end this practice of allotting reservation land, in 1936 Grand Ronde voted to confederate and accept an Indian Reorganization Act (IRA) government. This was a major turning point in the development of a unified national identity for Grand Ronde, and under the IRA they adopted a constitution and by-laws modeled after the US government.

Grand Ronde was run by the confederated IRA government until 1954, when the US Congress "terminated" the tribe. Hearings were held on February 15, 1954, before the 83rd Congress, concerning Senate Bill 2746 and House Resolution 7317, which would become Public Law 588, known as the Western Oregon Termination Act. Rhetoric employed to promote the concept of termination to Native nations forwarded the idea that this would free Native people from the federal government and the oversight of Indian agents. However, this "freedom" effectively severed Grand Ronde's government-to-government relationship with the United States, dissolved the tribal government, and broke apart remaining reservation lands that were sold primarily to non-Native land speculators and settlers.

Grand Ronde was one of over sixty western Oregon tribes identified by federal employees and politicians as good candidates for sweeping termination legislation. The factors used to judge a tribe's level of competency and self-sufficiency were typically their similarities to their white neighbors or level of assimilation into white communities.[40] In Oregon, one champion of termination was former governor Douglas McKay, who was the US secretary of the interior at the time and seemed intent on showcasing federal Indian policy in his home state.

The process that led to the termination of western Oregon tribes was dubious at best. E. Morgan Pryse, the area director of Indian affairs for the Portland office of the Bureau of Indian Affairs, was the main person representing western Oregon Indians at the congressional termination hearing in 1954. He provided most of the testimony and submitted documents of support for termination from sources including Native nations in Oregon, judges, attorneys, and Secretary McKay. Pryse's role as a voice for Native people was highly problematic, to say the least, given that Pryse's job had been created specifically to facilitate the termination of Native nations in Oregon.

The documents Pryse submitted as evidence of western Oregon tribes' consent to termination are highly suspect. These consisted of three resolutions passed by the Grand Ronde Business Committee and its document titled *Economic Development Program and Statement of Plans and Policies Which the Grand Ronde Business Committee Proposes to Follow in Conducting Its Credit Activities, Using Rehabilitation Funds Available to the Community*. The economic development plans and one of the resolutions (one that had passed in November 1949) were used to establish that the Grand Ronde community was self-sufficient and economically stable. The other two resolutions (passed in June and August 1951) were used as proof that Grand Ronde had voted to approve federal termination.[41]

Even if the Grand Ronde Business Committee had possessed the authority to speak for the whole nation on this matter, which it appears it did not, the June 1951 resolution states that Grand Ronde wanted their lands to be fee-patented and the supervisory powers of the secretary of the interior terminated. The resolution also illuminates the circumstances under which this vote was taken by recording that only 30 percent of the Grand Ronde population participated, with twenty-five individuals voting against termination and forty-eight voting in favor—hardly a majority of the community.[42] The August 1951 resolution states that "the response from said membership has been reluctance to accept said program of termination and withdrawal, on the grounds that no provision has been made therein to compensate the membership for loss of alleged rights to hunt and fish, believed to have been retained by the Indians when their lands were ceded by them, or when appropriated by the Federal Government without their consent."[43]

The Business Committee's resolution highlights the fact that Grand Ronde people were concerned about protecting hunting and fishing rights and would consent to vote on tribal termination only if the language in Section 7 of the bill was changed to say that "nothing contained in this act shall be construed to deprive any Indian of any hunting, fishing, or other right or privilege under federal law, treaty, or agreement."[44] The final version of the legislation that became Public Law 588 does not include such language, however, or any provision to address hunting and fishing rights. Furthermore, it turns out that all three resolutions were written not in response to S. 2746 and H.R. 7317 but in response to earlier versions of those bills. When responding to questions regarding these discrepancies, Pryse argued that because the resolutions had never been withdrawn from the public record, it should be assumed that their "approval" could transfer to S. 2746 and H.R. 7317. There were no tribal members present at the hearings, yet Pryse defended the situation with reasonable-sounding arguments, saying, "It is not believed the tribes will send delegates to appear before the committee. They approve the bill in principle, are conservative with their funds, and are busy making a living."[45] However, it is likely that many tribal members never heard about the hearings until after they were over.

Jurisdiction over tribal lands was another important issue discussed at the 1954 hearings. Public Law 280, passed the previous year, had transferred jurisdiction over tribal lands from the federal to some state governments, thereby dramatically shifting the way Native nations could exercise their legal authority.[46] Oregon was one of the states that the law mandated to assume jurisdiction over tribal lands. When Senator Arthur Watkins (R-UT) asked Pryse about the State of Oregon's willingness to assume jurisdiction over Native nations, Pryse pointed out the fact that Oregon had assumed jurisdiction over tribal lands in the state some time prior to the passing of Public Law 280: "The State has been more or less assuming that responsibility for some time, a good portion of it, although in reality it was a question of whether the State had legal authority to do so. But, they do now, in a recent act of Congress [referring to Public Law 280]."[47]

Though Pryse acknowledged that there was some question as to whether or not the State of Oregon possessed the legal authority to assume this jurisdiction, for him (and for all in attendance) the matter seemed to be cleared up simply by the passing of Public Law 280 after the fact. And once it was established that Oregon was willing to assume this role without compensation from the federal government, the matter was put to rest.[48] Clearly this raises serious questions about the role of Indian agents in manufacturing tribal consent, the absence of trust protection for Grand Ronde rights and lands, and the problematic process and rationale used to write and administer US Indian policy. Nevertheless, the 83rd Congress passed the Western Oregon Termination Act in August 1954. This single piece of legislation effectively ended the government-to-government relationship between the United States and sixty-one tribes named in the law.[49]

Tribal elder Robert "Bob" P. Tom (Grand Ronde) recalls that "being a terminated Indian at one time was the ugliest thing you could say about somebody. The tribes that weren't terminated looked at tribes that were terminated as selling out and that a terminated Indian was a negative, an ugly word."[50] The period following termination was a devastating time for the people of Grand Ronde. Recalling that period, Soderberg remarks, "I never did understand termination. I always thought it was very unjust. My grandfather had sixty-three acres, a house, a nice barn, and two outbuildings that were in good shape. And they gave him $3,500 for all of that. That was stealing. They terminated our tribe and gave our property to the white man. I'm telling you that they gave our land away. Probably the most harmful thing that has ever happened to this tribe was termination."[51]

Lewis, who conducted research on the termination of Grand Ronde, further explains the impact of termination on the community: "After termination the tribe lost all services and the rights to their land; the land had to be sold out. Many people didn't have a lot of money, they'd been used to living in a system where they didn't have to pay taxes, and they had certain services paid for by the government."[52] After termination, Grand Ronde's landholdings were a mere 2.5 acres.[53] The tribe's economy was destroyed, and Congress declared western Oregon free of Native nations.[54]

Although the termination period was devastating to Grand Ronde and caught some tribal members by surprise, Lewis points out that termination did not occur suddenly. It had been discussed for more than a decade by some members of the tribe. According to Lewis, "Many people decided to move away before it happened because they didn't want to be caught off guard. And so there was a gradual moving away from the tribe even before termination."[55] Some Grand Ronde families had anticipated vastly depleted resources, services, and economic opportunities and made the decision to move to other parts of the country over a period of several years.

A few tribal members, such as elder Leon "Chips" Tom (Grand Ronde), signed up with federally funded relocation programs. In the program, Tom and his family were relocated to Colorado. While Tom felt that relocation was the best option for his family under the circumstances, he was unprepared for life away from Grand Ronde, and he recalled that the program was severely underfunded and participants often left with little support once they relo- cated. Tom and his daughter Kathleen Tom describe their experience with relocation and their return to Grand Ronde:

> Kathleen: People don't talk about relocation, the devastation to families, and how it affected people who were relocated. And when you came back home [to Grand Ronde], things were different. There were people that stayed behind here, who had land or family, and didn't take the opportunity Dad thought [relocation] was. We lost our footing here, at home. We're kind of looked at as outsiders.
>
> Chips: When you say "Native American," we have an image of not being able to cope out there in the public. Well, I have an answer for that: we were rounded up and kept in the bushes while everyone else had the opportu- nity to go to school. Although we're in our own country, our resources were diminished right and left. Then we're supposed to get out in the world and compete with the other cultures, and they're all frowning at you, and they're frowning worse when you're out there trying to do some- thing and you don't have the background or the education to compete.[56]

The testimony of the Toms illuminates the alienating experience felt by Grand Ronde people who left Oregon before and after termination, finding themselves transplanted into strange and even hostile environments. Even when Grand Ronde members moved back home, the effect of termination and relocation was division of families and erosion of tribal cohesion. Reflecting on the policy of termination, Thorsgard points out that it was an "attempt by the federal government to break down tribes and bring them into the fold of the American dominant culture, and it was the last in a bunch of futile attempts to destroy Indian people."[57]

In the 1970s, terminated Native nations from coast to coast began to demand that their government-to-government relationship with the United

States be restored. Shortly after, encouraged by the success of the Siletz Tribe's restoration in 1977, a group of Grand Ronde people gathered for a public meeting at a Grand Ronde bank and voted in favor of working toward restoration.[58] Once it was decided that Grand Ronde wanted to work for restoration, a small handful of community members worked diligently to get the nation restored. They met in a small building where their cemetery was situated—the only land collectively retained after termination. Throughout the late 1970s and early 1980s Grand Ronde members filled out paperwork, held fund-raisers, solicited and received letters of support from all Native nations in Oregon, networked with tribal organizations, and gained the support of US Senator Mark O. Hatfield (R-OR), US Representative Les AuCoin (D-OR), and then lobbyist Elizabeth Furse (who would later become AuCoin's successor). Grand Ronde activists made trips to Washington, DC, to lobby and testify. Tribal elder Kathryn M. Harrison remembered her efforts to get support from other Native nations in Oregon:

> I made up my mind to go to every tribe in Oregon. I thought how nice that would be to say that every tribe supports us. Each time I'd go up worried, saying my prayer, the same one I said all the way through: "Oh, God, help me to say the right thing to help my people." And it always worked. It was the only time I'd be able to tell about my people, so, boy, I'd just pour my heart out. Sometimes I'd tell about the march to Grand Ronde, and I'd have to stop because I'd start crying. I'd have to gain my composure and apologize. One time a young man from one of the tribes came forward afterwards, and he said "I just want to tell you, ma'am, don't apologize for those tears. Those are tears of valor."[59]

Harrison also recalls,

> I had to go to Affiliated Tribes of the Northwest Indians, which consisted of forty-five tribes of the Northwest. And got to talk to the president. I remember sitting down with him before the meeting, and I said, "I wanted to tell you that I'm here to get a letter of support from this organization. I'm scared to death because it seems like when I come into a room full of tribal people, I feel like I have a T-shirt on that says 'Terminated. No land.'" He looked at me and said, "No Indian should feel that way." I said, "Well that's what I'm trying to say. We're trying to get recognized—it's a justice issue." I said, "If we

could get every tribe to come on board and support us, gosh, that would be helping our dream come true." So he said, "Okay, it's on the agenda." Each time I talked I got a little bit stronger.[60]

Harrison remembers that there were times she felt like other Native people were the hardest to convince. Federally recognized tribes sometimes expressed worry about limited federal funding and services, and in some conversations, she says, some Native people accused Grand Ronde of choosing termination, a misconception Harrison tried to correct.[61]

On November 22, 1983, House Resolution 3885 (known as the Grand Ronde Restoration Act) became law, restoring federal recognition status to the Confederated Tribes of Grand Ronde. On September 9, 1988, House Resolution 4143 returned 9,811 acres of land to Grand Ronde—only a small part of what had originally been the Grand Ronde Reservation. Today reservation land is used almost exclusively for timber, recreation, and traditional food and medicine harvesting practices. This land was taken into trust for the Grand Ronde people for their use and economic development, but the Grand Ronde people—like those of many other Native nations—were compelled to give up something important to regain it. The federal government insisted that, in order for the land to be restored, the Grand Ronde people waive their claim to hunting and fishing rights that their ancestors had retained in the treaties of 1855. Grand Ronde leaders agreed to this stipulation, believing that the most important thing for the tribe at that time was to have a land base. Present leaders and members are now working to get these inherent and treaty-retained rights restored.[62]

Illustrative of Grand Ronde's experience, tenacity, and resiliency is the story of Chachalu, or the "place of the burnt timbers." This was the name given to the Grand Ronde Valley by the Yamhill Kalapuya people following a devastating fire that decimated the region prior to the removal era in which many Native peoples were forcibly marched to the valley from their various homes in western Oregon in the mid-nineteenth century. While the fire devastated the bioregion, over time the land was renewed and its life forms revitalized, paralleling the restoration story of the Grand Ronde people.[63] Since restoration the growing tribe has endeavored to build a strong economic base. Some Grand Ronde people returned home, and Grand Ronde opened cultural centers in Portland, Salem, and Eugene for their citizens who live there, away from the reservation.[64] Economic success, primarily in the casino industry, has made it possible for Grand Ronde to provide low-income housing, elder housing, health-care facilities, and a language program that teaches Chinuk Wawa. As this section has shown, Grand Ronde nationhood was targeted for destruction many times, yet, despite intense and violent demands that the Grand Ronde people assimilate, the nation lives and has grown strong again.

WARM SPRINGS: IN IT FOR THE LONG HAUL

The Confederated Tribes of Warm Springs incorporates Wasco, Warm Springs, and Northern Paiute peoples whose historical territory spanned much of the Columbia River and land east of the Cascade Mountains.[65] Wasco, Warm Springs, and Northern Paiute peoples were different culturally, each with unique primary language, customs, and worldviews. Warm Springs people moved over the course of the year between winter and summer camps in the Columbia Plateau near the river, Wascoes lived primarily in permanent villages near the river, and the Northern Paiutes traveled the high desert region of eastern Oregon, following a seasonal itinerary. Both Wasco and Warm Springs people developed an extensive trade network, with communities dotting both sides of the river's length, from where the mouth met the ocean to the upstream connections with the Snake and Deschutes Rivers.[66] Both relied on fishing, hunting, and harvesting as central to their economies.

The Treaty with the Tribes of Middle Oregon (1855) was negotiated between Wasco and Warm Springs leaders and Superintendent of Indian Affairs Joel Palmer. Tribal leaders ceded ten million acres of land to the United States but reserved a 640,000-acre reservation in central Oregon for "exclusive use" by Wasco and Warm Springs peoples. The treaty stipulated that the tribes reserved rights to fish, harvest foods, and hunt game in their "usual and accustomed stations."[67] While the retention of these rights was significant, relocation to the reservation was not easy, and the decision to move there was made with great trepidation and under duress. Adjustment to reservation life was difficult, and many people died from disease, while the traditional tribal economy faltered and the tribes' cultural ways were challenged.[68] As Wasco elder Elijah Miller points out, "Indians made a good living before they were forced onto the reservation, but had hard times there."[69] White settlers destroyed many of the tribes' traditional fishing spots, building fences and erecting fish wheels along the Columbia River to increase their commercial catches.[70] The treaties contain unambiguous evidence of the inherent fishing rights reserved

MAP 2.4. Ceded lands claimed by the Confederated Tribes of Warm Springs

by Native peoples, but private, non-Native land ownership and state-recognized property titles often made their access to usual and accustomed sites "a fictional and distorted thing."[71]

As early as 1865, J. W. Perit Huntington showed gross abuse of his position as superintendent of Indian affairs in Oregon. Huntington did not support Native fishing rights and wanted Warm Springs people confined to the reservation. In Huntington's view, Warm Springs people would spend so much time at the Columbia River fisheries that he would have "no control over his 'wards.'" Indians "infest the towns along the Columbia River," he wrote in one report.[72] Such racist expressions were widespread in the city of The Dalles, located alongside the Columbia. George W. Aguilar Sr. remembered being denied service at a barbershop as late as 1952 and seeing signs that read "no Indians and dogs allowed."[73] Capitalizing on public sentiments against Native peoples, Huntington played on the very rational fears of the Warm Springs tribe and convinced them that written passes issued to prove that they were "good" reservation Indians would benefit them by keeping them from being seen as "hostile" Indians. Garnering seven leaders' signatures on one version of the treaty agreement, Huntington then destroyed the original document, fastening the signatures to a new treaty that he sent to Washington for ratification. In this way he was able to "negotiate the sale of the Indian fishing rights for only $3,500 or $3.50 per Indian person."[74] William Chinook (Wasco) and other Warm Springs leaders fought to have this fraudulent treaty overturned. Though this treaty is widely rejected today as fraudulent, it was nonetheless used to expel Warm Springs members from significant fisheries, exclude them from lawsuits, justify arrests, and deny compensation.[75]

In 1879, an estimated thirty-eight Northern Paiute people were settled on the Warm Springs Reservation by the US government; around seventy more Paiutes relocated there in 1884. This settlement was an uneasy arrangement since the Warm Springs and Northern Paiutes had historical conflicts.[76] Some Paiutes have argued that the Warm Springs Reservation itself is partly located on ancestral territory claimed by the Northern Paiutes.[77] While the three tribes today function as a nation with a unified government, many tribal members strongly affiliate with only one of the three.

From 1871 to 1972 there was contention over the reservation boundaries, which has become known as the McQuinn Strip boundary dispute. In 1871, a surveyor named T. B. Handley found the reservation boundaries to enclose far less land than Warm Springs people knew had been agreed upon in the Treaty of 1855. In 1887, a government surveyor, John A. McQuinn, found that Handley had surveyed the land incorrectly and that the true boundaries were where Warm Springs leaders had claimed them to be. By this time, settlers had moved onto the disputed land, and the government offered the tribe a cash settlement for it. Warm Springs people refused to relinquish their land and instead continued to fight for it. This dispute lasted 101 years, but finally Public Law 92-427 (1972) restored ownership of 61,360 acres to the Warm Springs Reservation.[78]

As was true elsewhere in the United States, Warm Springs cultures, languages, religions, and systems of governance were the targets of various assimilationist projects. Christian missionaries for a number of denominations participated in attempts at assimilation, and boarding schools both on and off the reservation specifically targeted Native children—among the most disturbing of the methods developed to erase tribal worldviews. For example, some of the brightest students were removed from Warm Springs and taken to Chemawa Indian School in Salem, Oregon.[79] This contributed to the undermining of tribal coherence and community wellness.

Another disruption to the fishing economy of Warm Springs occurred in the 1930s with Columbia River dam-building projects, part of President Franklin D. Roosevelt's response to the Great Depression. With the construction of the Bonneville Dam beginning in 1933, just downriver from Cascade Locks, Columbia River tribes were left with many flooded fishing platforms and fisheries. Riverbanks that had "provided game, medicinal herbs and other plants" were also destroyed.[80] In the 1950s, when the Dalles Dam was built, Celilo Falls, a critical tribal fishery upriver, was submerged. Columbia River tribes were devastated by the flooding of their crucial fisheries but did not possess the power to stop the dam projects. Prior to construction of the Dalles Dam, various tribes affected by the damming of the falls made agreements with the Army Corps of Engineers for compensation. The Warm Springs tribes received a total of $4,047.80, which came out to about $145.50 per individual. However, this kind of compensation was woefully inadequate, and the final agreement failed to compensate for the flooding of the Five Miles Rapids site or the Spearhead Fishery, both of which were also destroyed by the Dalles Dam.[81]

In 1937, the Warm Springs tribes voted to confederate under the Indian Reorganization Act, adopting a constitution and by-laws, and officially became known as the Confederated Tribes of Warm Springs Indians. Today's director of governmental affairs Lewis "Louie" E. Pitt Jr. explains how distinct and separate nations and bands that reorganized as confederated peoples (by choice or by circumstance) often saw solidarity as a strategy:

> The confederacy that we have now at Warm Springs was a tool of survival. We were trying to figure out how to work with [settlers], since they're taking everything that we used to live off of. They're taking our lands and our access to those lands. In the thirties, folks had a real challenge to try to figure out "Which way do we go to preserve who we are as a people?" My dad used to tell me about the ends and the means. "Don't think the tribal government as it exists now, that confederacy is the ultimate; that's only the means. The end is our Indian way of life, whatever that be, Warm Springs, Wasco, or Paiute." To me, that really made a wonderful model to work from. This confederacy is a tool for us to figure out how to work together peacefully, and our constitution says we want unanimity in the vote. It presumes kind of a traditional process where everybody gets heard in the longhouse, everybody gets their chance to say something, and in the end, that folks can generally live with that decision that's made for the larger group.[82]

For many Native nations in the United States, an IRA government meant some significant changes to traditional tribal governing practices. While the form and character of an IRA government authorized by each Native nation varied greatly from tribe to tribe, Warm Springs incorporated both traditional and constitutional models in its government. The Warm Springs Tribal Council (an eleven-member body that includes eight elected members who serve three-year terms and three traditional chiefs who serve for life) became the central governing authority of Warm Springs. There are three districts on the reservation, with a chief from each district; the Simnasho (Warm Springs) and Agency (Wasco) Districts each have three elected representatives, and the Seek-seekqua (Paiute) District has two elected representatives.

Conflicts over access to Columbia River fishing sites that remained led to judicial deliberations to determine Native nations' treaty rights to fish. Chief Delvis Heath (Warm Springs) explains the Warm Springs people's connection to the river: "Our people still respect the people that have gone on before, that have led the way to our being here. They didn't want to lose the fishing sites, because that's the way of life of our people. The water, the salmon. Our people lived along the river; they did everything along the river. Everything."[83]

Previous contention regarding access and site locations gave way to the determination of equitable shares of the fish harvested. Yakama tribal attorney Tim Weaver points out that Oregon was managing the fishing areas in a way that allowed non-Native people to catch all of the fish before they reached Native sites.[84] In 1969, Judge Robert C. Belloni (US District Court of Oregon) ruled in *United States v. Oregon* that Indians had a right to a "fair and equitable share" of the Columbia River fish and retained their treaty-reserved right to fish at their usual and accustomed places.[85] "Fair and equitable" was contested until 1974, when Judge George H. Boldt (US District Court of Washington) ruled in *United States v. Washington* that Native nations with reserved rights treaties were entitled to 50 percent of all harvestable fish.[86]

Though deeply affected by settler colonialism, the Warm Springs people have demonstrated, in several important cases, their ability to fend off devastating laws and policies that would transfer reservation lands and jurisdiction to the state.[87] Additionally, Warm Springs was the only Native nation in Oregon exempted from the mandate of Public Law 280, which transferred jurisdictional authority from Indian Country to states, and they were one of only two Oregon tribes that avoided termination in the 1950s.[88] This distinction remains important for understanding how the Warm Springs relationship with the state has been significantly different than the state's relationship with all other Oregon tribes. All criminal and most civil jurisdiction over the lands of the other Oregon tribes was transferred to the state with Public Law 280, laying the groundwork for the termination legislation later in that same decade.

Much of the success of Warm Springs in defending itself against post-1855 land cession and termination can be attributed to strong tribal leadership. Chief Heath remembers conversations that took place in Warm Springs about the policy of termination: "All of us were against termination, because we didn't know what termination meant. Warm Springs people could tell about the lands that were already taken away by the United States; we didn't want to lose any more land. That's all the United States wanted—they wanted the land. The people said the United States can't take more. They're asking us to give it up, and we don't want to do that."[89]

Pitt believes that "those who sought to terminate tribes were unable to attack the unity of the Warm Springs leadership."[90] Tribal member Wendell Jim further explains that "we just had good leaders who were connected to what strong Indian sovereignty truly meant, had good vision, and who could comprehend and foresee this as the best deal for us."[91] The Warm Springs people have never been terminated. They own and administer 99 percent of their reservation, and they maintain their own courts and police force. As Tribal Council Chairman Ron Suppah Sr. notes, "I think that the values of being an Indian have remained fairly well intact here on the Warm Springs Reservation because we still speak our language[s], we still practice our traditions, we still practice our culture, and we still exercise our treaty rights."[92]

The Confederated Tribes of Warms Springs now invest in many economic endeavors though Warm Springs Ventures, including a timber company, Kah-Nee-Ta Resort and Spa, Indian Head Casino, Warm Springs Power and Water Enterprises, and the Museum at Warm Springs. Wasco, Warm Springs, and Northern Paiute people continue to maintain distinct cultural identities, despite the fact that many have intermarried.[93] Although the languages are severely at risk, there are still a few speakers of all three Warm Springs languages: Kiksht (Wasco), Numu (Paiute), and Ichishkiin (Warm Springs). They have endured much, but as tribal member Pitt explains, "We're in it for the long haul. You take care of the waters and the lands, and it'll take care of you. You only take what you need. You think about, some people say, seven generations. Well, it's seven generations both ways."[94] Despite the economic downturn that has plagued the tribe since the 1980s, tribal members are often heard saying that "we are poor, but rich in culture," a testament to Warm Springs people's fortitude and determination to survive as a distinct nation.

COLONIZATION AND DECOLONIZATION

Colonization is an ongoing, unfinished project. Native people struggle to resist the forces of colonization and survive as Native nations. The process that Native nations engage in to restore their land, resources, government, cultural ways of knowing, and right to self-determine their children's future is rightly known as decolonization, which is also an ongoing and unfinished project. The diversity of Grand Ronde and Warm Springs and their unequal treatment by the United States becomes all the more striking when one considers that these two Native nations live within a day's drive away from one another within the boundaries of Oregon.

One must only look at the practice of treaty-making in Oregon to see the discrepancies in tribal experiences with US diplomacy. The treaties made in Oregon between individual tribes and federal agents were not uniformly written, and circumstances surrounding negotiations varied greatly. While the tribes that would become Grand Ronde negotiated several treaties, many of these were never ratified by the US Congress, a political body that was under pressure to make more land in western Oregon available to settlers hungry for the resources of the region. The treaties that finally were ratified lacked the strong reserved rights language that some of the Columbia River tribes have obtained. Further, the Grand Ronde treaties that were ultimately ratified did not explicitly name the location or size of the reservation that the many tribes and bands would retain after they ceded their lands. Meanwhile, the Wasco and Warm Springs tribes successfully negotiated a treaty with reserved rights language and an explicitly designated reservation in central Oregon.

After Native people in Oregon were forcibly relocated to reservations, Grand Ronde people had the difficult task of forging a national identity out of the traumatized survivors of twenty-seven distinct and diverse tribes and bands from western Oregon while simultaneously experiencing ongoing threats from nearby settlers and unscrupulous Indian agents. In contrast, two Warm Springs tribes, the Wasco and Warm Springs peoples, negotiated in 1855 the sole Warm Springs treaty, which was ratified by Congress. After relocation to the reservation, Warm Springs people were fairly isolated from the settler society, with three distinct communities living together. They too had problems with dishonest Indian agents and experienced extreme resistance by the settler society when they tried to exercise their reserved rights to hunt, fish, and harvest in their usual and accustomed places. In the 1950s, the Grand Ronde and Warm Springs experiences with federal Indian policy diverged again, as the Grand Ronde experienced termination, which resulted in the tribe becoming landless but for a few acres. Conversely, Warm Springs was able to successfully defend against the same fate and retained their land base. In the 1980s Grand Ronde joined other terminated tribes seeking to restore their federal recognition status. In regaining this status, Grand Ronde was able to restore a small portion of their original land base.

While Grand Ronde and Warm Springs have some shared experiences, there have been a number of significant events that have made each distinct from the other. The unique events that have formed each tribal community affect the way each perceives and responds to economic opportunities, such as those available through the tribal casino economy. Both Grand Ronde and Warm Springs considered the tribal casino economy in the 1990s, and they did so from dramatically different standpoints, which will be explored in the following chapter. Ultimately community stories of cultural rupture, resistance, and survival have played a key role in how each Native nation has approached this economy and eventually participated in it, and all of this factored into debates over the proposed Bridge of the Gods Casino.

Out of the Blue Someone Said, "Well, Let's Build a Casino"

Eagle was a Klamath man, and he came to the Columbia
River on a sporting expedition—to gamble. At first he won
all the games. . . . After that Eagle lost everything that he
had won and all that he had brought with him. He gambled
off his buckskin dress, his moccasins, arrows, everything.
Then he bet one arm, lost; lost the other arm; bet one leg,
lost; bet the other leg, lost. He lost one whole side of his body,
one eye, one ear, all of one half of himself. Then he played
and lost the other half of his body. His life was now in the
hands of those with whom he gambled. They cut off his head.
Then his people at home discovered where he was and what
had become of him.

—Wasco story, as recounted in Donald M. Hines, *Celilo Tales*

THE DECISION TO ENTER THE GAMING INDUSTRY IS NOT NECESSARILY
an easy one for Native nations. Oral teachings include cautionary tales about
gambling in excess and the potential dangers of living a life out of balance.
Consequently, Indian gaming in Oregon provides hope but also elicits concern.
Native nations that are successful generate income with which they can create
cultural retention programs and language classes and provide health care,
elder services, and greater educational opportunities for their children, and
in some cases they are able to distribute supplementary income to their members. Nonetheless, Native people have expressed concerns over the potential
social ills associated with gambling, including addiction and organized crime,
and others have worried about the financial risks of operating a business of
this kind.

In this chapter, I examine aspects of national debates concerning the tribal casino economy, early histories of tribal casinos in Oregon, and the complex response to the tribal casino economy by Grand Ronde and Warm Springs members. Grand Ronde and Warm Springs were motivated and influenced by distinct needs and concerns as they considered entering into the tribal casino economy. The approach of each nation as they considered, entered, and participated in this economy became central to the debates and divides over the Bridge of the Gods Casino. Contributing to the intertribal conflict that ensued was each tribe's articulation of cultural identity, proximity to Oregon's settler population, experience with termination legislation, historical success in economic endeavors, possession or lack of a substantial land base, and business practices in the tribal casino economy.

"WE HAD TRIED POVERTY FOR 200 YEARS. WE DECIDED TO TRY SOMETHING ELSE."

Oregon tribes are not alone in facing the dilemmas associated with Indian gaming. Nationally, critiques of the gaming industry are visible in Native American scholarship, art, and literature. Rejecting a popular rhetoric, which argues that Native nations' participation in the casino economy is merely an extension of the gambling traditions of Native societies, literary scholar and novelist Gerald R. Vizenor (Anishinaabe) has countered that "pull tabs are not moccasin games and bingo is far from a traditional tribal giveaway to counter materialism."[1] Artist Judith Lowry (Mountain Maidu, Hamawi Band Pit River, and Washo) represents the casino industry as both seductive and destructive in her painting *Jingle, Jingle*, which depicts a Native woman wearing jingles (and not much else) and kneeling in front of a slot machine. Coins from the machine fall from between her spread legs. Many other authors and artists are likewise concerned that casino-owning Native nations are lured by the promise of wealth into an industry that lacks virtue and damages culture. Such concerns have led some Native nations to reject Class III gaming. For others, a high-stakes casino economy is viewed as a powerful tool with which to advance culturally specific projects of self-sufficiency and self-governance.

The tribal gaming economy has its fair share of critics, but there are also many proponents. Director of research for the National Indian Gaming Association (NIGA) Katherine A. Spilde asserts that Indian gaming has mostly been a success story for the Native nations that engage in it.[2] Others note that the tribal casino economy is a means to an important end, a notion highlighted by

Jingle, Jingle, by Judith Lowry

tribal chairman Ray Halbritter (Oneida). Halbritter asserts, "The casino is not a statement of who we are, but only a means to get us to where we want to be. We had tried poverty for 200 years, so we decided to try something else."[3] Public criticism of tribal casinos is often articulated as concern for the danger of Native peoples losing their culture through accumulating wealth, but a countering view is that financial wellness has resulted in increased political and cultural distinctiveness for Native nations who have been successful in the industry.

Research has shown mixed social and cultural effects of gaming. Thomas D. Peacock (Fond du Lac Band of Lake Superior Chippewa) explores the noncommercial costs of Indian gaming in a study conducted on reservations in two Minnesota counties. The study provides insight into polarized communities, with individuals either strongly in favor of gaming or strongly in opposition. Some interviewees raised concerns that gambling could lead to diminishment of social and family life and an increase in addictions. While some envisioned gambling replacing traditional social activities, others thought that gaming would have a positive effect on the collective consciousness, increasing individual self-worth through employment and providing a means for breaking down negative stereotypes. Peacock found that many Indian people hoped that gaming revenues would restore them to a precontact status of stability and self-determination and concluded that the impact of gaming on culture is still to be determined.[4] In any case, as Spilde argues, questions about the impact of gaming on tribal culture should be "left to Indian nations" to address.[5]

External influences, whether from state or federal government, actions of Native nations, or shifts in public opinion in the broader society, also contribute to Native nations' decisions in the casino era. State governments have worked to formally and informally limit gaming expansion, largely to find ways to profit from tribal gaming. States and Native nations must develop and agree on compacts in order for Native nations to operate casinos. These formal agreements outline negotiated limits, including the number and kinds of games allowed, as well as the percentage of profits that are redistributed to the state, directly or through community funds or services. Through compacting negotiations in the 1990s, Oregon governor Barbara Roberts articulated an informal policy of one casino per tribe, located on the reservation. This policy contributed to the discord between Oregon tribes and figured prominently in the debates about the proposed Warm Springs Bridge of the Gods Casino in Cascade Locks alongside the Columbia River.[6]

At the federal level, Supreme Court cases can complicate the tribal casino industry. In 2009 the Court held that the secretary of the interior did not have the authority to take land into trust for Native nations that were federally recognized or acquired land after 1934.[7] The decision in *Carcieri v. Salazar* has been called an "anti-Indian sovereignty" ruling that "put a halt to 75 years of Indian land restoration."[8] The decision led to uncertainty for Native nations that were not federally recognized in 1934 but that have since gained or regained this status. Moreover, it led to conflict between Native nations. Grand Ronde, in their efforts to protect their economic interests, legally challenged the authority of the secretary of the interior to take land into trust for the Cowlitz Indian Tribe of Washington State for the purpose of building a tribal casino, noting that in 1934 the federal government did not formally recognize the Cowlitz Tribe.[9] When decisions of the Court negatively affect Native nations, the nations often seek remedies from the other branches of the federal government to resolve resultant problems. For example, the US Congress is debating the possibility of a "Carcieri fix" that would amend the language in the Indian Reorganization Act in order to reestablish the authority of the secretary of the interior to take lands into trust for Native nations recognized after 1934 (when the IRA was passed).

The tribal casino economy in Oregon has been informed by this history. In the late 1980s and early 1990s, Native communities around the nation learned about the Supreme Court's affirmation of Native nations' rights to operate casinos on their sovereign lands. In 1992 the Cow Creek Band of Umpqua Tribe of Indians was the first Native nation in Oregon to open an Indian gaming facility, locating a bingo hall in Canyonville. Prior to that, the Confederated Tribes of Siletz Indians and the Coquille Indian Tribe had each run small-scale weekly bingo games but had no permanent facilities.[10] Native nations in Oregon had talked among themselves about whether a high-stakes gambling economy was feasible in their state. Don Hamilton of the *Oregonian* reported in 1991 that Native nations in Oregon were paying close attention to "about two dozen tribes across the country that quietly have started developing successful, sometimes multimillion-dollar, businesses."[11]

Once Native nations in Oregon decided to move forward to open casinos, the economic landscape changed swiftly. During 1992, Siletz looked at potential gaming sites in Salem and Troutdale, while Cow Creek negotiated new gaming facilities in Canyonville with then-governor Barbara Roberts. By 1994 six Native nations in Oregon, including Grand Ronde, were actively involved in securing locations for gambling establishments.

MAP 3.1. Tribally owned casinos in Oregon at present

THE WAY TO SPIRIT MOUNTAIN:

GRAND RONDE AND THE CASINO ECONOMY

Opportunities for financial stability for Grand Ronde have often been limited or heavily regulated. As tribal member Wink Soderberg told me, "We had a cemetery, and everything that we did revolved around there because we had nowhere else to go. When we were restored, [Congress] gave us part of our reservation back. Most of it was forestland for our timber. The other three thousand and some acres was all bought back piece-by-piece with money from our casino. The money from our casino went into our programs, endowments, and housing. And later on, the tribe provided per capita [payments] to tribal members."[12]

For almost thirty years, Grand Ronde existed as a terminated tribe without federal recognition from the United States, a status that led to devastation of their land base, economy, and social services. After termination, many Grand Ronde tribal members relocated around the United States for economic survival, and life was often difficult for those who remained in Grand Ronde. Tribal member John Mercier recalls the challenges faced by his community and explains, "Grand Ronde was going through economic hard times. The timber industry was failing, and the loggers weren't working, so Grand Ronde was in a severely depressed economy."[13] Further illustrating the conditions in the community after termination, reporter Foster Church of the *Oregonian* wrote in 1988 that nearly half the families were living below the poverty line and that "unemployment was three times the state average."[14]

After Grand Ronde people organized and succeeded in pursuing the reestablishment of federal recognition as a Native nation, they began to go about the business of rebuilding their community. According to the Grand Ronde Restoration Act (1983), the secretary of the interior was required to negotiate with Grand Ronde leaders regarding the establishment of a reservation.[15] By 1984 Grand Ronde had developed a reservation plan, which they submitted to Congress in 1985. This plan highlighted the goal of Grand Ronde: to regain a reservation to "provide a sufficient land base to establish a 'viable economy' in order to generate revenue." In addition, the plan reasoned that annual revenue from the timber industry would "enable the tribal government to financially respond to the economic, social, health and educational needs of its members."[16]

The need for the reservation went far beyond monetary considerations. The report noted that it was vital to Grand Ronde's well-being as a people and culture to have a "homeland":

> More than just a means of improving the economic health of their community, the re-establishment of a reservation is paramount to the strengthening of their culture, and the reinforcement of not only their Indian identity but their pride in their ancestors.
>
> The Reservation will restore to the Grand Ronde People a portion of their original reservation and will once again give them a voice in determining their future and ensuring that new generations will always have a place where their cultural traditions and values will be preserved in this their homeland.[17]

It wasn't until 1988 that Congress enacted the Grand Ronde Reservation Act, which restored 9,811 acres of Coast Range timberland (that was part of the tribe's original reservation prior to its termination) to the tribe's collective ownership.[18] Though the timber economy was still thriving in Oregon in the early 1980s, Grand Ronde's ability to use this resource was restricted by the land restoration legislation. Framed as a "compromise" with local sawmills, Grand Ronde agreed not to export raw logs overseas or process timber in their own mills for twenty years after the reservation was restored.[19]

Conditions for Grand Ronde were difficult then, and tribal members were generally poor, with severely inadequate economic opportunities. There were paltry services and insufficient and substandard housing, and the tribal government operated out of temporary buildings. Tribal member Reynold L. Leno, who worked for twenty-six years as a logger in the region before serving on the Grand Ronde Tribal Council, points out that his nation relied heavily on grants during that period to provide services and benefits to its membership.[20] Despite limited economic opportunity following restoration, those living at Grand Ronde worked to reconstruct legal, political, and cultural aspects of their nation.

In the early 1990s, Grand Ronde began to consider the gaming economy in earnest after Supreme Court cases opened the door for federally recognized tribes to own gambling establishments on their reservations. Raised in Grand Ronde, John Mercier worked for his nation for several years doing community planning and recalls some of the factors that led Grand Ronde to shift its focus to a Class III casino development: "We knew that the Cow Creeks down by Roseburg had started with a bingo hall, which appeared to be moderately successful. Their chairwoman had actually come to visit us and tell us some of the successes they had. The Grand Ronde tribe at first didn't express any interest in any high-level gaming, but then we were approached by people knowledgeable about the gaming industry and how it was helping tribes. Internally we decided that . . . the higher level of gaming that we have today [was] an opportunity that we just couldn't ignore."[21]

To learn more about the casino economy, tribal leaders visited the successful casino-owning Shakopee Mdewakanton Sioux Community in Minnesota and the Poarch Band of Creek Indians in Alabama.[22] The Shakopee Mdewakanton Sioux, owners of the Mystic Lake Casino, provided consulting services to Grand Ronde. This appears to have contributed to Grand Ronde's choice to finance their own casino instead of hiring a management group. Leno explains, "We were fortunate enough to have a tribal member [Bruce Thomas], and he started it up, and we didn't have to pay out that management cost," which "usually [amounts to] about 20–30 percent of your revenues."[23]

When Grand Ronde members first considered the casino economy, many people expressed complex reactions. The very idea that a cash-poor and land-poor Native nation like Grand Ronde would become the owners of a successful multimillion-dollar casino seemed unbelievable to many Grand Ronde people who had rarely known economic stability as a community. Wink Soderberg laughs a little when he thinks back: "I heard about it over the years as a kind of a joke, because we would never have a casino. We were never going to be rich enough to have something like that. I guess I first heard about Indian casinos in the late eighties. That's when I started hearing little bits about it, and then it just kept evolving as the nineties came in."[24]

Others raised concerns about the moral and ethical implications as well as cultural appropriateness of a gaming economy, the impact of this business on the community, and the financial risks involved. In a conversation about the concerns of the tribe, Tribal Council member Chips Tom and his daughter Kathleen Tom (Grand Ronde) acknowledged that some people were worried about addiction and debt, while others thought that operating a gambling establishment was not culturally appropriate.[25]

A number of tribal members remember being concerned that the broader non-Native society would respond poorly to any Native nation getting into gaming. For example, Chips Tom wondered if his nation would be able to conduct business on a fair playing field without additional scrutiny or regulation directly stemming from the fact that Native people were involved: "Out of the blue one day somebody said, 'Well, let's build a casino.' Well, me being a little bit cautious, I wondered if we were going to have the opportunity to start our own business out there with the other cultures, just like their businesses or their industries. Or if we were going to be looked at like, 'Well, what are you folks trying to do out there?'"[26] The risks seemed to be amplified, considering the history of Native relations with non-Natives in the region. There was no guarantee that this economic venture would be exempt from the dominant society's ongoing attempts to block tribal advancement as it had done in timber and other industries.

Today a number of Grand Ronde tribal members refer to the members of the Tribal Council who made the difficult, smart, and bold decision to enter the casino industry as "visionaries." Soderberg reflects, "You've got to stop and think about those people that were on Tribal Council in those days. A lot of them didn't even have a full elementary education, and yet they were smart enough. They had enough horse sense to know that certain things had to be done, like the endowments that were set up: invaluable. I often wonder, how did they know stuff like that? They had help, I'm sure, but they had enough sense when they heard it, to do it."[27]

Deciding to take the risk to open a casino in rural Grand Ronde was in no way easy for the leadership. A 1993 *Oregonian* article reported that "Mark Mercier, chairman of the Grand Ronde Tribal Council, said the tribes turned to gaming 'after long meetings and painful deliberations' in search for non-timber economic development."[28] Likewise the process of establishing a casino in Grand Ronde was complicated and took several years to negotiate after the Tribal Council had decided to proceed. In 1993 Grand Ronde made a compact with Governor Roberts and planned to open a gaming hall the next year. Plans were stalled when the secretary of the interior denied Grand Ronde's request "on grounds that the [chosen] site was not part of the tribes' reservation."[29] In order to move forward with the development plans, Grand Ronde sought clarification from Congress, and in 1994 Congress passed An Act to Make Certain Technical Corrections, which amended the Grand Ronde Reservation Act and confirmed the reservation status of the land where the tribe planned to build their casino.[30] With this clarification, Grand Ronde was able to move ahead with plans to construct Spirit Mountain Casino, and it was built in 1995.

While many Grand Ronde members tell me that they continue to have qualms about some aspects of the casino economy in their community, they generally feel that it has improved life for tribal members. David G. Lewis explains:

> When I first saw the casino come into Grand Ronde, I thought it would destroy the community and everything would turn towards gambling. In many ways it has. But at the same time it has enabled us to build infrastructure, support tribal government, offer jobs to the tribal people, and . . . to put people through school to do whatever they want to do. When the casino started making money, the tribe started giving per capita payments to tribal members, so we were able to get some money to help pay bills. There was some talk about how other casinos in the East had been taken over by gangs or the mob, and you have to keep certain illegal elements out, and I think we've done a good job with that.[31]

Acknowledging that there have been significant changes in the community as a result of the casino, some troubling and others positive, Lewis notes that many of the problems he initially associated with the gaming economy, like crime and disruption to the community, never manifested.

Although some individuals in Grand Ronde still think that there is too much centering of life around the casino, most believe that the casino business has provided economic and cultural opportunities for tribal members that were unimaginable a few generations earlier. In the words of Soderberg, "Once they got the notion that we could have a casino, then everybody was for having a casino. And it's probably the best thing that ever happened to this tribe . . . I mean, we'd be back there in the same place we were twenty years ago if it wasn't for that."[32]

A stable economy in Grand Ronde has reconnected members, even those who live outside of the immediate region. In 2018 Spirit Mountain is the largest casino in Oregon, and Grand Ronde is the largest Native nation in Oregon, with over five thousand members.[33] It is the closest to both Salem and Portland metro areas with their large populations, and the casino is Polk County's largest employer. Through their Spirit Mountain Community Fund, Grand Ronde annually donates 6 percent of profits earned at the casino to nonprofit and civic organizations in western Oregon, and as of 2017 Grand Ronde had donated over $75 million.[34]

The many nations that would become the Confederated Tribes of Grand Ronde survived horrendous violence before and during the reservation period. As a confederated tribe, Grand Ronde experienced generation after generation of assaults by the settler society that directly labored to remove all that was "Indian" from the people of Grand Ronde, using every possible tool of colonialism. Specifically, the 1950s policy of termination created a situation where many tribal members had to leave their homes to find opportunities elsewhere, which in turn ruptured tribal cohesiveness. Spirit Mountain Casino has given Grand Ronde economic security for the first time in generations, which has in turn improved the cultural and social health of the community. Money earned from the casino pays for government infrastructure, cultural programs, health care, elder services, and many other outstanding programs and services. Casino profits have afforded Grand Ronde tribal members access to higher education, opened doors politically at state and national levels, and given Grand Ronde opportunities to reconnect with culturally significant lands and resources.

TO "KEEP OUR INDIAN WAY OF LIFE":
WARM SPRINGS AND THE CASINO ECONOMY

Conditions at Warm Springs in the early 1990s were significantly different from those at Grand Ronde. Warm Springs had retained all but 1 percent of their original reservation land and had never been subjected to termination laws such as Public Law 280. Tribal member Wendell Jim explains, "We were known for lumber. Hydroelectricity was big on the Deschutes River. Warm Springs used to be known as the Big Dogs in economics. Federally recognized tribes from the United States, First Nations from Canada, and other sovereign nations from around the globe would travel to Warm Springs just to come and look at our model, look at our economy."[35] Throughout the 1970s, 1980s, and early 1990s, Warm Springs was nationally known as an economically and politically powerful Native nation with a stable government. Much of their strength came from a land base of 640,000 acres, much of it consisting of commercial timberland. The *Oregonian* in 1991 described Warm Springs as "one of the most economically successful tribes in the United States. The tribe employs 1,400 people in several operations including a resort, a lumber mill and a hydroelectric plant."[36] Together these factors help contextualize how Warm Springs entered the casino era.

Some people at Warm Springs were talking about the option of a formal gaming economy even before the Indian Gaming Regulatory Act (IGRA) passed in 1988. Tribal elder Faye C. Wahenika recalls that discussion of a possible casino at Warm Springs began as early as 1972. Wahenika worked at Kah-Nee-Ta, the Warm Springs resort and hotel, and remembers when its manager held a meeting there: "One day Ed Mannion said, 'Well, you know, we could have a casino on the reservation.' And I said, 'Well, isn't it illegal to have a casino?' He said, 'No, not on an Indian reservation. We could have anything.'" Wahenika notes that the idea didn't gain much traction in the 1970s and early 1980s: "We didn't talk too much about the casino. Every now and then it would sneak in, and we'd wonder how would it go, or where would we set it, how would we set it, what would be our return, or how would it be accepted—there were a lot of questions."[37] Though Warm Springs didn't pursue gaming in the 1970s or 1980s, Warm Springs members were already conceptualizing the scope of their sovereignty as it would apply to gaming.

Warm Springs members learned about Indian gaming and the casino economy as Native nations around the United States opened their high-stakes gaming operations. Tribal member Gerald J. Danzuka Jr. heard about this new opportunity while attending college, and he specifically notes that it was California Native nations' involvement with the casino economy that first caught his attention. Later Danzuka worked in legal aid for his community, and he recalls becoming acquainted with the possibility of Warm Springs getting into the gaming economy: "I would go to different trainings and would hear people asking, 'Well, what do you think about gaming or gambling in general?' The discussion really was about 'Is gambling bad for you? Does it create dependence?

Is it addictive? Does it create more problems than not?' And I said, 'Well, I don't know whether it does or not. I do know gambling has been around our people for a long time, because we've participated in things like stick game.'"[38]

Though Warm Springs was widely seen to be more economically stable than other Native nations in the early 1990s when conversations about gaming began, Danzuka thinks that this would nonetheless have been the best time to diversify the tribal economic portfolio: "I think our financial condition in Warm Springs was good to very good. We had decent timber revenues. Although I think times were good, I felt like it was more important for the tribes to diversify and not rely on timber, because the times were good. I felt like that was when we should have been looking at other sources of revenue."[39] Danzuka's statements reflect conversations taking place in many tribal communities grappling with the idea of a casino that would provide economic development.

Despite the fact that some members wanted Warm Springs to consider the gaming economy in the late 1980s, Warm Springs leaders expressed very little interest when they were first approached by the Bureau of Indian Affairs (BIA). Louie E. Pitt Jr. remembers the response from the Tribal Council when this opportunity was first presented: "When the BIA asked, 'Well, you've got the right to have some lands set aside in trust, are you interested in Indian gaming lands that could be for a casino?' 'No,' was the answer that came from Warm Springs."[40]

Tribal Chair Ron Suppah Sr. recalls, "Our tribe was pretty much late in the game, simply because we didn't understand the industry very well, and our people were a little bit afraid to go into something such as gambling."[41] In just a few years, however, the economic circumstances of Warm Springs changed dramatically. By 1994 the *Oregonian* was reporting that, due to a "drastic decline in timber revenue," Warm Springs had, "cautiously," entered into discussions about a casino economy.[42] With large reductions to their annual income, tribal leaders became understandably concerned and more open to getting into the casino business.

Warm Springs people have expressed strong and mixed feelings about the casino economy. Jody Calica, who worked for the Tribal Council for more than thirty years, says, "I heard about it in the late eighties when the tribe started talking about getting into gaming. I heard a lot of success stories, so I think a lot of people became attracted to the idea of gaming. However, there was also a fair amount of hesitation here in Warm Springs about getting into gaming."[43]

Calica identifies three primary concerns that his community had about the tribal casino economy. First, people wondered whether that economy was in line with the beliefs and values of the community. Second, they were concerned about the stereotypes associated with gaming and speculated that Oregon might end up looking like Las Vegas or Reno. Third, they worried about the impact of a gambling economy on their own people, including gambling addiction, alcohol and drug addiction, and other negative effects on families.

As the economies that had supported Warm Springs faltered, tribal leaders began to educate themselves on the laws that regulated Indian gaming and the operating systems of the business in order to formulate the best plan possible for moving forward with opening a casino on the reservation. Chief Delvis Heath Sr. recalls this change from a leadership standpoint: "Our timber revenues were going down. We had to look for something else. Since we are so far away from major cities, we didn't think the casino would work. We thought, 'It won't help us.' But then we decided that we could temporarily try it. We asked the people if they wanted to build it to fund education. So we would have a way to educate our people."[44]

In 1994 Warm Springs leaders surveyed tribal members and asked them if they believed that a gaming enterprise would be "an acceptable form of economic development." Although there were only 341 responses out of 1,800 eligible members of voting age, 78 percent of those responses were favorable to a gaming enterprise in Warm Springs, with half indicating that they would want it located at the Kah-Nee-Ta Resort.[45] Suppah remembers, "The council at that time made a determination that we were going to assemble a three-member point team. Their charge was to go and visit other tribes, other casinos, even public casinos, maybe Vegas or Reno and things like that, to see what might be the potential."[46]

This team, composed of Tribal Council members Jacob Frank Sr., Joe Moses, and Warren "Rudy" Clements, was given the task of gathering information by visiting tribes with casinos such as Mystic Lake in Minnesota. As Pitt points out, "Warm Springs is known for its methodical, cautious approach to new things." However, he laughs a little when remembering how fast Warm Springs proceeded into gaming once they decided to take the opportunity: "I still got the tire marks on my back after that. Once the leadership felt it was safe, within years we were talking very serious about gambling. But we're going to do it our way!"[47] More generally, Pitt states, "We are Warm Springers. We are going to look at it for ourselves. We are going to look down the road to see which way we're headed and what we need to keep our Indian way of life. We need to keep our community going as an Indian people, while being consistent with our values from the past."[48]

Warm Springs tribal attorney Dennis C. Karnopp explains that when tribal leaders began to seriously consider entering into the gaming industry, the issue needed to be voted on again by the people.[49] In Article VI of the Warm Springs constitution and by-laws there is a provision that says, "Whenever a matter of great importance comes before the Tribal Council, the councilmen shall, by resolution duly passed, submit the matter to the vote of the people."[50] Tribal Chair Suppah remembers, "The Warm Springs casino was placed before the people in a tribal referendum. I did vote in support of it because there was a sunset clause contained in the compact. Basically this meant, 'We don't know if this is really a good idea for Warm Springs, so for five years we'll allow the casino to be, to exist, but after five years there needs to be a follow-up referendum to decide, *Now what?*'"[51]

The Warm Springs people voted in 1994, with 606 in favor and 229 against, to establish a casino on the reservation at their Kah-Nee-Ta Resort, which already had infrastructure to support this new business in a temporary facility.[52] The tribal vote also approved a sunset clause, which extended the authority to run the casino on the reservation for only five years. After five years, the people would again have to vote on whether Warm Springs would stay in the casino business, following an assessment of the costs and benefits of the casino according to two major criteria: first, the casino would need to generate a projected amount of revenue; second, it would be determined whether there were any "significant negative impacts on the community."[53] Expectations for revenue generations were modest. A study ordered by the tribe showed that a small casino at Kah-Nee-Ta could generate $3–6 million in profits annually.[54] According to Karnopp, the figure was this small in part because the casino would be located fourteen miles off the nearest through road, US 26.[55]

As these perspectives highlight, participation in the casino economy was not a foregone conclusion for the Warm Springs people. Not only were there concerns about social ills, but also some tribal members noted that there were many practical and logistical considerations to address. For instance, Wahenika explains that in order to successfully operate a casino, tribal members had to be taught new skills and receive extensive training: "Every now and then they'd talk about, 'Well this tribe is going to build a casino. If they're going to build a casino we could have built one long before them.' Other reservations were looking into it. I began to hear and wonder, 'Well, if we build a casino, we'll have to train people on how to repair machines. They'd have to learn how to deal, and what would be the hours, and where do you get profit to run the thing?' There are a lot of things that to me are still unanswered, I still don't know."[56] Wahenika expresses uncertainty about how successful a casino would be at providing good jobs for tribal members if they failed to receive the training needed to fill the better-paying jobs, which required particular skills.

Once it was decided that Warm Springs would pursue opening a casino on the reservation, tribal leaders and their lawyers had to work quickly with Governor Roberts to make a state-tribal compact before her term ended. This sense of urgency was driven in part by the fact that other Native nations in Oregon had already made compacts with Roberts, so Warm Springs leaders felt that they knew what to expect when negotiating with her. In contrast, it was anyone's guess what the next governor's position on Indian gaming would be. However, the fact that other Native nations in Oregon had negotiated compacts before Warm Springs affected the outcome of the negotiations. Tribal member Aurolyn Stwyer, who was gaming consultant (and later general manager) for the Warm Springs Indian Head Casino, recalls, "We took a number of trips to Salem and met with Governor Roberts's staff to discuss the components of our state-tribal compact agreement. Unfortunately, we were the third tribe to have a casino in Oregon, so there was already a cookie-cutter state-tribal compact in place. We had a difficult time diverging from the other compacts that were already reached with the State of Oregon."[57]

Warm Springs officially entered into a compact with the State of Oregon on January 6, 1995. Significantly, the compact included a provision that would allow Warm Springs to move the casino to another location on the reservation in the future. That provision reads as follows:

> If the Tribes elect to conduct gaming at the Kah-Nee-Ta Facility first, they agree to discontinue gaming at that facility before opening a Permanent Gaming Facility at another location.
>
> 1. The Kah-Nee-Ta Facility authorized under this Compact shall be located on the Warm Springs Indian Reservation at the site of Kah-Nee-Ta Lodge.
>
> 2. The Permanent Gaming Facility shall be located on Indian lands that qualify for Class III Gaming under 25 USC §2701 *et seq.* within the boundaries of the Warm Springs Indian Reservation at a site, other than the Kah-Nee-Ta Lodge, to be designated by the Tribes.[58]

Once the Kah-Nee-Ta casino was running, many of the community's fears diminished. Though some people note that there was an increase in the time that tribal members spent gambling because of the new casino, many of the social ills feared by members never materialized.

In 1999, tribal members formally voted in a referendum on whether to continue with the casino economy. This referendum passed easily, with the majority voting for the continuation of the casino. Warm Springs attorney Karnopp remembers that this referendum passed with more popularity than the first because Warm Springs people had by then seen the casino bring revenue into the community: "It's my belief that the people of Warm Springs, the vast majority, didn't see it as a negative thing. They saw it as a positive thing to produce revenue and improve the economy and to provide jobs."[59]

However, several Warm Springs members I interviewed told me that they had voted against Warm Springs opening a casino at any location. One was Wendell Jim: "Casinos—I don't like them, because it has changed Indian Country. It's fast money; it's like drugs. But one thing about casinos, those more successful tribes are trying to re-buy or purchase their lands back. They're building museums and trying to learn the cultures that were lost. So in a positive way they're trying to repurchase or re-buy what was lost."[60] Other interviewees disclosed that casinos went against their personal values, and they articulated serious concerns about addiction. Another pointed out that quick money had created problems for other Native nations. At the same time, all these individuals acknowledged that they could also see the potential benefits that casino profits would fund.

The location at Kah-Nee-Ta was not considered the best long-term location for the Warm Springs casino, however. Chairman Suppah says, "The casino at Kah-Nee-Ta started off fairly well. We were maybe making about five million dollars a year annually for the general fund. That paid for some governmental services, but since then it has dropped off. It's kind of a downward trend right now. I think that's part of the reason that we decided to look for an alternative location that would ensure a better return on our investment."[61]

Warm Springs considered their options in the tribal casino business. Another point team was put together, this time to assess and evaluate other possible locations for a Warm Springs casino after the five-year initial period. Studies showed that building a casino at another location on the historic reservation (the contiguous reservation lands in central Oregon reserved by Native nations in the Treaty of Middle Oregon) was not going to generate the revenue Warm Springs needed. According to Karnopp, two major findings of the studies were that the remoteness of Warms Springs, even though it is along

US 26, limited the number of potential patrons who would visit the casino and that there was very little infrastructure to support the building of a casino on the reservation. Once Warm Springs ruled out locations on their reservation, they began to explore viable locations on eligible trust lands outside of the reservation.[62] One of the most attractive parcels of land Warm Springs owned was forty acres located just east of Hood River, Oregon.[63]

As early as 1998, Warm Springs had begun to gauge public response to the possibility of a tribal casino on their Hood River trust land. The suggestion that Warm Springs might build near Hood River was met with high levels of public resistance, foretelling the struggle Warm Springs would face in trying to situate a casino at Cascade Locks. Initial disapproval came from the Hood River community as well as mainstream media. For example, the *Oregonian* editorialized, "The casino shouldn't go there. That property lies in a place too beautiful, too unspoiled, too important, to mar with a 75,000-square-foot casino, acres of blacktop and thousands of cars and motor homes."[64] By November 1998, signs could be seen in Hood River: "No Casino."[65] Some opposed to the location pointed out that the land was within the boundaries of the Columbia River Gorge National Scenic Area Act.[66] They argued that the site was far too environmentally sensitive for such development and that building a casino would negatively affect the beauty of the area, which would not be in line with community values, and they said it would bring social ills to the region.[67] Though Warm Springs did take into consideration environmental concerns regarding their Hood River trust lands, tribal leaders believed that the lands were exempt from the provisions of the Scenic Area Act due to their trust status.[68]

Warm Springs leaders held a series of formal meetings to inform local communities of the tribe's intentions to build on the Hood River site. As a participant in those meetings, Karnopp recalls that they received intensely negative reactions: "We ran into a buzz saw in the City of Hood River over that casino. The first couple of public meetings we went to reminded me of the hearings during the early years of the fish litigation, where there were demonstrators with signs that said, 'Save a Salmon, Spear an Indian.' We really ran into a buzz saw."[69] Karnopp refers back to 1960s and 1970s anti-Native protests by non-Native commercial and sport fishers when Columbia River tribes fought for their treaty-reserved rights to fish.[70]

During late 1998, non-Native residents from Cascade Locks who had attended some of the public meetings in Hood River invited Warm Springs to consider their community as a location for the new casino. Like Warm Springs, Cascade Locks was attempting to reverse an economic downturn as a result of the dwindling timber economy. While not everyone in Cascade Locks was open to the idea of a casino being built there, Karnopp describes the majority of the Cascade Locks community as welcoming the project.[71]

The themes discussed above and the perspectives shared by Grand Ronde and Warm Springs members and their employees do not tell the whole story of the tribal casino economy in Oregon or even the full span of Grand Ronde and Warm Springs perspectives on these topics. Native nations are not single-minded. However, the Grand Ronde and Warm Springs people I interviewed provide a broad understanding of their tribes' histories, rights, and experiences in the casino era, and a picture of multifaceted and complex communities begins to form. Falling under the designation of tribe or Native nation in contemporary confederated form, both Grand Ronde and Warm Springs have within them multiple cultural communities, religious affiliations, and worldviews that coexist even as they differ. Despite the differences, however, there can also be cohesion, with shared identity and shared visions. Even after the community values of a tribe seem to have led to consensus on a particular topic, this can reflect uneasy arrangements, compromises, and even acquiescence. Like other communities and nations worldwide, Native nations are made up of individuals who have thoughtful debates and vying political and family affiliations. They struggle over differences of opinion and dream beyond present circumstances.

Tribal Casino Discourse

"Who Tells the Story Is a Mighty Piece of Information"

> Self-representation was almost unheard of, stereotypes and
> biases were bleeding into American culture freely. So *who* tells
> a story is a mighty piece of information for the listeners; you
> must know what that storyteller has at stake. Demanding to
> know who is telling your story means asking, "Who is invent-
> ing me, for what purpose, with what intentions?"
>
> —Deborah A. Miranda, *Bad Indians: A Tribal Memoir*

THIS CHAPTER EXPLORES THE EMERGENCE OF A TRIBAL CASINO DIS-
course in the United States, the ways that images and narratives of Native
people and Native nations are shaped within this discourse, and the manifestation of this discourse in Oregon, specifically as it relates to the proposed Bridge
of the Gods Columbia River Resort Casino and tribal relations in the state.[1] A
discourse analysis of more than two decades of journalism in the *Oregonian*
highlights moments that shaped both Native and non-Native people's views
of the participation of Native nations in Oregon in the tribal casino economy,
looking specifically at how the Confederated Tribes of Grand Ronde and the
Confederated Tribes of Warm Springs are framed in this discourse.[2] Following
Deborah A. Miranda, I ask: who is telling the story of the tribal casino economy,
and with what intentions?

When it comes to the tribal casino economy, the public is exposed frequently to fixed images, stories, and narratives. These powerful representations of the casino economy have the ability to affect policy debates and legal
outcomes. Political scientists Jeff Corntassel (Cherokee) and Richard C. Witmer II explain that "distorted images of indigenous people are pervasive in
the United States. One can readily see Natives depicted on products ranging

from butter to chewing tobacco. These are not harmless depictions. Manufac-
tured images of the bloodthirsty savage, the noble savage, the childlike Indian,
the spirit guide, the militant protestor, and, now, the rich Indian that reduce
indigenous peoples to one-dimensional stereotypes have become embedded
in U.S. educational and governmental policymaking institutions."[3]

These stereotypes affect how the larger non-Native public understands
the contemporary issues facing Native people. Since the late 1980s, one of the
most heated public debates regarding Indian Country has entailed the tribal
casino economy. Everyone has an opinion on tribal gaming, and views range
dramatically. For some, the tribal casino economy represents a profound irony
and is a turn of events that might work in small ways to make amends for the
violence of colonization. For others, the casino economy raises concern over the
corrupting influences of capitalism and this economic system's potential threat
to "authentic" tribal cultures. A few articulate their belief that the casino economy is a manifestation of Native nations' special and undeserved privileges.
Still others fret that the casino economy will invite addiction and crime into
Indian Country and surrounding communities. These represent just a few of
the strong opinions held by the general public concerning the tribal casinos.

While the general public has much to say about this issue, most non-Native
and some Native people understand little about Native nations' histories,
rights, and contemporary politics, including the complex milieu that gave rise
to tribal casinos and the contemporary regional manifestations of this economy. As Walter R. Echo-Hawk articulates, there is a scarcity of accurate information available to the mainstream public: "Most Americans have never met
or talked to an Indian, have never been on an Indian reservation, and know
very little about Native Americans in general. . . . Shortly after dining with the
Pilgrims, the Indians often disappear from schoolbooks or become a sidebar
when necessary to tell the story of popular American heroes, like Andrew
Jackson or Lewis and Clark—a role not unlike that of the Lone Ranger's side-
kick, Tonto." Echo-Hawk concludes that the "widespread lack of reliable information about Native issues is the most pressing problem confronting Native
Americans in the United States today."[4]

Public conceptions—or rather misconceptions—of Indigenous peoples
have played a central role in the process of colonization. For generations, popular cultural texts and imagery have been created to describe "Indianness,"
casting Native people in wide-ranging but always one-dimensional roles as
savages (noble or not), heathens, wards, drunks, and mystics, to name just a
few stereotypes.[5] The power of Indian imagery prompted C. N. Gorman

Museum curator Veronica Passalacqua to state that photography is "one of the most pervasive and effective weapons of colonialism."[6] Professor of law Rennard Strickland (Osage/Cherokee) maintains that media-promulgated images of "the Indian" can "profoundly impact every aspect of contemporary American Indian policy and shape both the general cultural view of the Indian as well as Indian self-image."[7] Visual literatures including Hollywood movies construct colonial logics that rework the realities of Native life into fantasies maintained by the dominant society.[8] As anthropologist Jessica R. Cattelino notes, "Images of indigenous peoples long have been central to how settlers imagine and play out their nationalized politics and culture."[9] These "fantasies" often depict unresolved anxieties of a settler society that has yet to come to terms with its colonial past.[10]

While not replacing these old stereotypes, new depictions of casino-owning rich Indians entered the national media landscape in the 1990s.[11] Since then, the tribal casino economy has been examined, debated, and otherwise represented in film, television, newspapers, and other cultural texts that are popularly consumed, thereby controlling how the story of tribal casinos is told, shaping popular perceptions of Native people, and, by extension, influencing policies and laws that regulate Native people's lives. Native people are among the consumers of this discourse and participate in it, sometimes using it to influence political outcomes. However, while Native people contribute their perspectives and opinions to national and local conversations on the tribal casino economy, they are rarely in control of how the story of Native nations' participation in the gaming economy is told.

What the public know or (think they know) about Native peoples makes a difference, whether the topic is the myth of the "discovery" of the Americas by Christopher Columbus, the reserved-rights language embedded in treaties, or tribal casinos. As Europeans and Indigenous peoples encountered each other in the sixteenth and seventeenth centuries, the notion of the Indian was drawn, etched, painted—and distorted—for a European public back home.[12] Public excitement and support fueled the push for global exploration and the possibility of new resources to enrich the competing monarchies of England, Spain, Portugal, and France. This enthusiasm was coupled with an unhealthy dose of fascination and fear at the very thought of non-Christian "others" who lived, it was imagined, without God or civilization. Far from simply manifesting a benign curiosity, these representations contributed to ideological perspectives globally, and they functioned to justify worldwide land dispossession, the transatlantic slave trade, ethnocide, and genocide.[13]

In the eighteenth century, the United States was a fledgling settler state looking to justify its takings of Native peoples' lands and lives. Ideas were developed about rights, civilization, morality, and race that served as justifications for the abridgment of Native peoples' sovereignty by the US government and its citizens. In his book *Like a Loaded Weapon: The Rehnquist Court, Indian Rights, and the Legal History of Racism in America*, Robert A. Williams Jr. (Lumbee) describes the language of inferiority embedded in federal Indian law, just as Echo-Hawk explains that colonial nations created mythological arguments or legal fictions that became the basis of federal Indian law and policy.[14] From the first contact onward, European nations produced records of their observations of Native nations, contributing to ideological justifications for Manifest Destiny, white supremacy, and other forms of domination and violence against Native people. Historian James J. Rawls contends that imagery created about Native people by non-Native people was not static but changed over time and that "the engine in this evolution of attitudes and images was the changing needs of the white observer."[15] Along with Rawls and other scholars, Corntassel and Witmer argue that there is a well-documented history of "invented images" of Indians that have directly contributed to popular perceptions of Indigenous peoples and influenced laws and policies "from the colonial period to present."[16]

As Corntassel and Witmer assert, "Among these images and social constructions of indigenous peoples, the legal fiction of the 'Doctrine of Discovery' is probably the most notorious example of a colonial stereotype used to establish official policy."[17] When Chief Justice John Marshall articulated this doctrine in *Johnson v. M'Intosh* (1823), he rationalized that the United States held absolute title to America, while Native nations were merely occupants on the land. His argument drew from invented images of Indians, framing them as savages and uncivilized heathens, and applied religious justifications for Christians to dispossess non-Christians of land. Thus, "heathens lack[ed] property rights," as Echo-Hawk sums up, and "the discovery of Indian land by Europeans operates to transfer legal title from the Indians to the [US] government."[18]

Prevailing images of Indians have changed over the years in correlation with federal Indian policies. As Corntassel and Witmer write, "Historical patterns suggest that every twenty years or so a new U.S. policy shift emerges that attempts to eliminate indigenous nations altogether or to assimilate Native peoples into the U.S. System." Drawing from previously conducted studies on the correlation between popular Indian imagery, federal policy, and federal Indian law, Corntassel and Witmer link these policy shifts with changes in the "dominant images and social constructions of indigenous peoples."[19]

From the 1830s onward, Native people were widely depicted as war-making savages, a notion that helped justify the financing of wars with Native nations and provided the rationalization behind the Indian Removal Act of 1830. Imagery that showed Indians as simultaneously savages and wards in need of protection became pervasive from the 1850s through the 1870s, when the federal government was under significant pressure to clear lands for American settlers, which contributed to the rationale for making treaties and creating reservations. The continuation of imagery that portrayed Indians as wards and children, in need of European tutelage, correlated with the federal policy of assimilation from the 1870s through the 1930s and the development of laws such as the 1887 General Allotment Act (Dawes Act), which led to more alienation of Native nations' lands.

In the 1930s, Commissioner of Indian Affairs John Collier, promoting the ideology of cultural pluralism, relied on imagery of the "noble savage" to gain support for the Indian Reorganization Act (IRA). This legislation was meant to strengthen a romanticized version of tribalism and put governing power back into the hands of Native nations. When reorganization didn't resolve the US "Indian problem" quickly enough, termination legislation, beginning in 1953 and extending into the 1960s, was supported by imagery of Indians as noble savages and US patriots in need of emancipation from federal oversight.[20] In response to the Red Power movement of the 1960s and 1970s, Native people were portrayed as militant protesters, spirit guides, and environmental stewards, paralleling an era of self-determination and the creation of legislation such as the 1975 Indian Self-Determination Act.[21] Although popular imagery representing Native people has thus changed over the years, "the primary premise of that imagery is the deficiency of the Indian as compared to the White," Corntassel and Witmer assert.[22] Whether stereotypes are essentializing or reductionist, law, politics, and society professor Renée Ann Cramer writes, "Racism is a matter of power—the power to include or exclude, the power to stereotype and set apart, and the lack of power to resist the separation and stereotyping."[23] Although essentializing and reductionist stereotypes continue in the casino era, new depictions of "casino Indians" and "rich Indians" became pervasive additions to the stereotypes.

Like other topics that spark the public imagination, the tribal casino economy eventually made it to prime-time television. In 2000, twelve years after the passing of the Indian Gaming Regulatory Act (IGRA), the *Simpsons* episode "Bart to the Future" aired, and the "casino Indian" entered the public consciousness.[24] The creators of this episode were not concerned, of course, with an in-depth examination of the tribal casino economy. Rather, humor was intended to derive from the very idea of rich Indians, Indians who own casinos. After being thwarted by mosquitoes on a family camping trip to Larva Lake, the Simpson family spies an Indian casino. Homer cries "God bless Native America!" and reroutes their trip, passing a billboard that shows a teepee, a mechanical waving cowboy, and the words "Caesar's Pow-wow / Now Appearing: Carrot Scalp." After the Simpsons are out of view, the cowboy tips over at the waist, exposing three arrows lodged in his back. As this occurs, a caricature of an Indian (like the Cleveland Indians mascot Chief Wahoo), with a single feather and headband, peeks out from behind the teepee with a huge grin on his face and holding a bow and arrow. The message is clear: casinos are Indians' way of getting back at the "white man" for the wrong he has done to the Indian.

Stereotypical ideas about Indians are reflected and propagated in this *Simpsons* episode. Upon entering the casino's sliding front doors, Homer and Bart are stopped by a security guard who bars Bart's entrance because he is a minor. Homer kneels down to Bart's level and says, "Although they seem strange to us, we must respect the ways of the Indians." Homer then proceeds to dance his way past the guard, singing "Hi-How-Are-Ya, Hi-How-Are-Ya" to a mock Indian tune, imitating halting powwow dance moves as he passes people playing blackjack and feeding slot machines.[25] When Bart tries to sneak into the casino, he is promptly caught by security guards and tossed into a room full of a hodgepodge of Indian items, such as Southwest pottery, a dream catcher, images of Kokopelli, a huge buffalo nickel, a hand drum, a picture of a tomahawk, woven rugs, baskets, and a buffalo skull. In conjunction with the notion that the Simpsons are everywhere at all times (aided by the generic name of the Simpson family's hometown, Springfield), it is fitting that there is a hodgepodge of Indianness represented in this room. The mishmash of Indian things exactly reflects the views of an uninformed public who do not see differences between Native peoples. The nicely dressed and bolo-tie-wearing (but unnamed) casino manager who has to deal with Bart's misbehavior speaks halting English and says things like "Your linen service has broken many promises to us, laundry bill soar like eagle." The many such examples that appear in this episode reflect commonly assimilated tropes and frames of reference that have persisted as part of the public imagining of Native peoples, most recently through the prism of the tribal casino economy.

The pairing of Indians and casinos has been, and continues to be, a strange juxtaposition for many. In *Indians in Unexpected Places,* Philip J. Deloria (Dakota Sioux) describes the spontaneous laughter he evokes when he shows people a picture of a Native woman in full regalia getting her nails done at a hair salon.[26] The humor derives from the seeming unnaturalness of the pairing: a Native woman, who is supposed to represent the past, in a beauty parlor, which represents modernity. Deloria notes that the laughter says more about the viewers' misinformed or skewed perceptions concerning Native people than about the picture itself. He argues that the general public has expectations when they imagine Indians and that images that place Indians outside of these expectations are viewed as anomalies.

After 2000, other television comedies began to include story lines about casino-owning Indians. One notable example is the 2003 episode of *South Park* entitled "Red Man's Greed," a play on the notion of white greed.[27] In this story, wealthy casino-owning Indians want to buy South Park, demolish it, and build a superhighway so that they can continue to increase their profits, without regard for the people of South Park. The episode is meant to be ironic, an inversion of events: now Native people are the ones who are powerful and greedy for land. Now they are the ones who heartlessly want to dispossess the South Park residents from their land and homes. In her book *High Stakes: Florida Seminole Gaming and Sovereignty,* Cattelino points out that this *South Park* episode merely offers a reversal of the stereotypical roles of Indians and whites, a reversal that "simultaneously call[s] attention to the colonization of Native America and problematically render[s] this past as something *of* the past by drawing a historically equalizing parallel between it and Indian casino power over small-town white Americans."[28] In comedic portrayals of casino Indians, the tribal casino economy is often portrayed as a form of justice or revenge for historical wrongs done to Indians, while it simultaneously works to absolve the settler society of having to take responsibility for the violent history of colonization and its ongoing manifestations.

In more recent television drama representations of the casino Indian, the message has changed. More disturbingly, popularly produced and consumed stories of the casino Indian increasingly question the ethics, legitimacy, capability, and authenticity of Native nations participating in the casino economy. For example, in a 2010 episode of *The Glades,* homicide detective Jim Longworth is dispatched to the Seminole Indian Reservation in response to a murder of a tribal leader at the tribe's casino.[29] As the story unfolds, it becomes clear that the Seminole Tribe is embroiled in conflicts over money, and unscrupulous white men are taking advantage of tribal leaders. In order to circumvent tribal jurisdiction, Longworth lies about the victim's time of death long enough to get her body off the reservation and back into state jurisdiction, where he presumes the case will be handled more properly than it would have been by tribal authorities. Despite the fact that the Seminole Tribe has a successful business, maintains their own tribal police force, and provides numerous opportunities to tribal members, the narrative works to propagate the impression that casino money has corrupted the tribe and that tribal police are easily fooled and therefore lack the competency to run their own affairs.

In 2011, *The Killing* introduced the character of Chief Nicole Jackson, and the tribal casino discourse took a turn towards the bizarre. Chief Jackson is both the feared totalitarian leader of the fictional Kalimish Tribe located on a Puget Sound island and the executive officer of the Wapi Eagle Casino, where she accumulates wealth by stealing from her own people while the rest of her tribe lives in abject poverty. Violently abusive to her lover, Roberta Drays, Chief Jackson provides a troubling and fascinating addition to the tribal casino discourse. Tribal sovereignty over Indian land is called into question as main character Detective Sarah Linden works to circumvent tribal authorities when investigating a murder on the reservation. In several scenes, Linden refers to head of security Drays and her team as "goons," invoking (for those who know the history) the image of corrupt Oglala Lakota tribal chair Dick Wilson, who terrorized his own people in the 1970s. But instead of showing the tribe responding to such a situation, as when Oglala Lakota people and the American Indian Movement led the resistance against Wilson's violence, the Native community is represented in *The Killing* as either complacent or colluding, thereby justifying the detective's ongoing trespass onto Native land.[30]

As is the case in both *The Glades* and *The Killing*, there is a strong theme of corruption of tribal leadership as a result of casino wealth in the Netflix original series *House of Cards*. After the second season aired in 2014, Dina Gilio-Whitaker (Colville), research associate at the Center for World Indigenous Studies, notes, "In *House of Cards*, the Indians are portrayed in two ways: as both ruthless business people who use their sovereignty claims to evade responsibility for their part in dirty dealings, as well as underprivileged people ever victimized by those more powerful, even their own kind. Both are familiar tropes in Hollywood's Indian representations: the greedy money-hungry Indian and the impoverished victim. Nothing about them is neutral or inconsequential."[31]

Led by a greedy tribal chairman, the fictional Ungaya Tribe of *House of Cards* not only disenrolls their own tribal members, they are also involved in an international money-laundering scheme connected to an attempt to influence high-ranking White House officials. While the issue of disenrollment is a very real and often deeply painful concern for many Native people, story lines like the one developed in *House of Cards* frame the casino Indian as concerned solely with profit and power. Though the characters and story lines in both *The Killing* and *House of Cards* are multifaceted and deserve a deeper analysis, their plots nevertheless omit and obscure the ongoing efforts of Native nations around the United States to provide for the basic needs and services of their members, build infrastructure, and retain and revive ways of life.

Most early representations of casino-owning Indians appeared in comedies, reflective of a public that saw the juxtaposition of Indians, casinos, and wealth as something abnormal and ironic and therefore funny. More recent representations of the casino Indian in television dramas may reflect a growing resentment toward or uneasiness with the growth in the tribal casino economy over the years. The juxtaposition of Indians, casinos, and wealth is now often represented as something corrupt, inauthentic, and even dangerous. The casino Indian has been a particularly difficult image for the public to consume, as the notion of wealthy Native capitalists challenges the constructed notions of Indianness that the public has developed over generations.[32] The dialectic embedded in cultural texts surrounding the tribal casino economy reflects the troubled mind of the public concerning this reordering.

As early as 2000, Katherine A. Spilde, director of research for the National Indian Gaming Association, articulated the emergence of "rich Indian racism." In many ways, Spilde explains, the tribal casino economy is a great success story, and, "like many stories of success, it is also a story of jealousy and conflict. And in this case, the jealousy and conflict threaten the success."[33] Misrepresentations of Native people and the tribal casino economy—primarily under the misconception that all Native nations are now rich as a result of casinos—have encouraged a backlash from the public and, by extension, states and the federal government. According to Spilde, some of the most troubling assumptions held by the non-Native public include beliefs that Native nations are a front for the Mafia, that Native nations don't pay any taxes, that Native identities are manipulated for political purposes, and that "tribal people cannot handle the intricacies of federal recognition, land management, and casinos on their own."[34]

Rich Indian imagery has been used to attack tribal sovereignty, challenge tribal governments' claims of economic need, and raise doubts about "authenticity" of casino-owning Native nations. According to Spilde,

> "Rich Indian racism" is often combined with quasi-concern about the threat that Indian gaming presents to "traditional tribal values"—the paternalistic argument that tribes should resist offering gaming "for their own good" because it somehow threatens traditional culture. This is nothing short of ironic considering that in the 1800s the justification for Federal management of Indian resources was because they were "too Indian" and not "civilized" enough. It is a fact that very few people are concerned about the impact of poverty, or diabetes, or unemployment on "traditional tribal cultures" and there are very few Federal policies targeting these conditions, which are ultimately a real threat to Indian nations. Now, it seems, having money diminishes a claim to Indian cultural authenticity.[35]

Drawing a comparison to the colonial perspective that Native nations had too much surplus land, which led to the Donations Land Act and the Allotment Act, Spilde argues that non-Native people now feel that Native peoples have too much wealth and that Native nations should relinquish some of their revenue to the non-Native public. While a relatively small number of Native nations have truly become rich from Indian gaming, "rich Indian" imagery and the racist attitudes it represents pose a threat to all Native nations, even those that are not fiscally successful in their gaming operations and those that do not participate in gaming at all. Although Native nations' rights and sovereignty are inherent—and legally recognized by federal contracts, court cases, and legislation—there is often a negative reaction from the dominant society when Native nations exercise their rights.

Although sometimes entailing views in support of the gaming economy and at other times views opposed to it, the tribal casino discourse serves as a mechanism to control the economic opportunities available to Native nations. The discourse both informs and reflects public opinion (as well as, to a lesser degree, the positions advanced by tribes), and this can lead to changes in policies and laws that have a direct impact on Native people's lives. For example, along with the discourse concerning the tribal casino economy, gubernatorial power to negotiate for a larger percentage of tribal casino revenues appears to have increased. In the case of Warm Springs, it seems that the narrative that framed tribal relations and casino discourse in the *Oregonian* and other Oregon media helped shape the negotiations for the Bridge of the Gods Casino. When representatives of Governor Ted Kulongoski and Warm Springs negotiated the state-tribal compact for the proposed Bridge of the Gods Casino, they agreed that Warm Springs would share 17 percent of their annual revenue with the state, 11 percent more than in any prior Oregon tribal-state compact. Newspapers primarily written from a non-Native perspective, like the *Oregonian*, will continue to have significant impact not only on the public's understanding and support for tribal casino economies in Oregon but also in framing tribal relations.

FRAMING TRIBAL RELATIONS IN THE *OREGONIAN*

The rise of the tribal casino economy put Oregon tribal politics unquestionably back into the public sphere. Contending Native nations are not always represented equally or with great fidelity. As Justin Martin (Grand Ronde) articulates, "The media frames us in a warring fashion. It's always tribe against tribe. It makes for a good story. However, they don't make clear, precise distinctions about the differences between the tribes. They don't explain cultural differences. They don't explain economic differences. They don't explain geographic differences. We are always just kind of lumped together."[36]

Reflecting national discourse on the subject, Indian gaming discourse emerged in Oregon during the early 1990s as Native nations in the state began to make preparations to open their own gaming establishments. As tribal casinos became more permanent and lucrative, Native nations of Oregon became the focal point of an increasing number of articles in the *Oregonian*.[37] The *Oregonian* serves as a primary source of news not only to a readership in the Portland metropolitan area but also elsewhere in the Pacific Northwest.[38] Written from a predominantly non-Native perspective for a primarily non-Native audience, the paper wields substantial power in shaping and reflecting the broader public's perspectives on tribal economic opportunities and Native people. However, tribal members express concern over how they are represented in the paper. Gerald Danzuka Jr. is one who is frustrated: "The *Oregonian*, I've lost a lot of faith in it over the years. Do they support the tribes? No, they generally don't. They're generally reflecting the attitude of people in Portland and the legislature in Salem."[39] This is the sentiment that emerges from the perspective that there have been years of misrepresentation or under-nuanced reporting on the issues that affect tribal communities and their participation in gaming.

This frustration has not been limited to Oregon but is nationwide. Historian Alexandra Harmon explains, "Remarkable Indian financial gains triggered unusual public discussion of economic ethics, and the discourse plainly owed its distinctiveness to the moneymakers' Indian identity. If the prospering people had not been Indians, the discourse might have been as unconcerned with social ideals as the buzz surrounding dot-com millionaires."[40]

When Congress passed the IGRA in 1988, during the Reagan administration, reporting in Oregon on tribal casinos was sparse, as were articles that reported news of any sort from Grand Ronde and Warm Springs. Articles about the possibility of Native nations in Oregon opening gaming establishments began to appear in the *Oregonian* in the 1990s as Native nations began to show interest in gaming and were reportedly paying attention to the success of other tribes engaged in the industry around the United States.[41] In 1993, Roberta Ulrich became the *Oregonian*'s primary reporter on tribal issues. Her articles were generally thoughtful about efforts by tribes to develop reservation economies while also reflecting nuanced perspectives of tribal people. Nonetheless, by employing the rhetoric of "self-sufficiency" Ulrich contributed to the nationwide paternalistic narrative that effectively defined appropriate tribal use of funds earned through gaming. By the 1990s the rhetoric of self-sufficiency was strongly linked to the ideals set forth by President Reagan, in which greater self-sufficiency equated to reduced dependency on the federal government, which was a move toward the cutting of federal funding to Native nations.

Most of the articles in the *Oregonian* were sympathetic to the tribes' need for economic development yet expressed concerns over morality, ethics, and the possible social problems associated with casinos (gangs, organized crime, and addiction). For example, a number of articles included the assurance that "no alcoholic beverages will be served."[42] It was made clear that the Native nations were limiting the sale and consumption of alcohol at the casinos—directly responding to issues of morality and illuminating the public's deeply ingrained stereotypes of Indians as drunks or addicts.[43] The focus on morality in the discourse indicates an effort by journalists to influence public opinion to support Native nations' economic endeavors, in part by assuring the public that Native peoples in Oregon will not be *those* kinds of Indians. Nevertheless, it simultaneously enforces the validity of these pernicious stereotypes.

Tribal representatives too were active in shaping aspects of this discourse, acutely aware of the importance of public opinion and the politics of public perception. For example, in 1994 Siletz tribal chair Delores Pigsley told reporters that "the goal of the gaming is to provide jobs and services so that no tribal member must rely on food stamps."[44] *Oregonian* reporter Courtenay Thompson wrote that Native nations in Oregon that participated in the gaming economy had a heightened awareness of their image in the public eye and reported that a coalition of them had run ads as part of a campaign titled Helping Oregon by Helping Ourselves, showing the positive things that gaming could do for the state. The main message of the campaign was that strong tribal communities contribute to a stronger Oregon. According to Pigsley, the impetus for the campaign was "mostly from the bad publicity, getting a bad rap for not having to pay taxes. . . . We may not be paying property taxes, [but] we're paying fees. We're paying a lot of other things."[45] Grand Ronde also independently produced an ad, Turning Things Around, that aired during coverage of the Olympics, Thompson reported: "The 15-second spots featured college scholarships for tribal members, a health clinic open to the public, a revamped city chamber of commerce and land donated for a new community high school—all financed by tribal gaming."[46] Native nations in the casino era often are expected to defend their right to participate in the casino economy, and Corntassel and Witmer argue that this places onus on tribes to prove that they still need or are deserving of their right to self-determination as distinct tribal governments.[47]

By the mid-1990s, Native and non-Native people alike were offering profuse commentary on the values they said should be motivating the tribal casino economy. In preceding years, as Harmon describes, "moral judgments of economic behavior merged with ideas about Indians." In one example she provided, Native nations resisted the demand from the State of California for a larger cut of casino profits in 2004.[48] In response, Governor Arnold Schwarzenegger ran a campaign ad that relied on public outrage when he said that Native nations were making billions and paid no taxes to the state and argued that it was time Natives paid their "fair share." The powerful rhetoric of "fairness" influenced a widespread belief that Native nations had special, unearned rights that exempted them from paying taxes and that states were owed something from the Native nations participating in gaming.

Within this national political climate, Grand Ronde opened Spirit Mountain Casino in 1995. Grand Ronde then took major steps to achieve control over their business interests and to shape the tribe's economy according to the needs and interests of their community. Grand Ronde made headlines for becoming the first tribe in the nation to finance a casino project, which they did with a $19 million loan.[49] As Grand Ronde's economy began to stabilize, the tribe took over the administration of several federally funded programs, including the

Indian Health Service, which had been financed and operated through the Siletz Area Office of the Bureau of Indian Affairs.[50] Also in 1995, Warm Springs opened a temporary casino at their Kah-Nee-Ta Resort. Like Grand Ronde, Warm Springs financed their own gaming establishment.[51]

Oregonian articles that appeared during this time reflected public anxieties about the scope of tribal casinos and the extent to which they would operate autonomously. In one, James Long and Steve Mayes detailed many public concerns about the tribal casino economy, noting that "for the most part, the tribes' gambling income won't be taxed, regulated or even disclosed." The major areas of concern included the lack of federal and state oversight, foreseen problems with tribal oversight and possible incompetency, the possibility of money funneling from casinos to professional gambling companies, tribal corruption, and off-reservation casinos in cities and metropolitan areas.[52] Rhetoric of tribal corruption served to undermine tribal leadership, as it suggested that Native nations were not capable of handling their own affairs. The implication was that tribal leaders would either be swindled or would mismanage their businesses.

In 1997, the *Oregonian* published numerous articles and editorials about the tribal casino economy. Most concentrated on Grand Ronde, and many focused on Grand Ronde's renegotiation of their state-tribal compact, signed by Governor John Kitzhaber and Tribal Chair Kathryn Harrison. During compacting negotiations, Grand Ronde agreed to establish a 6 percent revenue-sharing agreement through the Spirit Mountain Community Fund and promised to limit their participation in the casino economy to one casino on their reservation (adjacent to Oregon Highway 18). In exchange, the governor agreed that Grand Ronde had the option of running high-stakes table games at their casino, including craps, roulette, and sports betting. The inclusion of high-stakes table games gave rise to new concerns about the morality of tribal casino wealth and introduced rhetoric that tribal casinos would remake Oregon in the image of Las Vegas. Reporter Thompson was one who wrote in this vein: "Though it still lacks showgirls and wedding chapels, Oregon moved one step closer to Las Vegas on Friday as Gov. John Kitzhaber signed a pact with the Grand Ronde tribe to bring a new level of gambling to a tribal casino."[53]

Thompson, quoting a public statement by Harrison, wrote that "the agreement fulfilled a promise made to the people of Oregon when the state helped restore [Grand Ronde's] status. 'This shows that we have kept our word and that by helping ourselves, we are helping the community.'"[54] Harrison's statement reflects the degree to which tribes—particularly those that had been terminated and that needed to work with allies to get support for restoration—were aware of the importance of managing public opinion and generating support from surrounding communities for their endeavors. In another article Thompson quoted Bruce Thomas, Grand Ronde member and manager of Spirit Mountain Development Corporation, saying that Grand Ronde was "already giving back to the community through a variety of programs, including funding for special education teachers for local schools, radar guns for state police, and money for local Head Start programs."[55] Thomas explained that the Spirit Mountain Community Fund merely formalized the arrangement, as it directed funds to communities near the tribe as opposed to the state government—a nuance of the compacting agreement that highlights the continued practice of Native nations asserting their agency even when their tribal sovereignty comes under attack.

While other Native nations in Oregon staunchly disagreed that they should be held to the same compacting provisions as Grand Ronde, this new compact marked a shift in state-tribal relations in Oregon, reflective of national trends that called for greater state control over the tribal casino economy. Citing tribal sovereignty and the differences between Native nations in Oregon (such as the locations of reservations and historical circumstances), other Native nations felt that the "one casino per tribe, on reservation" agreement that the Oregon Governor's Office had negotiated with Grand Ronde should not become the expectation for all Native nations in the state. Native nations of Oregon rigorously debated the revenue-sharing component, and many compared it to taxation. Thompson reported in January 1997, "Like many tribal leaders, Warren 'Rudy' Clements, chairman of the Warm Springs Indian Head Gaming Center's board of directors, said he was worried that the state would consider the foundation a precedent for future negotiations. 'If that becomes a requirement on the other eight federally recognized tribes, then I would be really concerned that that would be an intrusion' of sovereignty, Clements said. 'The state has no jurisdiction on our reservation.'"[56]

Kitzhaber and other state officials thought that the new compact with Grand Ronde would "serve as a model for other tribes expecting to renegotiate their agreements with the state."[57] Native nations were compelled to renegotiate contracts when they wanted to expand gaming enterprises. After Grand Ronde's agreement, other Native nations in Oregon were expected to have a revenue-sharing component in their renegotiated compacts. In addition, Grand Ronde leaders' agreement to limit themselves to one casino, on their reservation, provided the antecedent to Governor Kitzhaber's often-articulated policy.

In response to Grand Ronde's new compact, incoming state senate president Brady Adams (R–Grants Pass) stated that he was "disappointed to see the state expanding the scope of gaming in Oregon" but felt it "appropriate for the Indian nations, as a good-neighbor policy, to share those profits for all of Oregon." Adams was one of many who believed that "all Oregonians, wherever they live, should benefit from the tribe's largesse."[58] Articles continued to contribute to the underlying assumption that the state was giving something to Native nations as it negotiated compacts. Revenue-sharing components were framed as fair arrangements through which tribes "give back," "share," or act as "good neighbors" for the benefit of all Oregonians, in exchange for broader public approval and permission from the state to run gaming operations. Despite this acquiescence on the part of Native nations to federal, state, and local pressures to redistribute some of their profits to surrounding communities, some articles and editorials in the *Oregonian* expressed uncertainty about whether 6 percent was enough of a share or whether the state deserved a larger cut.[59]

In a January 1997 article, Courtenay Thompson wrote that sovereign Native nations were strategically repositioning themselves in relation to the state. Native nations in the casino era were becoming formidable and central participants in state politics.[60] Yet this transformation in the power dynamic between Native nations and states also illustrates the role of states in both limiting and offering economic opportunities to tribes. With the passage of the IGRA in 1988, Congress chose to acknowledge the sovereignty of both tribes and states and opened the door to increased state control over tribal development.[61]

The degree of state influence over outcomes affecting Native nations is troubling when it is understood that the state, through the governor, wields substantial power to move forward or block Native nations' goals during compact negotiations. As Warm Springs public relations consultant Greg Leo explains, "The State of Oregon has a funny, almost conflicted role here. They regulate Indian gaming through the compacts and through negotiations over the number of machines and that kind of thing. But at the same time they run the Oregon Lottery."[62] As Leo suggests, the state is arguably in direct competition with tribal casinos, because the state runs and relies on profits from its lottery. Partly in recognition of this fact, Native nations in Oregon increasingly understood that they needed to develop new relationships with the state in order to get support for their compacts.

While reflecting the national discourse on the tribal casino economy, a survey of articles, op-eds, and letters to the editor in the *Oregonian* from 1988 to 1998 highlights regional discourse entailing casino Indian rhetoric, narratives, and images. Reporting was initially highly sympathetic to the economic troubles faced by Native nations in Oregon, though there were concerns from the start about the morality of the economy, the appropriate way for Native nations to spend their profits, the lack of state and local regulation, and the amount tribes would "give back" or "share" with the citizens of the state from their revenues. Even in the early years of gaming in Oregon, commentary highlighted public concerns over casinos located off-reservation and the need for Native nations to develop "good neighbor" agreements with nearby communities.[63] The rhetoric around "off-reservation" casinos (along with the derogatory term "reservation shopping") served to limit Native nations' economic growth to particular geographic regions, while "good neighbor policy" became synonymous with the requirement that Native nations share casino wealth or risk being cast as inauthentic Indians valuing profit over ethics.

Over the years, coverage of tribal issues has shifted from focusing on sovereignty and rights to talk of special interests. As Chris Mercier (Grand Ronde) speculates, "When tribes start to throw in lots of money to influence the political process of this country, I think as far as the general public is concerned, tribes are going to end up not looking any different than guns, oil, cigarettes, all these different special interests that are kind of stigmatized."[64]

After 1998, there was a significant shift in the representation of Grand Ronde in the *Oregonian*. Earlier articles, though sparse, primarily explored Grand Ronde's reinstatement as a federally recognized Native nation and their efforts to become self-sufficient through the use of their new income from gaming. In news reporting after 1998, Grand Ronde began to be discussed almost exclusively in relation to their casino. An increasing number of reporters became interested in how much revenue was generated by Spirit Mountain Casino. As profits increased, so did journalistic scrutiny of Grand Ronde's expenditures, which primarily focused on three areas: the tribe's use of funds to build reservation infrastructure and support tribal members, the tribe's charitable giving, and the tribe's financial participation in politics.

The use of gaming revenue to build reservation infrastructure and provide services to tribal members was generally framed as an appropriate use of tribal gaming profits. For example, Courtenay Thompson wrote that the revenue from the casino "goes directly to tribal government, which uses the revenue to finance economic development, housing, health, education and other government programs. The tribe also distributes 25 percent of the profit among the tribe's 4,800 members, giving each member approximately $3,000 in dividends [in 2000]."[65] While statements such as these were framed positively, they illuminate the extent to which journalists, perhaps as reflective of the broader public, were becoming increasingly preoccupied with the financial gains of Native nations that were finding a measure of success in the tribal casino economy. In addition, by reporting on how Native nations spent their money, articles such as these continue to suggest that there are appropriate ways to do so, which conversely implies that there are less appropriate ways for Native nations to use money earned through the casino economy.

From 1998 to 2001, the vast majority of stories about Grand Ronde focused on the tribe's success in the gaming industry, and journalists reported on how the tribe was "giving back" to Oregon though the revenue-sharing component in their renegotiated state-tribal compact.[66] Grand Ronde dedicated 6 percent of their annual profits from Spirit Mountain Casino to develop the Spirit Mountain Community Fund, which awards grants to programs and organizations located in the eleven western Oregon counties that make up the ancestral homeland of the Grand Ronde tribes. Projects funded fall in the areas of arts and culture, education, health, historic preservation, public safety, environmental preservation, and "problem gaming" (i.e., addiction).[67] Articles often highlighted the tribe's charitable contributions to a wide range of projects, including $100,000 for the Lane Community College longhouse project in Eugene, $270,000 for a Portland-area battered women's shelter, and $450,000 annually to the Polk County Sheriff's Office.[68] Many Grand Ronde members assert that theirs is a "sharing" and "giving" tribe, and tribal representatives contribute actively to this discourse.[69] Like Native nations around the United States, Grand Ronde needed to manage the politics of public perception by attempting to generate positive associations with the tribal casino economy. Ultimately, Oregon communities benefited greatly from Grand Ronde's agreement to share a portion of their revenue. As of 2017, according to the Spirit Mountain Community Fund website, Grand Ronde has funded 2,522 grants, with support totaling more then $75 million.[70]

The image of Grand Ronde as a generous and giving tribal benefactor was challenged in 2000. Discourse on the subject exposed public anxiety over what many seemed to see as a radical shifting of economic and political power into the hands of Native nations. Articles and editorials in the *Oregonian* began to create a casino Indian discourse that recast Native nations with casino revenues as savvy political players in federal, state, and regional politics, capable of employing their resources to directly influence the outcome of a US Senate race, hire lobbyists to work at the state level, or "buy an occasional attack ad."[71] Framing Native nations as previously having been apolitical entities is a troubling aspect of this discourse. Casting Native nations as having become more involved in politics as a result of casino wealth obscures a long history of tribal political activism.[72] Grand Ronde's use of casino dollars to influence political outcomes favorable to Grand Ronde's goals in the casino era (including protecting their Portland-area market) led to an unprecedented examination and critique of the tribe's financial participation in the political process. Media attention primarily concentrated on three aspects of Grand Ronde's political activities, the first of which was their endorsements of and contributions to politicians.[73] A second area of focus was on tribal offers to fund large-scale projects of interest to Oregon in exchange for the right to build a casino closer to Portland.[74] Finally, extensive attention was given to Grand Ronde media campaigns meant to influence the public's views on the proposed Warm Springs Bridge of the Gods Casino as well as Grand Ronde attempts to highlight the records of politicians with whom the tribe disagreed.[75] The logic of "rich Indian" racism asserts the belief that Native nations with casino wealth no longer have a legitimate claim of economic need. Thus they should share their wealth with the state and no longer need assistance from the federal government. The logic of this racism argues that tribal sovereignty is an unearned and special right and that Native nations with wealth are no longer authentic Indians.[76] As such, Grand Ronde was often portrayed by the news media as an aggressive and greedy special interest group. The coverage of the tribe's activities was framed in a way that called into question the tribe's legitimacy and authenticity and undermined Grand Ronde's very real claims of economic need.[77]

After Warm Springs proposed to build a new casino in the Columbia River Gorge in 1998, more than a decade of debate followed in the *Oregonian*. Discussions focused on whether or not the casino should be built at all, and, if so, whether it should be built on Hood River trust land already owned by Warm Springs, on less environmentally sensitive land in Cascade Locks, or located on the Warm Springs reservation in central Oregon. Contributors to the debate, whether arguing for or against the casino, often invoked noble savage imagery to represent Warm Springs as traditionalists, environmental stewards, or impoverished people.[78]

However, a narrative of Warm Springs as despoilers of the Columbia River Gorge emerged in the discourse with an *Oregonian* article by Steve Duin in

September 1998.[79] Soon after, the paper's editorial board responded to the Warm Springs plan to locate their casino on their Hood River trust lands, arguing that a casino shouldn't "be built in any of the few relatively undisturbed sections of the gorge. It shouldn't sit right along one of the prettiest drives in Oregon," and "surely, the tribes must share this view. After all, the Warm Springs have more history and perhaps a deeper affinity for the Columbia Gorge than anyone. They, of all people, should not want to further damage the gorge."[80] While there is irony in the paper's statement that a casino would ruin "one of the prettiest drives in Oregon," Duin and the *Oregonian* were not alone in their indignation. In other *Oregonian* articles the Gorge was referred to as a "scenic wonderland," "pristine and beautiful," "nature in its glory," and "Oregon's greatest national treasure," while a casino in the Gorge was as "jarring as a neon beer sign in a cathedral."[81] One North Portland resident opined in a letter to the editor, "Because tribes can build a casino in a scenic area is no reason to do so. That most Native Americans traditionally respect and celebrate nature and the sanctity of natural resources makes this even more repugnant."[82] In the same issue, another Portland resident wrote, "Oregonians should do everything possible to stop this gross action. The tribes are always quick to decry and stop any activity that might impinge on their 'sacred sites.' They should show some sensitivity to the natural scenic areas so important to the rest of us."[83]

Those participating in this discourse employed shaming tactics, relying on oversimplified ideas about Indians and Indianness to formulate their dissent. The message blared: if the Warm Springs people were the environment-loving Indians the public imagined them to be, then they would never think to advance themselves economically at the expense of nature. What Duin and the others in the conversation failed to mention (or take responsibility for) was the damage already done to the gorge as a direct result of a century and a half of economic activities of the settler society that had displaced Native peoples from the region in 1855.[84] The discourse tended to obscure the fact that the continuous presence of Warm Springs and other Native peoples along the Columbia River has often resulted in greater protection for the river, particularly when Native nations have exercised their treaty rights to fish and harvest in the region.[85] Also embedded in the discourse was a paternalistic argument that if Warm Springs people sought economic development in the Columbia River Gorge, it would be at the risk of their own cultural ethics.

Discourse in opposition to the Warm Springs proposal moved beyond merely expressing displeasure at the idea of a casino located in the Columbia

River Gorge. A number of commentators actively worked to delegitimize Warm Springs people's claim that they had sovereign rights over their Hood River trust land.[86] For example, even as Duin grudgingly acknowledged Warm Springs tribal sovereignty, he also called it into question: "Technically, of course, this sovereign nation is well within its rights. The prospective casino site—dished out to a single Native American during the Harding Administration—has been back in tribal hands since 1978. It is clearly exempt from the stuffy requirements of the Columbia Gorge management plan."[87] Duin's article includes a thinly veiled subtext that questions the Warm Springs claim to the land as well as the tribe's sovereignty, which exempts them from the Columbia River Gorge Scenic Area Act.[88] Representatives of the environmental land-use organization Friends of the Columbia Gorge also challenged the Warm Springs claim that it had the right to build on its trust lands in Hood River.[89] The organization's conservation director Michael Lang argued in an *Oregonian* op-ed, "The Indian Gaming Regulatory Act and other federal laws prohibit casino development on the Hood River trust land. The proposed site is not 'Indian land' as defined in the federal act because the tribes have not exercised governmental powers over the land."[90]

Warm Springs attorney Dennis Karnopp dismissed this line of reasoning: "It's basically arguing that if you have land that you could make some use of, and you don't make that use of it, then it's not your land." He continued, "Deciding not to do something is exercising power over the land, too."[91] The argument that Native nations who don't make "proper use" of their land lose their power to govern that land is eerily reminiscent of the arguments in *Johnson v. M'Intosh* that reduced Native peoples to mere occupants of the land because they didn't "use" the land in a way that was considered productive by colonizing European nations. However, since members of the Friends of the Columbia Gorge commanded significant editorial space and were often quoted in articles and editorials on the issue in the *Oregonian*, they had a solid platform from which to get their perspective heard by the broader public.[92]

One of the primary proponents of the revised Warm Springs proposal—to build the casino in Cascade Locks—was the *Oregonian*. Many of its editorials, though somewhat hostile to all casinos, seemed part of a distinct agenda to oppose a casino on the Hood River trust land but support the Warm Springs proposal to build a casino in Cascade Locks. Often the editorials were directed to the Oregon governor, who had the power to negotiate a compact with Warm Springs for the Cascade Locks site. These editorials also relied heavily on the development of a narrative of Warm Springs as an environmentally minded, impoverished, and traditional people, evoking noble savage imagery but this time in service to Warm Springs goals in the tribal casino economy. For example, the paper wrote, "No one believes a casino belongs [on their Hood River trust lands], not even the Warm Springs, but the tribes would almost certainly build one there if that were their only choice. A confederation of poor tribes struggling with rampant alcoholism, child abuse and a child death rate more than twice the statewide average isn't going to walk away from tens of millions of dollars to help its impoverished people."[93]

Subsequent editorials highlighted that Warm Springs people "know and love this landscape; they spent centuries there before being pushed onto their Central Oregon reservation" and noted that they "roamed the Columbia Gorge for thousands of years and still have strong treaty rights there."[94] For more than a decade, *Oregonian* editorials were highly sympathetic to the needs and troubles of Warm Springs, recognizing their lagging economy, high infant mortality rate, and lack of adequate health care and educational opportunities.

GRAND RONDE AND WARM SPRINGS

After Warm Springs proposed to build a casino in the Columbia River Gorge, reporting in the *Oregonian* increasingly focused on the relationship between Grand Ronde and Warm Springs, which progressively became framed in terms of conflict and competition.[95] As Reynold Leno (Grand Ronde) points out, "I think the press tries to create animosity, like it is war, when it's just a basic disagreement over the off-reservation policy. It's not war or hatred. Thirty-eight years ago I served in Vietnam as a marine. That was war. That was hatred."[96] The newspaper harshly criticized Grand Ronde for opposing Warm Springs and portrayed Grand Ronde as a greedy competitor, hungry for the Portland metro market. The dispute between Grand Ronde and Warm Springs was framed as another instance of Native nations fighting over casino markets, as articles described Grand Ronde as a "rival Oregon tribe" who only wanted to defend their "money machine" and "may not care whether the Warm Springs are treated fairly under the law."[97] The relationship between the two communities was articulated as a "turf war," "challenge," "rift," "feud," "battle," and "fight."[98] This framing cast the tribes as embroiled in a conflict over gaming dollars and minimized what was at stake for both communities: their survival as Native people and their ability to function as sovereign nations.

Warm Springs director of governmental affairs Louie Pitt Jr. has this view of the *Oregonian*'s portrayal of relations between Native peoples: "It sells newspapers, Indian fighting Indian. It's entertaining at best, but [there's] not much substance in there about who we are and how Indianness works."[99] Faye Wahenika (Warm Springs) notes, "The media gets involved too much. Some of it is bitter, but to a certain extent it's as bitter as you want it to be. I'm not bitter. A lot of us are not bitter."[100]

With very few exceptions, Native nations in Oregon do not have direct control over how they will be represented in the media.[101] Native nations have become savvy with the media, however, and many have spokespeople who deliver strategic messages and promote ideas that tribal leaders hope will influence the general public on issues important to them. In the tribal casino discourse found in the *Oregonian*, tribal representatives have attempted, with varying degrees of success, to manage the politics of public perception, on rare occasions authoring editorials.[102] *Oregonian* reporters used quotes from Grand Ronde tribal representatives to give weight to the idea that there would be an "arms race" or a "free-for-all," with all nine Native nations in Oregon competing to build casinos near Portland if Warm Springs was allowed to build off-reservation. The term "arms race," from Cold War rhetoric, invoked an image of mutually assured destruction and served to incite public fear.[103]

Warm Springs was described in the *Oregonian* as "rooted in tradition" and bound by "traditionalism," and members were quoted as feeling "betrayed" by Grand Ronde, which had deviated from the usual protocol of Native nations supporting each other's endeavors.[104] This powerful narrative of Warm Springs as the victim of Grand Ronde's greed was supported by reporters and the *Oregonian* editorial board.[105] An unacknowledged perspective was that the Warm Springs plans, undertaken without significant consultation between the two nations, would likely cut into Grand Ronde's annual revenues, and so the Grand Ronde people were naturally concerned that their services and programs could be severely affected.[106] Instead Grand Ronde's concerns were often framed in the *Oregonian* as being without merit.[107]

The Warm Springs proposed casino in the Columbia River Gorge was the central story on the tribal casino economy through 2008, the year that the Bureau of Indian Affairs hosted five hearings to solicit comments from the public on its newly published Draft Environmental Impact Statement, an important step in the process for moving the land at Cascade Locks into trust for a Warm Springs casino. After the hearings, there was a significant drop in reporting on the tribal casino economy in the *Oregonian*, although an occasional story updated readers on the slow-moving process of the Warm Springs land-to-trust application for their Bridge of the Gods Casino.[108]

The tribal casino discourse evident in the *Oregonian* has, for the most part, insufficiently contextualized tribal motivations and historical events that led to the creation of the casino economy. Reporting seldom explains Native nations' limited economic development opportunities on reservations or the specific roles of the federal government and the State of Oregon in creating these circumstances. There has been paltry coverage, at best, of how Native nations in Oregon experienced disparate treatment during the treaty-making era, on their reservations and by federal Indian laws and policies such as termination. News articles focused on the topic of tribal casinos have rarely mentioned projects of colonization—such as federal and state support for illegal land disposition—that have contributed to the present-day circumstances of Native nations in Oregon. The complexities of the historical, cultural, and economic connections between Grand Ronde and Warm Springs, and of both to the Cascade Locks region, were also obscured within the discourse. All of these circumstances profoundly shape Grand Ronde and Warm Springs perspectives on issues that have arisen in the casino era.

In the epigraph at the beginning of this chapter, Esselen and Chumash poet Deborah Miranda asks, "Who is inventing me, for what purpose, with what intentions?"[109] Looking at the long history of Indian imagery and narratives, it is apparent that social constructions of Indians have most often been employed to justify land dispossession, deny Indigenous self-determination, and assert the claim of colonizer and settler supremacy. The imagery, narratives, and rhetoric of the casino Indian have likewise served these goals. Greg Leo explains how this has damaged the general public's perception of complex Native issues: "I wish we'd have been able to avoid the conflict because it has not been good from a public relations point of view. There are racist people in the world that say, 'Oh, look at those Indians fighting each other.' There are people who have pitted the tribes against each other for their own gain. There are people in the political world that are concerned about tribes getting a lot of power. So it would be better for all Indian people if this could be worked out in an amicable way without a lot of public conflict."[110] Leo's comments illustrate that the stories told about intertribal conflict in the casino era have real consequences, both economic and political, for Native nations and the well-being of Native people.

Native nations in the casino era spend a significant amount of time and resources working to shape the tribal casino discourse. As both Grand Ronde and Warm Springs did in responding to media coverage of their participation in the tribal casino economy, Native nations are often forced to spend their time responding and reacting to skewed and often inaccurate representations of Indians in this discourse. When Native nations are focused on managing the politics of public perception, their attention is drawn away from more critical issues facing their communities, such as acquiring land, defending reserved and retained rights, and other important tasks of nation building and cultural revival.

CHAPTER 5

A Risky and Uncertain Business

The Case of Cascade Locks

Nobody has to go through the crap Indian Country does. It's tradition in America to raise hell with the Indians. It's been happening from day one. And then, right in the middle of the game, what are they going to do? They're going to change the rules. Casinos are unfortunately one of the few options we have to try to acquire revenues that will support our sovereignty, not to build empires but just to be Indians.

—Louie Pitt Jr. (Warm Springs)

NATIVE PEOPLES IN THE UNITED STATES HAVE LONG BEEN EMBROILED in struggles to survive. Native nations resist, adapt to, and sometimes acquiesce to each new generation of federal laws and policies. They react to fluctuations in state and regional pressures and respond to dominant public perceptions and misconceptions of Native peoples. Over generations, policies that affect Indian Country have at times led to opportunities and simultaneously undermined or eroded tribal sovereignty and autonomy. In 1981 the US Supreme Court affirmed that tribes have the constitutional right to operate casinos, and Congress developed a regulatory framework for such operations in the Indian Gaming Regulatory Act in 1988.[1] Since 1988, tribes across the country—often lacking other economic development options—have chosen to establish themselves in this risky business. The tribal casino economy remains particularly uncertain as Native nations' rights to operate casinos are often contested, and the rules governing the industry are subject to quick changes that can derail tribal casino projects at any given moment.

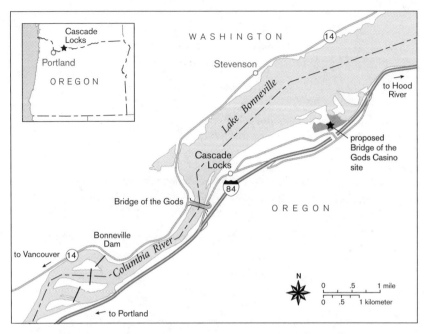

MAP 5.1. Proposed Bridge of the Gods Casino site in Cascade Locks, Oregon

For fifteen years the Confederated Tribes of Warm Springs worked diligently to open a new casino in the Columbia River Gorge in Oregon. The tribe first proposed to build the casino on tribal trust land near Hood River in 1998, but the Hood River community was adamantly opposed to the plan, as were environmental organizations such as Friends of the Columbia Gorge, which argued that the land in Hood River was too environmentally sensitive (a concern shared by Warm Springs). Representatives of the tribe therefore quickly reset their sights on a parcel of land in the nearby city of Cascade Locks. Warm Springs leaders hoped that by doing so they could respond to the concerns of the Hood River community while simultaneously leveraging their situation to gain access to an even better site in Cascade Locks: one located on less environmentally sensitive land, closer to the Portland metro market, and in a community that appeared to welcome the casino project.

A CASCADE LOCKS SITE

In 1998, Warm Springs began to refocus their plans to build the Bridge of the Gods Casino adjacent to the Columbia River in the city of Cascade Locks. To develop the relationship between Warm Springs and the city, Warm Springs purchased a tract of land on the eastern edge of Cascade Locks called Government Rock. Although Government Rock was the first site considered seriously by the Warm Springs development team, it was not seen as the ideal location for their casino, as the development of the necessary infrastructure to support a casino there would require significant effort. Warm Springs attorney Dennis Karnopp remembers that during a meeting between tribal representatives and Friends of the Columbia Gorge executive director Kevin Gorman, Gorman suggested that Warm Springs consider the Cascade Locks Industrial Park as a location for their new casino.[2] Karnopp researched that alternate site and found it a much more desirable location than Government Rock, as it already had utilities and was more accessible. Unlike the Hood River site, the industrial park, prior home to several mills, was not part of the lands covered by the Columbia River Gorge National Scenic Area Act passed in 1986 and amended in 2003 and would be less visible from the Washington side of the Columbia River.[3]

Despite the positive possibilities of this site, there were major barriers to Warm Springs building a casino in Cascade Locks. Even though lands identified in Cascade Locks were within the urban growth boundary of the city and technically not protected by the Scenic Area Act, the Warm Springs team understood that there could be controversy over this location.[4] The greatest obstacle was that the land in Cascade Locks was not on the Warm Springs Reservation, and it was not already held in trust for the tribe. After 1988, Native nations that sought to have land off their reservations taken into trust for gaming purposes had to meet the requirements for an exception to the policy outlined in the IGRA, a two-part determination that required, first, that the taking of land into trust would be in the best interest of the Native nation and not detrimental to the surrounding community. Second, approval was needed by both the secretary of the interior and the governor.

In state-tribal relations, one Native nation's actions or agreements made with a governor often directly affect other Native nations within a state or across the nation—by setting precedents, for example, that all will then be required to follow. As Warm Springs made plans to meet with Governor John Kitzhaber to discuss a casino at Cascade Locks, there were signs that other Native nations were concerned about the outcome of his decision. On May 7, 1999, Courtenay Thompson of the *Oregonian* reported that a casino in the Columbia River Gorge "could draw gamblers in Washington and Portland away from the lottery, or away from other tribal casinos."[5] In a subsequent news report, other Native nations in Oregon voiced their concerns over the possibility that the governor might make an exception for Warm Springs and were said to be "watching closely" to see how Kitzhaber would respond to the request.[6]

In late 1999, Warm Springs proposed to locate their casino in the Cascade Locks Industrial Park. In exchange for the authority to build in this location, Warm Springs would agree to close their Kah-Nee-Ta Resort casino and indefinitely give up the right to build on the Hood River trust site. Despite the significant public and media pressure on Governor Kitzhaber to approve the proposal in order to protect the Hood River site from becoming a casino location, this bid proved unsuccessful. Kitzhaber rejected the tribe's request on November 4, 1999, basing the decision on his much-articulated policy—one casino per tribe, on reservation land—that he had established during compact renegotiations with Grand Ronde two years prior.[7] Following Kitzhaber's rejection of the Warm Springs proposal to build their new casino at Cascade Locks, Warm Springs leaders worked to regroup and reassess their options, and a team reconsidered the Hood River site. News coverage directly following Kitzhaber's decision showed that the Hood River community and groups such as the Friends of the Columbia Gorge continued to advocate strongly against this location.[8]

THE TROUBLE WITH MADRAS

In addition to the Hood River trust lands, Warm Springs owned five acres of trust land in an industrial park north of the city of Madras. Located off the reservation fifteen miles southeast of Warm Springs on US 26, Madras shared similar economic conditions with Warm Springs at this time, and Courtenay Thompson reported that Madras and Jefferson County were showing some support for a tribal casino located there.[9] On May 23, 2000, however, Warm Springs members voted against building a new casino on their Madras trust lands.[10] Members cited a number of reasons for this outcome. Some expressed that they would like to see a new casino at a Columbia River Gorge location, and others felt that a new casino should be opened on the reservation, closer to tribal members who wanted to work there. Many explained that the fraught historical relationship between Warm Springs and Madras affected tribal members' decision not to support a casino in Madras. Warm Springs Chief Delvis Heath Sr. remembers, "The people said no. [The community of Madras] treated us rotten. . . . They never treated us right."[11] Karnopp shares his reflection on this decision: "It's hard to say why people vote one way or another, but I think it's because there's been an unfortunate, pretty sad history of relationships between Warm Springs and Madras, which is the nearest off-reservation non-Indian community. I think a lot of the tribal members thought that they wouldn't get treated right there, and that it would be a big boom for Madras, not for the tribe. In any event, people resoundingly said, 'No, don't do that.'"[12] Thompson echoed tribal perspectives on this issue: "In emotional public debates on the reservation, some tribal members brought up long-simmering feelings of resentment toward Madras, where some say they have been the target of prejudice and police harassment."[13]

Although the Madras site was rejected by the membership, Warm Springs still needed to generate new economic development. In February 2001, the *Oregonian* reported that "a budget shortfall of $1.6 million" had led Warm Springs to lay off "39 tribal government workers" and that "70 workers were laid off at the Warm Springs mill." The Warm Springs Tribal Council had voted unanimously to continue to pursue development of a casino on their trust lands east of Hood River.[14] Tribal member Brent Florendo explains the difficult conditions on the reservation that led Warm Springs to again work to locate a casino along the Columbia River Gorge: "After the timber sales went down, economically we were in dire straits. When there is poverty, there's abuse, drugs, and alcohol, and those same things that affect other places outside the reservation. When you put people in such an incomprehensible situation, there is going to be great conflict. That's a fact. We need money to invest in education and in innovative programs and to address the problems that we have in Warm Springs. We need the option to explore places we have never been. Opportunity—money should support opportunity."[15] As Florendo's analysis highlights, while Warm Springs experienced hardships similar to those faced by other communities around the state, they lacked the economic resources needed to address their challenges. Furthermore, the isolated nature of the reservation in central Oregon exacerbated social ills and limited the prospects for economic development that could generate enough money to support all a tribal nation entails: governmental infrastructure, social services, and natural and cultural resources.

A SECOND LOOK AT HOOD RIVER

In 2001, the Warm Springs newspaper *Spilyay Tymoo* featured a vibrant discussion about where the casino should be located. While the community appeared

to widely agree that Warm Springs needed to generate revenue and jobs for
the people, there was disagreement over the best route to achieve these goals.
In a letter to the editor, a Warm Springs member voiced his strong opposition
to the tribe's participation in the casino economy: "To me gambling is like
the Trojan horse or those smallpox infested blankets that those sick people
gave our Indian people."[16] He suggested that the tribe instead invest in an on-
reservation amusement park. Other members of the community argued that
the purpose of the casino was not just to make the most money possible; they
wanted to see the casino located on their reservation so it could provide jobs
to members as well as give them something fun to do.

While location of a casino on the reservation closer to Highway 26 could
have meant profits higher than those of the casino at the Ka-Nee-Ta Resort, a
tribally commissioned study conducted at that time showed that the most
lucrative location would be in the Columbia River Gorge.[17] Supporters of a
Columbia River Gorge location for the casino contended that Warm Springs
should invest in the location that would bring the most revenue for the tribe,
which in turn would be used to "develop businesses and jobs that people are
actually interested in pursuing."[18] Proponents of a gorge location pointed out
that tribal members only filled around 30 percent of the jobs at the Kah-Nee-
Ta casino and that this was perhaps an indication that tribal members desired
other kinds of economic opportunities. An active member of the economic
development team stated that Warm Springs "should look towards the option
that will generate the most revenue, which can then be used to create new
jobs in a variety of economic sectors" and in turn create higher-paying jobs
that would appeal to more tribal members.[19] Conversations in Warm Springs
reflected similar discussions throughout Indian Country about how casino
profits were meant to contribute to a strong reservation economy. While some
argued that casinos were supposed to be on-reservation businesses that
strengthened the reservation economy, others contended that the casino was
a tool for profit generation and could be located anywhere, even off the reservation, as long as profits were used to grow a healthy reservation economy.
Significantly, Indian gaming legislation can be interpreted to support either
of these views.

Though some community members had strong feelings about where they
wanted to see a Warm Springs casino located, others were undecided. During
the early part of 2002, leaders began an education campaign to inform the
membership about options available to the tribe. Informational meetings were

held in the different districts around the reservation, sometimes in the tribal longhouses, other times hosted in family homes. Surveys were then distributed to tribal members in order to gauge their views on gaming expansion.[20] The results showed that, of the 270 members polled, 90 percent were in favor of a Columbia River Gorge casino.[21]

Leaders in Warm Springs began again to consider building a casino on their Hood River trust lands, again raising concerns from other potential stakeholders on the issue, including the Governor's Office, various communities along the Columbia River Gorge, environmental organizations, and other Native nations in Oregon, such as Cow Creek and Grand Ronde. *Spilyay Tymoo* reporter Dave McMechan wrote, "Warm Springs tribal leaders have said that this opposition [from other tribes] comes as a surprise and a disappointment." According to one Warm Springs member whom McMechan quoted, "The opposition from Grand Ronde and Cow Creek goes against the long-standing tradition that a tribe does not interfere with the business of another tribe." Another member, Rudy Clements, part of the casino economic development team, was quoted as saying that "the opposition from Grand Ronde and Cow Creek does not appear to be popular with all members of those tribes" but that it "seems to come largely from younger members rather than the elder members." Clements continued, "The support that Warm Springs gave Grand Ronde and Cow Creek during reinstatement makes their opposition especially hard to accept."[22] In these statements, Clements articulated a number of common perspectives held by Warm Springs tribal members. Such views would become central rhetorical strategies used by Warm Springs to influence public perception on this issue.

A number of Grand Ronde leaders felt that they had good reason to be concerned about the Warm Springs proposal. While many said that they understood, respected, and supported Warm Springs leaders in their desire to take care of their members by developing a strong economic base, they felt that Warm Springs leaders failed to understand the position in which this proposal put Grand Ronde people. Justin Martin, Grand Ronde's intergovernmental affairs director, explains the pressure that Grand Ronde leaders felt at the thought of losing their sole source of revenue, which supported all the infrastructure, services, and programs on their reservation: "If you're on the Tribal Council and you've started these programs, you certainly want to see them continue. Politically, there is a lot of pressure on our elected officials to make sure that things stay the way they are or continue moving in a positive direction."[23] From the time it opened in 1995, Grand Ronde's casino had been the most successful in Oregon, which allowed leaders on the Tribal Council to use its revenues to fund endowments for health care and elders' pensions.[24]

At the Fifth Annual Government-to-Government Summit in 2002, Governor Kitzhaber's legal counsel explained that the Governor's Office believed that if the State of Oregon altered its initial gaming compact with Warm Springs to allow the tribe to locate a casino outside of their reservation, it would alter the gaming compacts that all Native nations in Oregon had signed with the state.[25] Though the point was debatable, the message was strongly conveyed that the Warm Springs plan would change the rules for all Native nations in Oregon. Kitzhaber's policy of one casino per tribe, on reservation land, had been in effect for five years at that point, and the possibility of a change to this policy continued to generate concern among Grand Ronde leaders. Grand Ronde's newspaper, *Smoke Signals*, reported on tribal leaders' evaluations of the potential consequences of a gorge casino. As Justin Martin was quoted as saying, "We've communicated with Warm Springs on numerous occasions before we ever went public with our objections [and] told them repeatedly that we stand behind them and would help them in any way we can as long as they build a replacement casino within their existing reservation lands."[26]

A central concern for Grand Ronde was the possibility of waning public support for tribal casinos. The *Smoke Signals* article cited a statewide poll (conducted by polling firm Grove Insight) that showed that "while most Oregonians have a positive impression of Indian gaming, especially for the community funded programs that are now established across the state, 80 percent don't want to see any further expansion of gaming." Grand Ronde leaders worried that if Warm Springs moved their casino off-reservation, all Native nations in Oregon would want to seek more lucrative locations for their casinos—closer to urban centers where the potential for profit would increase. Tribal Chair Cheryle Kennedy said, "If Warm Springs prevails, clearly we'd have to look at casino locations much closer to Portland. . . . I know that Siletz would look at Salem and Burns at Bend. Cow Creek would have to come closer to Eugene."[27] The fear was that if all Native nations in Oregon sought land closer to urban centers for their casinos, this would not only be costly for all the nations but also could turn the public against the tribal casino economy or open up the possibility of public support for non-Native gaming enterprises in Oregon.

In August 2002, Grand Ronde sent a letter to the Bureau of Indian Affairs in which they questioned whether the Warm Springs trust lands in Hood River "met the definition of Indian land" under the IGRA. Grand Ronde "urged the agency to consider what siting a casino in Hood River would do to other tribes." Regarding the latter point, Grand Ronde cited an analysis by ECONorthwest that "found that a casino in the gorge would have a significant impact on the Grand Ronde."[28] While Grand Ronde leaders were uneasy about the fiscal impact of a competing casino located in the Columbia River Gorge, they were also concerned that changes made to the Warm Springs state-tribal compact would affect their compact.

NEW VISTAS: CHANGING LEADERS AND SHIFTING POLICY

In late May 2002, anticipating upcoming gubernatorial elections and the prospect of a new governor with new views on the tribal casino economy, Warm Springs again turned to their members for a mandate on how to proceed with gaming and the development of a gorge casino. The tribe held a referendum on whether to again pursue a Columbia River location for a new casino. The referendum passed with 76 percent of the votes cast, 724 members in favor and 210 against it.[29] Tribal Chair Suppah recalls, "We ended up with a referendum where tribal members were asked, 'After five years, if you want the casino to continue, where would you want it?' And by 80 percent to 20 percent, with the biggest voter turnout for a tribal referendum, they said, 'Build it someplace in the Gorge.'"[30] This referendum included language that would allow Warm Springs leaders to pursue the Hood River site. According to an *Oregonian* article, however, "Rudy Clements, chairman of the tribe's gaming enterprise, said . . . [that] the Tribal Council 'left a little wiggle room' in the wording of the referendum should the political climate toward Cascade Locks change."[31]

This was an uncertain time for Native nations in Oregon. Kitzhaber was still governor, but his second term was coming to an end in 2003, and all of Oregon's Native nations understood that a new governor might have different perspectives about tribal casinos and could make changes to policies developed by Kitzhaber. When the gubernatorial campaigns began in October 2001, the *Oregonian* reported that "campaign managers for Ted Kulongoski and Beverly Stein said each candidate supports the governor but would welcome a dialogue with the tribes, leaving open the possibility of a Cascade Locks casino."[32] After a visit from gubernatorial candidate Kulongoski to the Warm Springs Reservation in December 2001, *Spilyay Tymoo* reporter Dave McMechan wrote, "Unlike Gov. Kitzhaber, Kulongoski indicated his willingness to support a casino at Cascade Locks. However, Kulongoski said he wanted to be sure that approval of a casino at Cascade Locks would not open the door to other Oregon tribes building casinos around Portland."[33] This perspective is perhaps telling of the role that Kulongoski would play in the generation of divisiveness among tribal communities in Oregon concerning off-reservation casinos. Kulongoski's position on the issue did not remain consistent during his campaign, which left those concerned uncertain about the future.

Reporting on Kulongoski's views regarding a Cascade Locks casino continued to highlight his uncertainty, although in January 2002 the *Oregonian* reported that "Kulongoski, a former state Supreme Court justice and attorney general, has opposed allowing a casino in Cascade Locks."[34] But even after Kulongoski became governor-elect, his stance on the question of the Warm Springs proposal to build a casino in Cascade Locks was unclear. *Oregonian* reporter Janie Har reported three contradictory positions held by the governor-elect and wrote, "Kulongoski has stayed mum on the topic of a Cascade Locks casino proposed by the Confederated Tribes of Warm Springs. This, in turn, has upset state Sen. Rick Metsger, D-Welches, who said Thursday that Kulongoski assured him in a face-to-face conversation shortly before the election that he supported the project." In the same article Har quoted Scott Ballo, a spokesman for Kulongoski, as saying that "[Kulongoski] has not made a final decision on a casino at Cascade Locks." But she also reported that "Kulongoski has agreed with Kitzhaber's position on where to allow casinos. Kitzhaber said in 1999 that he would not allow a casino in Cascade Locks because he thinks tribes should be limited to building casinos on land they owned prior to the passage of a 1988 federal law on tribal gambling. Casinos on land acquired after that date require the approval of the governor."[35]

While these contradictory stances may have reflected a new governor learning about the complex issues of Indian Country, Kulongoski's public and private indecisiveness on this issue nevertheless created anxiety and frustration for many Native nations in Oregon, particularly Grand Ronde and Warm Springs. Throughout Kulongoski's first term, it was unclear what his decision would be on the proposed Bridge of the Gods casino in Cascade Locks and how he conceptualized the parameters for off-reservation gaming in the state. On March 16, 2003, the *Oregonian* reported, "The question that remains unresolved is whether the state will depart from longstanding policy and allow a casino on nontribal land."[36] While Warm Springs leaders hoped that Kulongoski would make an exception to allow them to build a new casino in Cascade Locks, Native nations such as Cow Creek said that they wanted to see him continue with the policy of one casino per tribe, on reservation land.

Although Grand Ronde was also officially against changing the existing policy, a number of leaders felt that they had to make sure they were prepared in case the policy changed. In order to test their potential options to expand gaming, they proposed to finance "a $350 million [baseball] stadium if allowed to build a Portland-area casino."[37] Grand Ronde was sometimes criticized for opposing the off-reservation casino projects of Warm Springs and the Cowlitz tribe while simultaneously looking for their own off-reservation opportunities.[38] Tribal member Justin Martin responds to the reproach:

> Grand Ronde passed an ordinance in '96 saying that we're against off-reservation gaming. Our position has always been clear on that. But if the rules of the game change, our council has a responsibility to our tribal members. So it's a question of "what if?" You can say, "Oh, isn't that hypocritical to be doing that?" Well, no, because, again, we've got the responsibility of adapting to changes in policy, especially when you're looking at losing significant profits and potentially looking at losing an industry.
>
> You can't overturn 150 years of not very good conditions on the reservation, 29 years of termination, health issues, drug and alcohol abuse, domestic violence, or a lack of education overnight. We're starting to make some strides in these areas, but these things take time. The uncertainty of a potential change in policy makes tribal members very uncomfortable, with the prospect of, "Maybe we will have to move off the reservation. Maybe we will have to go somewhere else within our ceded lands. Maybe the investment we made at home is all for naught, because the rules of the game are going to change." In terms of the general public, I think they're very uncomfortable too.[39]

As Martin's statement highlights, Grand Ronde leaders felt that they had a mandate to protect their tribal members, the services they relied on, and the economy that supported these goals.

Warm Springs leaders publicly declined to take an official stance on Grand Ronde's attempt to get approval from the governor to open a casino in Portland. Warm Spring member Olney Patt Jr. stated that "it is a policy of the Confederated Tribes of Warm Springs not to comment on other tribes' efforts to provide economic development and to become economically self-secure." However, he went on to say that as a result of the Grand Ronde proposal, "There can be no reasonable objection by Grand Ronde in the future to off-reservation gaming."[40] Ultimately, Governor Kulongoski denied Grand Ronde's proposal to fund a stadium if allowed to build a casino in Portland, on the grounds that "it's not good public policy to link baseball to gambling."[41]

In 2004, Warm Springs tribal chair Garland Brunoe sent a letter to Kulongoski requesting to begin tribal-state compact negotiations for a new casino in the Columbia River Gorge. Citing a 60 percent unemployment rate on the reservation, Brunoe explained the Warm Springs leaders' stance that they had the right to build on their trust lands east of Hood River but that the residents there opposed a casino at that site. He went on to note that another option would be to build on lands in Cascade Locks, which would require approval from the governor.[42] The Friends of the Columbia Gorge opposed any casino in the Columbia River Gorge and argued that the Warm Springs position—that they could build a casino on their Hood River trust lands—was invalid because "the proposed site is not 'Indian Land' as defined in [the IGRA] because the tribes have not exercised governmental powers over the land."[43] Warm Springs representatives, on the other hand, believed that it was the tribe's right to build in the Hood River location, pointing out that not developing land is also an exercise in governmental power. Several state and local officials, including Hood River county commissioner Carol York and former Oregon governor Vic Atiyeh, issued statements supporting a Cascade Locks casino and encouraging Kulongoski to move forward with meeting with Warm Springs and making a decision on the issue.[44]

In 2004, the first of several non-Native gaming interests attempted to open up Oregon's gaming market. The *Oregonian* reported that two men from Lake Oswego, Bruce Studer and Matthew Rossman, proposed to build a one-million-square-foot private casino.[45] They eventually proposed to locate the casino at the Multnomah Greyhound Park in Wood Village, twelve miles east of Portland.[46] For the proposal to move forward, voters would have to approve an amendment to Oregon's constitution that would make it legal for nontribal entities to operate casinos in the state. Governor Kulongoski opposed the ballot measure. While the idea of nontribal casinos has never gained much support in Oregon, proposals from non-Native interests continue to constitute a threat to the tribal casino economy in Oregon—particularly in light of the decision made by New York voters in 2013 to amend the New York State constitution to allow up to seven private casinos in the state.[47]

After several years of meetings and negotiations, Warm Springs representatives and Governor Kulongoski signed a state-tribal compact for the Cascade Locks Bridge of the Gods Casino on April 6, 2005. This agreement outlined the percentage of annual dividends that Warm Springs agreed to pay to a nonprofit community fund and the amount that they would contribute to local services such as road maintenance and law enforcement. It also stated that Warm Springs would close Indian Head Casino and relinquish rights to build on the Hood River trust lands in the future.[48] *Spilyay Tymoo* reporter Dave McMechan covered the compact signing held at the Marine Pavilion at the Port of Cascade Locks and noted that this agreement "quite possibly could lead to the most important development program in the tribe's history." McMechan added, "The coincidental timing of the Cascade Locks casino compact is interesting to think about: In the year of the 150th anniversary of the Treaty of 1855, the tribes have signed another agreement, one that should lead to the first major tribal presence at the Columbia since the creation of the reservation, and especially since the flooding of the mighty Celilo Falls."[49]

Other Warm Springs tribal members and people from Cascade Locks felt genuine excitement (as well as relief) that the compact was finally agreed upon and signed. The process was not over, however. For the project to proceed, the compact and the land-to-trust transfer still needed to win approval from the secretary of the interior, a process that promised to be long and costly.

Governor Kulongoski's decision to negotiate a state-tribal compact with Warm Springs in support of a casino at Cascade Locks upset Grand Ronde tribal members. Many Grand Ronde representatives felt that Kulongoski had lied to them, saying in meetings with Grand Ronde that he would not allow off-reservation casinos in Oregon. Grand Ronde public affairs director Siobhán Taylor says, "All I know is that the governor told [Grand Ronde leaders] prior to his election that he would not allow tribes to move off-reservation for gaming." She continues, "I'll be blunt. We were lied to. And that's the sense of this Tribal Council because of that one-on-one meeting they had with the governor. I just can't explain to you the sense of dismay and disbelief that this tribe felt with Ted Kulongoski's switch of policy."[50]

Taylor went on to clarify that the decision that Grand Ronde leaders made to officially oppose a Warm Springs casino in Cascade Locks was directly related to the actions of the governor: "Our disagreement is with the governor. It's not with the Warm Springs people. This governor established a policy that allows one tribe to move off-reservation to open a casino to the detriment of all the other tribes."[51] As this section highlights, the relationships developed with and political positions forwarded by a state's governor have a significant impact on the ways in which Native nations orient themselves in the tribal casino economy and influence how they engage in politics and alliance building with state interests.

On May 20, 2005, in response to what many at Grand Ronde viewed as a radical and detrimental shift in Oregon's public policy on tribal casinos, Grand Ronde held a special Tribal Council meeting at their governance center. At this meeting, the Tribal Council voted to join the Coalition for Oregon's Future, an alliance of small businesses, environmentalists, and pro-family organizations that opposed the casino in Cascade Locks. Grand Ronde council members also voted to move one million dollars from the tribe's Land Acquisition Contingency budget to the Tribal Council Diversification Project budget, "to fund the campaign opposing off-reservation gaming in Oregon."[52] However, as in any Native nation, there were differences of opinion within Grand Ronde about the best way to respond to the proposed Warm Springs casino in the Columbia River Gorge. Grand Ronde Tribal Council vice-chair Angela Blackwell, who has worked for Grand Ronde since she was fourteen years old, explains:

> There is not a unanimous consensus with our five thousand tribal members or even within the council over which path we should or shouldn't be taking as far as our approach to the Cascade Locks casino. The same is true for Warm Springs. Not everybody in their tribe wants to be engaged in this perceived battle over gaming dollars. Some of their tribal members want to see their casino in Hood River, or Cascade Locks; some of them want to see it at home. Same thing is true here—some tribal members want to see us continue to defend what we believe is our right to have a say and some of us don't.[53]

Blackwell's statement highlights that tribal members and those seated on tribal councils are not always in consensus. The latter must carefully weigh the concerns, needs, and goals of their tribal members alongside their desire for intertribal coalition and the ever-present pressure to manage public perception of tribes' participation in the casino economy.

On May 20, 2005, a letter from Department of the Interior associate deputy secretary James E. Cason notified Warm Springs tribal chair Ron Suppah that the tribe's state-tribal compact had been denied. A principal explanation for the rejection was that the lands at Cascade Locks had yet to be taken into trust for Warm Springs. Cason stated that the IGRA "does not authorize the Secretary to approve a compact for the conduct of Class III gaming activities on lands that are not now, and may never be, Indian lands of such Indian tribe." Referring to the two-part determination process outlined in the IGRA, Cason explained that Warm Springs still had to undergo a "rigorous process" in order for the lands at Cascade Locks to be taken into trust for gaming purposes. Cason acknowledged that the Department of the Interior had changed its position: "We are aware that the Department has previously approved compacts for the regulation of Class III gaming activities before the specified lands qualified as Indian lands under IGRA. However, on closer examination of the statute, we have concluded that the Secretary's authority to act on proposed compacts under 25 U.S.C § 2710(d)(8)(A) is informed by section 20 of IGRA. Thus the proposed gaming lands are subject to a two-part determination and State Governor concurrence under section 20. These two conditions must be complete before Departmental action on a compact can occur."[54] This letter illustrates the shifts in conditions that can occur within federal agencies, including varying interpretations of the law and changing procedural requirements. Administrative changes at the federal level—like politics at the local and state levels—can result in changes in philosophies and approaches toward Indian gaming.

Although the decision was disappointing to Warm Springs, the denial of the state-tribal compact did not mean that the project had been denied altogether. Governor Kulongoski sent a letter to the BIA stating that he would concur with a decision to approve the taking of the Cascade Locks lands into trust for Warm Springs.[55] Warm Springs turned their attention to preparing an environmental impact statement, a requirement of the National Environmental Policy Act (NEPA), which is intended to aid the secretary of the interior in deciding whether or not to take land into trust for a Native nation for gaming purposes.

CONTENTIOUS GROUND: FROM RESERVATION
TO OFF-RESERVATION GAMING

When Native nations have wanted to build casinos away from what they (or others) perceive as their historical reservations, they have often been met with strong opposition—from Native and non-Native communities alike. Louie Pitt Jr. (Warm Springs) doesn't mince words about this:

> They called it the "Indian problem." What are we going to do with these folks
> that require such a large expanse of land to be able to live their lives. Put
> them in a small area—it was just a very sad joke—then cut people off from

going to their areas to travel, to carry on their way of life. Our folks always have gone off-reservation, right from day one. They can document that. Non-Indians don't understand what we have to do to be Indians out here and our rights. And of course non-Natives would turn it the other way around and say, "No, you don't understand, you gave that land up." But we didn't. We put our reserved rights in the treaty. Indians were pretty smart in those days, and strong, to keep up the battle. So we have it pretty clear that part of the Indian problem was that we were supposed to have looked at the reservation as a prison, to go there and stay and be happy. Hell no![56]

The IGRA primarily limits tribes to building and operating casinos on their reservations, but Native nations can also seek a determination from the secretary of the interior to build on other "Indian lands" that were already held in trust for the Native nation on or before October 17, 1988 (when the IGRA was enacted). Native nations with existing reservations at the time of the IGRA's enactment were given the option to request that land "within or contiguous" to the tribe's current reservations be taken into trust for gaming purposes. Native nations that were recognized but did not have reservation lands in 1988 were also given the option to request that lands be taken into trust for gaming purposes, as long as the lands were within "the boundaries of the Indian tribe's former reservation" or "the Indian tribe's last recognized reservation."[57]

The IGRA sets out exceptions to the general regulatory framework, and Native nations that can meet these exceptions (articulated in Section 2719) are provided with a route to open gambling establishments on lands acquired after 1988. These are often called "after acquired" or "newly acquired" lands. According to the American Gaming Association (AGA), Native nations can request that "after acquired" lands be taken into trust by the following means:

1. Obtaining local support and seeking a "two-part determination";

2. Obtaining a finding that the land was received for a settlement of a land claim;

3. Obtaining a finding that the land was taken into trust for a tribe that was recognized after the passage of the 1988 law; or

4. Obtaining a finding that the land was restored to a tribe that was wrongfully derecognized by the federal government.[58]

Native nations that want to bring lands into trust after passage of the IGRA have a number of routes available to them, but the process can be daunting, and there are a number of barriers to tribal applications, including opposition from other parties potentially affected by the outcome, such as other tribes, states, and public interest groups.

While some exceptions allow Native nations to regain land for gaming operations on their reservations or former reservations, at times nations such as Warm Springs must make the case that, because of special circumstances, they require trust land for gaming that was never a part of their reservation. When Native nations request that land off their reservations be taken into trust, they must pass a "two-part determination" test. First they must prove that the "gaming establishment on newly acquired lands would be in the best interest of the Indian tribe and its members, and would not be detrimental to the surrounding community" (including non-Native communities and other Native nations in the region). Second, after the secretary of the interior approves an application, the governor of the state must concur with the findings.[59]

Warm Springs was not the first Native nation in Oregon to propose building a casino on lands that would have to meet the requirement of the two-part determination test outlined in the IGRA. The Confederated Tribes of Siletz endeavored to get sixteen acres taken into trust for the purposes of opening up a gaming establishment in Salem.[60] On November 6, 1992, Secretary of the Interior Manuel Lujan Jr. found that the Siletz proposal was in the best interests of the tribe and not detrimental to the surrounding community, meeting the first requirement of the two-part determination test. However, the secretary ultimately denied the tribe's request after Oregon governor Barbara Roberts declined to concur. According to the editorial staff of the *Oregonian*, this "affirms the important veto power a state's governor should have over off-reservation gaming centers."[61] Siletz contested the constitutionality of the governor's concurrence requirement but was ultimately unsuccessful in this challenge.[62]

During the Warm Springs attempt to gain trust lands in Cascade Locks under the exceptions outlined in the IGRA, there was a great deal of confusion among Native and non-Native people alike over what was meant by "off-reservation" within the context of this debate. Some individuals argued that a Warm Springs casino in Cascade Locks would be the first off-reservation casino in Oregon. Others countered that there were already several Native nations in Oregon with off-reservation casinos. Some Native nations, including Grand Ronde and Siletz, were regularly accused in the media, in public hearings, and by Warm Springs supporters of having off-reservation casinos, which added to the confusion and contributed to the contentious relations. Part of the problem seems to have stemmed from differences in the ways that tribal leaders and their legal counsel understood and interpreted legislative history. During early talks with soon-to-be-governor Kulongoski in 2001, Warm Springs leader Rudy Clements made the case that most of the other Native nations in Oregon had been able to get lands taken into trust for gaming purposes even well after 1988. He argued that "each casino was provided through a specific act of Congress" and said that Warm Springs merely wanted the same opportunity: "Allowing the Confederated Tribes of Warm Springs to construct one off-reservation casino, at Cascade Locks, would be fair and equal treatment."[63]

In a 2005 article in the *Spilyay Tymoo*, Warm Springs attorney Dennis Karnopp pointed out that only three Oregon tribal casinos—Wildhorse (Umatilla), Old Camp (Burns Paiute), and Kah-Nee-Ta Resort and Casino (Warm Springs)—were built on lands that had reservation status in 1988. Karnopp noted, "In view of the circumstances of how six of Oregon's casinos came to be established on land that was not part of an established Indian reservation in 1988, the Warm Springs Casino at Cascade Locks will not be Oregon's 'first off reservation casino.' Rather, it will be Oregon's seventh off reservation casino."[64]

Karnopp described the various legislative or administrative routes the other six Native nations in Oregon (Grand Ronde; Siletz; Coos, Lower Umpqua, and Siuslaw; Coquille; Cow Creek; and Klamath) had undertaken to get the lands on which their casinos are situated taken into trust. In the cases of the first four, the lands were indeed restored to reservation status but *after* the 1988 date outlined by the IGRA. Cow Creek's and Klamath's casinos were situated on lands taken into trust for these nations, but these lands did not have reservation status.[65]

Several Native nations in Oregon that had been terminated and then restored, such as Grand Ronde and Siletz, successfully lobbied Congress to make corrections to their restoration legislation. These corrections brought lands that had been part of the tribes' historical reservations back into reservation status, which made them eligible for gaming operations. In response to questions about the status of the parcel of land on which the Grand Ronde Spirit Mountain Casino is situated, Siobhán Taylor explains, "The land that the casino is on was all originally reservation land. When the tribe was terminated, they were left without almost any reservation land. When the tribe looked for a way to grow and develop an on-reservation economy, they built the casino. At that time the land that the casino is on was taken into trust for the tribe, and then it was restored to reservation status."[66]

Both Grand Ronde and Siletz built their casinos on land restored to reservation status as a result of the Technical Corrections Act signed by President Bill Clinton in 1994. The act made corrections to Public Law 96-340, which had established the Siletz Reservation in 1980, and to the Grand Ronde Reservation Act, which had established the Grand Ronde Reservation in 1988.[67] In early 1994, the Department of the Interior denied Grand Ronde's state-tribal compact for Spirit Mountain Casino, "on the grounds that the site was not part of the tribes' reservation."[68] The Technical Corrections Act was the legislative mechanism through which this land-status issue was resolved for Grand Ronde. At the time the IGRA was enacted, both Grand Ronde and Siletz were engaged in ongoing processes to restore land and rights that had been stripped away during the termination era. The process they followed to get lands restored to reservation status for their gaming operations was different from what Native nations went through to acquire trust lands for gaming purposes after 1988, as outlined in the IGRA.

Following the passage of the Technical Corrections Act, reporting compounded confusion over this distinction. For example, *Oregonian* reporter James Long wrote in 1995 that Oregon congressman Mike Kopetski had "tacked an amendment on a bill in November 1994 to let the Siletz build on another off-reservation site in Lincoln City" and that "President Clinton was persuaded to sign an amendment to the Indian Law Technical Corrections Act allowing the Grand Ronde tribe to build a casino on nonreservation property southwest of McMinnville."[69] In this case, Long misread the purpose of the Technical Corrections Act, which was actually to restore the lands to reservation status. This in turn made them eligible for casino development in accordance with the IGRA. Although the legislative history of Grand Ronde and Siletz reservation land acquisition in this case is fairly straightforward, coverage of off-reservation casinos continues to be muddled in the media, and a false notion that these are off-reservation casino sites is perpetuated.

The location of tribal casinos on off-reservation sites continues to be one of the most hotly debated aspects of the tribal casino economy. Critics often accuse Native nations of unscrupulously "reservation shopping" to procure lands closer to metropolitan centers with their large populations of potential gamblers.[70] This argument works to undermine tribal sovereignty and discredit tribal leadership, and it fails to recognize that in many cases Native nations are seeking land within historically and culturally important regions. The exception in the IGRA provides a way for some Native nations to reclaim and reconnect to land that was forcibly taken or ceded during highly coerced treaty negotiations. In the case of the Warm Springs bid to take land into trust for a casino in Cascade Locks, it was often articulated by tribal membership that opening a casino in the Columbia River Gorge was important for the community beyond the economic relief it would have provided. The Columbia River has always been and continues to be central to Warm Springs spiritual, cultural, and economic life. Even after Warm Springs ceded most of their territory in 1855, Warm Springs people continued to practice their treaty rights and maintain an active presence along the river. Throughout the Warm Springs efforts to locate a casino in Cascade Locks, many members expressed that the area was a part of their home and a place that they never wanted to be separated from, and many felt that to regain land near the Columbia River would have increased their political sovereignty and strengthened cultural ties to the region that were already strong. In the casino era, however, economic considerations most often overshadow these spiritual and cultural aspects of the land-to-trust exception under the IGRA.

The Warm Springs proposal faced new challenges in 2006. House Resources Committee chair Richard W. Pombo (R-CA) introduced H.R. 4893, Restricting Indian Gaming to Homelands of Tribes Act, which would have created new regulations limiting off-reservation gaming. Senate Indian Affairs Committee chair John McCain (R-AZ) introduced S. 2078, which would have amended the IGRA to repeal the two-part determination test and create new rules for Native nations seeking to take lands into trust for gaming purposes off their reservations. Concerned that these bills would permanently derail their work to build a casino in Cascade Locks, Warm Springs leaders traveled to Washington, DC, to testify at a hearing before the House of Resources Committee on November 9, 2005.[71] Warm Springs leaders hoped that the final versions of both bills would include a "grandfather clause" that would allow the Bridge of the Gods Casino project to move forward. On September 13, 2006, the Pombo Bill failed. Even though the House of Representatives voted in favor of the bill by a 247–171 vote, it did not meet the required super majority needed.[72] Senator McCain's S. 2078 never made it out of committee for a vote.

At the same time, Governor Kulongoski was up for reelection in 2006, an event of particular interest to both Grand Ronde and Warm Springs. Kulongoski had been clear that he would continue supporting the Cascade Locks location for a Warm Springs casino if he won. If he lost, Warm Springs would have to start negotiations for a Bridge of the Gods Casino all over again with a new governor. During the gubernatorial primaries, Grand Ronde received a substantial amount of media attention in response to ads they ran highlighting various aspects of the Kulongoski's record. One Associated Press article noted that Grand Ronde had spent $850,000 on ads in the primary and stated that the tribe would run another round of ads "targeting Kulongoski in the general election, if he persists in backing the Cascade Locks casino plan of the Confederated Tribes of Warm Springs."[73]

Several Grand Ronde Tribal Council leaders recalled that they were concerned about what they saw as increasing tensions between Grand Ronde and Warm Springs. In the hope of finding a middle ground that would be mutually beneficial and that might end the conflict that had arisen between the Native nations over the gorge location, Grand Ronde representatives made an offer to Warm Springs to assist them in financing a casino at the location of Warm Springs tribal members' choice, on the Warm Springs Reservation. According to Grand Ronde Tribal Council member Wesley "Buddy" West,

> Our primary concern was the changing of policy to off-reservation gaming. The Grand Ronde Tribal Council discussed it and said, "Hey, let's offer Warm Springs a good deal. Let's say we'll help finance a casino anywhere on their reservation." We wanted to keep the good relationship—they're our family members—and show them that we are not fighting them, we're fighting a policy change. Of course they declined it, and I can see it from their point of view. They saw Cascade Locks as a good source of revenue, and they've invested a few million dollars in this outfit. I am sure they had a lot of discussion about it before they declined. But this offer was us extending our hands and saying, "Listen, we want to do this for you. We see what you're trying to do to help your tribal members. Here's what we'll do to help you."[74]

A group of Grand Ronde leaders headed efforts to meet with Warm Springs leaders, sending them a letter detailing the offer to finance a Warm Springs casino. Grand Ronde tribal chair Chris Mercier explains,

> We saw that Grand Ronde probably wasn't going to change its stance on off-reservation gaming, and the tribe was willing to fight for that. We saw that Warm Springs wasn't really going to back away from their stance. So the whole point was really to try and develop a situation where the two

tribes could compromise. It would be an opportunity for us, and it would be an opportunity for them. I felt it would have been a win-win for the two tribes. I was chair during that time, and we actually sat down with some members of the Warm Springs Tribal Council and with [Governor Kulongoski] in Portland and tried to just hammer out an agreement, but it ended up just not working.[75]

Tribal leaders from Grand Ronde and Warm Springs met twice, and Warm Springs ultimately decided to decline the Grand Ronde offer.

Warm Springs tribal member Gerald Danzuka Jr. remembers,

I participated in family meetings with the Heath family, the Danzuka family, my own sisters, my uncle, and a few other close friends that we all worked quite closely with. We all talked about it, and I think it was a reasonable offer. Given the circumstances, Grand Ronde was attempting to negotiate a deal that they felt was good for everyone. I don't believe it was in our best interests to adopt it, and I agree with the council leadership that said, "Thank you, but no thanks." I don't perceive that as a negative thing. Grand Ronde was honestly trying to represent their people the best way they could, and it came out in that proposal.[76]

Individuals from Warm Springs share a variety of reasons for their decision not to accept the offer made by Grand Ronde. Several tribal leaders explain that Warm Springs had already invested a significant amount of time and resources in the tribe's bid to build in the Columbia River Gorge, and they had the mandate of their membership to follow that course of action to completion. Warm Springs representatives also felt that the proposed deal, even with its favorable terms, was not in the best economic interest of Warm Springs, a position that was supported by an analysis of the proposal conducted by gaming economist Bob Whelan of ECONorthwest.[77] According to Whelan's analysis, as the Grand Ronde offer stood, Warm Springs was likely to lose money while Grand Ronde would make money on the deal. Chairman Suppah says, "Faced with this analysis of the proposal made by Grand Ronde, we declined to participate."[78] Suppah notes, however, that economic considerations were not the only concerns: "Warm Springs has pretty much always liked to be independent and to pay their own way."[79]

When Kulongoski won reelection in 2006, it solidified the Warm Springs decision to continue to pursue the gorge location for a casino at Cascade Locks.

Although the tribe decided to turn down Grand Ronde's offer, Louie Pitt Jr. notes that Warm Springs made a counteroffer to Grand Ronde, inviting them to be investors in the Bridge of the Gods Casino project, which Warm Springs studies showed would bring both nations greater returns than the Grand Ronde proposal offer could.[80] Individuals from both Grand Ronde and Warm Springs involved in the discussion over the Grand Ronde offer to fund an on-reservation casino in Warm Springs stated that these conversations were fairly amicable. The matter soon became a point of contention between the two nations, however, when Grand Ronde made public their offer to Warm Springs and incorporated information about it into rhetoric opposing the casino. In response, Warm Springs publicly expressed their frustrations with Grand Ronde's opposition to the casino and with their decision to go public with details of the conversations about the Grand Ronde offer.[81] Relations between the two nations were strained after this.

New perspectives and positions typically accompany changes in administration at the federal and state level. Each incoming US president can appoint new people to such positions as secretary of the interior, which can directly result in changes to rules, policies, and laws that regulate the gaming economy. As Wendell Jim (Warm Springs) explains regarding the Bridge of the Gods Casino project, "Federal barriers kept creeping into place with the change of the secretary of the interior and the assistant secretary for Indian affairs and new rules coming about. All of those things were like a perfect storm for a casino in the gorge."[82] While Warm Springs had resolutely weathered threats to their economic endeavor posed by legislation and the gubernatorial election, new challenges to the Bridge of the Gods Casino emerged in 2006 when Dirk Kempthorne became President George W. Bush's appointee for secretary of the interior. Native nations seeking off-reservation locations for their casinos had good reason to be concerned about this appointment since Kempthorne had opposed off-reservation casinos when he was governor of Idaho.[83]

Kempthorne issued a new rule that required off-reservation casinos to be within a reasonable commuting distance from the reservation, making it more difficult for Native nations to meet the exceptions outlined in the IGRA. Though what would be considered reasonable was not defined in the rule, Assistant Secretary of Indian Affairs Carl Artman gave testimony in which he stated that forty miles was the farthest a Native nation could build a casino away from its reservation.[84] The memo containing this new rule, issued at the beginning of 2008, directly affected the Warm Springs attempt to build a casino in Cascade Locks, as Warm Springs leaders then had to argue that their proposed location was a reasonable commute despite the fact that the drive from Warm Springs to Cascade Locks was much longer than the seemingly arbitrarily chosen forty miles.[85]

In 2005, the BIA Northwest Regional Office initiated the two-part determination process by scheduling a series of public information meetings to inform the public about the proposed Cascade Locks casino and solicit public input on the issues that would need to be analyzed in an environmental impact statement (EIS) as required by the National Environmental Policy Act (NEPA).[86] As noted in the draft EIS that would be published three years later by the BIA, the act "mandates that the EIS determine, characterize, analyze, and document the project's environmental impacts, as well as specify possible mitigation of adverse effects. The EIS is used, along with other relevant information, by federal officials in making decisions."[87] Once input from state, local, and tribal officials had been solicited and the comment period was over, Warm Springs submitted a "45-page report, with hundreds of pages of supporting exhibits" to the secretary of the interior for review.[88] From 2006 to 2007, the BIA facilitated the EIS study of the Cascade Locks casino project, as well as an analysis of possible alternatives to the preferred site.

During this period, many in the Warm Springs community were becoming impatient with how long Secretary Kempthorne was taking to release the draft environmental impact statement (DEIS) and to publish the dates for public hearings in the *Federal Register*, a requirement to proceed with the process. They were not alone in such concerns. On November 8, 2007, the *Spilyay Tymoo* reported that the St. Regis Mohawk Tribe of New York had filed a lawsuit accusing Kempthorne of "undue delay and acting in bad faith on the tribe's application to put into federal trust land for a proposed casino," while "letting his personal opposition to off-reservation Indian gaming interfere with his legal responsibilities."[89] After significant delays, the BIA received confirmation in February 2008 that the Warm Springs environmental review process could move forward, and in March the DEIS was released for a ninety-day public review period. The next step required the BIA to hold a series of public hearings on the impact study's findings, with the goal of collecting public comment on the document. As a requirement of the NEPA, the DEIS included an analysis of the proposed Cascade Locks casino project as well as a "reasonable range of alternatives," including a no-action alternative, a Hood River alternative, and a Warm Springs on-reservation alternative.[90] The DEIS indicated that Cascade Locks was the best location for the casino because it would address the financial needs of the tribe and have the least impact on the environment. It also showed that the other alternatives either had greater environmental impacts or did not generate revenue sufficient to address the long-term economic needs of Warm Springs.[91] In the spring of 2008, five public hearings (discussed in chapter 6) were held to collect public input on the DEIS. All comments on the document were due by May 15.

The final EIS, published in August 2010, identified the Cascade Locks site as the preferred site for the Warm Springs casino, and another public input period of forty-five days followed the release of the report. Although Warm Springs had reason to hope that their project would be approved by new secretary of the interior Ken Salazar and approved by Governor Kulongoski, by 2010 Oregon's new gubernatorial candidates had already begun to voice their opposition to a Columbia River Gorge casino, and the election was fast approaching. The leading Democratic candidate was former governor John Kitzhaber, who had solidified the "one casino per tribe, on reservation" policy and had staunchly opposed the Warm Springs proposal in his previous terms. Secretary of the Interior Salazar approved the Warm Springs state-tribal compact on January 7, 2011, but no decision had been made about the Warm Springs fee-to-trust application for the lands at Cascade Locks. On January 10, John Kitzhaber became Oregon's thirty-seventh governor, which resurrected a long-term barrier to the tribe's goals. That year, Warm Springs decided to close the Kah-Nee-Ta casino and reopen what many saw as a temporary casino along US 26 in Warm Springs. In 2013 the Warm Springs Tribal Council voted to end efforts to open a casino in Cascade Locks, at least for the time being.

A LANDSCAPE OF POSSIBILITIES

As the case study detailed in this chapter highlights, the process Native nations must negotiate to situate a casino off their reservation in accordance with IGRA can be a long, daunting, and frustrating experience. An examination of the fifteen-year process of Warm Springs efforts to open a casino in the Columbia River Gorge illuminates the complex and quickly changing landscape of this economy. Native nations must be attentive to policy changes and challenges to the tribal casino economy at the federal level. With each new US president, alterations are made to policies and approaches forwarded by the secretary of the interior. Additionally, calls for IGRA reform often come from Congress. State and regional politics also can create access or barriers for tribes, depending on shifts in public opinion and differences in approaches and philosophies from one state governor to the next. Greg Leo, like many I spoke with, strongly believes in a different approach:

> Frankly, the United States government policy has been prejudicial toward Indians since the beginning. It's important for the people of the United States that the government works with tribal people—not get in their way, not tell them what to do—but to let tribal people do what they feel they need to do. The United States needs to be an aid and not a hindrance to the pursuit of tribal rights. How we treat Native Americans is super important to who we are as people, and if we act in a discriminatory way towards Indian people, it does not reflect well on us or our democracy or our way of life.[92]

Relations within and between Native nations also contribute to the landscape of possibilities in the tribal casino economy. As an examination of Warm Springs efforts suggests, tribal communities also have significant struggles over where, when, and how best to participate in the gaming economy. The long, convoluted, and uncertain process to situate an off-reservation casino can impact relationships between Native nations and leave leaders of both in limbo, without the ability to know how best to plan for their tribes' future or protect their membership. The highly regulated but inequitable tribal casino economy entails complex political systems as well as differences in circumstance that place Native nations in direct competition over what many believe are limited resources and opportunities, and it can contribute to intertribal conflict. In addition, disputes that arise between tribes can cost each community significant amounts of money spent on lawyers, lobbyists, and other consultants. Although the leaders of the competing Native nations described here may have disagreed with each other's perspectives, approaches, or tactics, they were both actively exercising their sovereign rights to determine their own future and take care of what they perceived as the best interests of their own citizens.

CHAPTER 6

Intertribal Relations and Conflict in the Casino Era

The most important thing as you're looking into the whole
Cascade Locks debate between Warm Springs and Grand
Ronde—and even how it's impacted Grand Ronde's relationship with other tribes and [the] Warm Springs relationship
with other tribes—is there's not a good answer. Warm Springs
leaders have a responsibility to look out for the economic via-
bility of their community. Grand Ronde's tribal leadership has
that same responsibility. And there's never going to be a good
answer.

—Eirik Thorsgard (Grand Ronde)

The federal and state government are very good at setting up
fights between tribes, because if tribes are fighting amongst
themselves they have very little time to focus on what's happening at the state level or the federal level, or even at the other
tribal levels, to do anything that would be useful.

—Ron Suppah Sr. (Warm Springs)

IN THE PART OF THE COLUMBIA RIVER THAT NOW FORMS THE BORDER
of Oregon and Washington is a location known as the Cascade Falls. The Cascade Falls were identified in two 1850s treaties negotiated between the United
States and Native peoples who would subsequently become the Confederated
Tribes of Grand Ronde and the Confederated Tribes of Warm Springs. The river
runs alongside the city of Cascade Locks, Oregon, where Warm Springs proposed to build their Bridge of the Gods Casino, a bid that lasted fifteen years
(1998–2013). After Warm Springs proposed to build the casino, Grand Ronde,

located a little over sixty miles Southwest of Portland, raised objections to the plan. As the case study in chapter 5 highlights, independent sovereign Native nations such as Warm Springs engaged in the tribal casino economy must navigate complex relationships with state and federal governments and bureaucrats and negotiate with a revolving cast of political players, a cast that may change quickly with each new election. While these shifting relationships are important to explore, it is also critical that the intertribal relations and conflicts that arise in the tribal casino economy are likewise interrogated.

In the spring of 2008, tensions ran high during the Draft Environmental Impact Statement (DEIS) public hearings on the proposed Bridge of the Gods Casino. Beginning on March 3, the Portland-based Bureau of Indian Affairs Northwest Area Office hosted five hearings: at the Kah-Nee-Ta Resort in Warm Springs; the Gorge Pavilion in Cascade Locks; the Rock Creek Center in Stevenson, Washington; the DoubleTree Hotel in Portland; and the Hood River Middle School. It was standing room only at each meeting as interested parties—including leaders, lobbyists, and community members from Grand Ronde, Warm Springs, other Oregon and Washington tribes, and the cities of Cascade Locks, Hood River, and Portland—came to show their opposition to or support for the Bridge of the Gods Casino. As individuals who testified at the DEIS hearings proclaimed their stances on the issue, some indicated where they thought the casino could or should be built; some questioned the morality of the casino economy; and others articulated their support for Indian gaming as a way to help cash-poor Native nations and other economically depressed communities such as Cascade Locks. Although the morality of gaming, environmental considerations, and the casino location were the central issues discussed, heated and emotionally charged testimony illuminated existing and growing tensions between Grand Ronde and Warm Springs. While many Grand Ronde and Warm Springs members gave heartfelt and thoughtful testimony about why they supported or opposed a gorge casino, a number of individuals used their time at the microphone to state their frustration, disappointment, and even anger with the other tribe's position on the subject.

For example, several Grand Ronde tribal members articulated their dismay and disbelief that Warm Springs would propose a casino that they believed would so clearly have a negative impact on Grand Ronde's economy and people. These Grand Ronde citizens argued that the BIA had a responsibility for the needs and well-being of Grand Ronde. They also stated that Grand Ronde too had claims to the area of Cascade Locks and that their claims needed to be recognized as legitimate as well. Many Grand Ronde tribal members said that they were worried that changes to Oregon's policy of one casino per tribe, on reservation, would lead to all Native nations in Oregon rushing to find better casino locations closer to metropolitan areas or would shift public opinion away from supporting tribal casinos, opening the door to non-Native gaming in Oregon. In addition, individuals argued that Warm Springs was historically privileged in ways that Grand Ronde was not, based on the fact that Warm Springs had never been subjected to termination, had a relatively large and intact land base, and had other economic options that were not available to the Grand Ronde people.

Conversely, a number of Warm Springs members expressed that they felt betrayed by Grand Ronde after Warm Springs had supported Grand Ronde during their restoration process. Speakers also stated that they resented Grand Ronde's well-funded opposition to the proposed casino when Warm Springs so desperately needed the economic boost the Bridge of the Gods casino would provide. While some agreed that the casino might affect Grand Ronde initially, many believed that both nations could have successful casinos and held that even if the new casino had a negative impact on Grand Ronde's Spirit Mountain Casino, this should be viewed as simply healthy competition between two businesses. Furthermore, it was clear that many Warm Springs people were frustrated by Grand Ronde's political claims to Cascade Locks. Based on the Treaty with the Tribes of Middle Oregon of 1855, Indian Claims Commission decisions, and the acknowledgment of their claim to the area by Governor Kulongoski (confirmed when he signed the state-tribal compact with Warm Springs), a number of individuals asserted that Warm Springs was the only one of the two Native nations who maintained an exclusive legal claim to the Cascade Locks region.[1] Other Warm Springs citizens argued that the state policy of one casino per tribe, on reservation, should not be viewed as a static, unchangeable policy but one that is a matter of tribal sovereignty—not the concern of all Native nations in the state—that could be modified through nation-to-nation negotiations. In addition, some members of Warm Springs felt that Grand Ronde was privileged by their close proximity to the Portland market and thought that their members were only concerned with protecting their own casino economy, even to the detriment of other Native nations.

No matter the arguments for or against the Bridge of the Gods Casino, both Grand Ronde and Warm Springs leaders made it clear that they were trying to do what they felt was in the best interests of their citizens. At times, however, the official positions taken by tribal representatives worked to delegitimize the needs or concerns of the other tribe. In the years of debate over the proposed gorge casino, tribal leaders, spokespeople, and members of both Native nations at times accused those from the other tribe of not acting the way they thought Native people should act or of having a colonized mentality. Though not representative of all of the complex positions that tribal members took on this issue, these statements of frustration, disappointment, and even anger reflect common sentiments articulated by tribal members and tribal employees over the years.

INTERTRIBAL CONFLICT ON THE NATIONAL STAGE

Intertribal casino politics have changed drastically since 1988, when Congress enacted the Indian Gaming Regulatory Act. Beginning around 1998, the United States witnessed a shift in intertribal relations as some casino-owning Native nations began to take oppositional approaches to other Native nations' gaming pursuits. From 1988 to 1998, tribes were most often unified in their support of tribal rights to own and operate gaming establishments, including casinos, while using their economic and political capital to resist state encroachment on these rights. In the years following, tribes—particularly ones that had experienced success in this economy—more regularly began to align themselves with states, elected officials, federal administrators, nongovernmental organizations, and citizen groups and to seek legal remedies in the courts to block other tribes' efforts to open casinos that might affect their own gaming markets. And this continues to the present. As Ian Lovett of the *New York Times* reported in 2014, "After decades of nearly uniform tribal support for Indian gambling—fighting in court and at the ballot box against state governments and anti-gambling politicians who sought to close their poker rooms—casino-owning Indian tribes have emerged as some of the most powerful and dogged opponents of new Indian casinos."[2] In several cases, Native nations that opposed new tribal casinos began to adopt some of the anti–Native casino rhetoric used by non-Natives to curb the growth of the casino economy. Some even conceived unprecedented tactics designed to obstruct their competitors' economic opportunities, including the practice of allowing the non-Native public to vote on the economic activities, supporting political campaigns, filing lawsuits to stop new casino projects, and partnering with state politicians against other Native nations.

Intertribal conflict in the casino era is not only news in Oregon but has shaped the gaming narrative on a national stage. For example, California has been the site of a growing number of intertribal disputes.[3] Lovett described a developing conflict between the Picayune Rancheria of Chukchansi Indians and the North Fork Rancheria of Mono Indians as "one of the most pivotal and expensive" and one of the "first times that tribes have turned to the ballot to fight another tribe's gambling plans."[4] Since the Chukchansi and North Fork peoples are historically and culturally interconnected through cultural and family relations, this conflict is personal and painful. In addition, it brings into sharp focus the fact that there are landless Native nations in California, as well as Native nations located in regions without many economic opportunities. In response to the North Fork's plans to have lands taken into trust for a casino in Madera County, the Chukchansi, who allied with Table Mountain Rancheria and Stand Up for California (a group that "monitors" gaming in the state) accused North Fork of being interlopers in the region and invoked the rhetoric of "reservation shopping" to argue that North Fork had no right to build a casino in the proposed location.[5]

In order to frustrate North Fork's plans, the Chukchansi and Table Mountain spent $2 million to get the issue on the November 2014 ballot, which put the question of whether or not the North Fork should be able to build a casino into the hands of California voters.[6] North Fork had successfully met the IGRA two-part determination test in 2011, negotiated a state-tribal compact with California governor Jerry Brown in 2012, and had land taken into trust for their casino and gained compact approval from the secretary of the interior in 2013. However, when it was put to a popular vote on November 4, 2014, 60.96 percent of California voters chose not to approve the North Fork compact.[7] In the past, California citizens have supported ballot initiatives in favor of tribal casinos in the state. In one notable example, in 1998, 62.4 percent of voters supported Proposition 5 to amend California state law to allow for tribal casinos and mandate the governor to negotiate tribal-state gaming compacts.[8] After the California Supreme Court deemed Proposition 5 unconstitutional, California citizens in 2000 again voted to support tribal casinos in California by approving Proposition 1A with 64.4 percent of the votes.[9] In these examples, California voters chose to support Native nations in their economic goals. However, while the Chukchansi and Table Mountain tribes are arguably within their sovereign rights to pursue all routes available to them to protect their tribal membership, the practice of allowing the non-Native public to vote on the economic activities of federally recognized Native nations could be interpreted as a violation of tribal sovereignty.

One of the most public intertribal conflicts in Arizona has involved the Tohono O'odham Nation and two neighboring and culturally related tribes, the

Salt River Pima-Maricopa Indian Community and the Gila River Indian Community. In the 2014 *New York Times* article cited above, Lovett argued that in response to the slowed growth of the Indian gaming economy, successful casino-owning Native nations in Arizona have concentrated efforts to "stifle the competition," including "lobbying lawmakers, contributing generously to political campaigns and filing lawsuits to stop new casino projects in their tracks."[10] A *Phoenix New Times* reporter attested to this, writing that "Gila River officials have maintained an exhaustive and costly campaign."[11] In an attempt to quash the Tohono O'odham bid to locate their West Valley Casino near Phoenix, Salt River and Gila River sought a remedy in the courts by filing a lawsuit.[12] In addition to the lawsuit, Gila River representatives employed anti–casino growth rhetoric to incite opposition to Tohono O'odham plans, warning citizens of the state that the casino would turn Phoenix into another Las Vegas. Gila River also lobbied Arizona residents via Facebook, asking them to support the federal Keep the Promise Act (H.R. 1410), which would have, if passed, prevented establishment of any new casino in the West Valley region of the Phoenix metro area until 2027, when current gaming agreements expire.[13]

Wisconsin has also been rife with intertribal conflicts over casinos. For example, in response to the Menominee Indian Tribe proposal for a Kenosha casino 150 miles away from their reservation, the Forest County Potawatomi tribe lobbied Governor Scott Walker to oppose Menominee. In addition, the Potawatomi tribe made contributions to both Republicans and Democrats.[14] Peter d'Errico, legal scholar and columnist for *Indian Country Today*, commented on the phenomenon of Native nations partnering with state politicians against other Native nations: "Strange as it may seem, the casino-owning Nations are appealing to state governments and politicians to help them fight rival casinos!" After comparing the new trend, in which tribes align with states against other Indian tribes, with the early colonial era, when tribes would sometimes ally themselves with European colonizing forces against other Indian tribes, d'Errico warned tribes to be wary of states: "Before an Indian Nation asks a state to help fight one of its enemies, it should ponder who its friends really are."[15]

While economic stability is desperately needed in Indian Country, the conflicts between Native nations that are historically, culturally, and politically interconnected can be particularly heated and painful. Although the casino economy itself, with the concomitant wealth that some Native nations accumulate, has been viewed as the cause of conflict, citing greed as the only explanation obscures important historical, political, and cultural circumstances and realities. As the Grand Ronde and Warm Springs conflict over the Bridge of the Gods Casino highlights, these disputes are often very personal to the Native peoples involved, shed light on complex and shifting relationships, and expose unique perspectives on and responses to economic development opportunities available through the casino economy. Further, such conflict reveals the ongoing reordering of tribe-to-tribe relationships that are constructed each generation in response to sometimes similar and sometimes disparate experiences with settler encroachment and federal Indian policy.

INTERTRIBAL RELATIONS: INTERCONNECTED PEOPLES

Grand Ronde and Warm Springs are distinct and separate sovereign nations, yet they are deeply interconnected historically, culturally, geographically, and politically. In 2014, when I asked Grand Ronde and Warm Springs tribal members about the tribes' historical relationship, most noted that the ties predated contact with settler societies and that both nations include Chinook-speaking peoples, such as the Wat-La-La, Clackamas, Wishram, and Wascoes, who lived along or near the Columbia River. These Native peoples controlled key rapids in the river, including ones at Cascade Falls, an important geographical boundary in the Treaty with the Tribes of Willamette Valley and the Treaty with the Tribes of Middle Oregon (both dating to 1855), negotiated between the United States and the Grand Ronde and Warm Springs tribes respectively. Warm Springs Tribal Council chair Ron Suppah Sr. explains that particular segments of each Native nation are related directly through kinship, and "the strongest connection probably here [in Warm Springs] with the Grand Ronde is the Wascoes because they shared territories to the north and west of [the Warm Springs Reservation]."[16] Tribal communities such as the Kalapuya, Chinook, and others who lived along the Columbia River, the Cascade Range, or the Willamette River, were also more broadly connected to each other in diverse social and economic ways.[17]

Native societies in Oregon were significantly altered after contact with European colonial forces, in large part because of the multiple epidemics that devastated tribal populations and the immigration of settlers who forced Native peoples onto small tracts of land. By the treaty-making period in the 1850s, Native peoples in Oregon had undergone some degree of reordering, and the removal period created further confusion as tribal communities were sometimes arbitrarily divided and removed to different reservations. Grand Ronde elder Bob Tom reflects, "When reservations were established they were established in the most remote places in the country, the places where farmers, ranchers, miners didn't want. So Indians were put in very remote places away from settler populations."[18]

The removal of Native peoples to reservations radically reorganized tribal life and further reordered relationships within and between Native nations. Tribal communities that shared geographic and cultural connections (including language) were often divided, and at the same time Native peoples who were vastly different had to find ways to live together on reservations.[19] The creation of reservations—and later the reordering of Native peoples into confederations—changed the ways that Native nations organized themselves and forced them to create new alliances.

Several Grand Ronde and Warm Springs people I interviewed stated that there were examples in their own families of relatives who became members of different Native nations in Oregon or Washington during the removal period. Though the details were often vague, interviewees suggested that tribal peoples living near Cascade Locks and the Cascade Falls were divided during the treaty and removal era, with some removed to Grand Ronde and others removed to Warm Springs. To complicate matters further, narrators also noted that individuals from this region might have been removed to other Oregon or Washington reservations, while others chose to remain along the Columbia River instead of relocating to a reservation.

Most of those I talked with discussed how tribal members continued to intermarry, maintain friendships, and conduct trade after reservations were created, explaining that these relationships took place not only on their reservations but also at important geographical locations along the Columbia, Willamette, and Santiam Rivers. Grand Ronde member Eirik Thorsgard shares, "At one point there were really close ties between the communities. Having been able to look through our tribal rolls, there's a great deal of intermarriage and intercommunication, and I have historical documents in my family of people going from Grand Ronde to Warm Springs to Yakima to Umatilla, and then back. And even to Siletz, and moving in this general circle of people that were all interrelated."[20]

Another individual who recognizes the deep connections between the two Native nations is elder Faye Wahenika (Warm Springs), who explains, "We traded a lot in the early years, and we were friends forevermore."[21] Also invoking this history of trade relations between these Native nations, Grand Ronde Tribal Council member Reynold Leno says, "I always remember people from

Warm Springs coming to my Grandpa and Grandma Leno's. They would have a trunk load of ice and salmon and would trade for deer meat. There were always people from Warm Springs here. The first time my dad left the reservation at seventeen was when he went up to what they called the CCC [Civilian Conservation Corps] camps up at Warm Springs where he could work because we had family up there. So, yeah, they did interact back and forth."[22] As these statements highlight, relations between Grand Ronde and Warm Springs continued in a variety of ways even after reservations began to form both Native communities into new legal, political, and cultural entities.

Although Native nations in the region continued to interact, the facts of resettlement and tribal confederation also placed new barriers between them. Jody Calica (Warm Springs) explains that to understand some of the issues that come up between Grand Ronde and Warm Springs in the casino era, it is vital to understand the history of how Native peoples were settled. According to Calica, Native nations' traditional identities were transformed during that era: "That sense of the traditional connection between our people has been lost over time, because of legal considerations, political considerations, economic considerations. That relationship is broken down."[23]

These new social and political configurations also created new relationships based upon Indianness in relation to the Oregon settler society. Native peoples within the state began to know one another in these new forms as their identities solidified in relation to the dominant society. Members of Grand Ronde and Warm Springs see themselves as kin, political allies, business competitors, and as individuals motivated by self-interests. The relationship between Grand Ronde and Warm Springs can be framed as any of these alone, but it is commonly seen by the members of these Native nations as a combination of all four.

"QUARREL AND FIGHT": THE BRIDGE OF THE GODS AND INTERTRIBAL CONFLICT

On November 16, 2013, famed traditional storyteller, poet, and playwright Ed Edmo (Shoshone-Bannock) sat on the stage at Mt. Scott Community Center in Portland and told his adaptation of the Bridge of the Gods legend for a Native American Family Days event. Through tone, inflection, repetition, and expressive hand gestures, Edmo brought the story of Wy'east, Klickitat, and Loo-wit alive:

Long time ago there's the Bridge of the Gods legend. There were two brothers who wanted better land for the people. One was named Wy'east, and
the other was Klickitat. They were chiefs of the tribes, but they were really,
really poor. The Great Spirit brought them asleep to this part of the country.
He woke up the brothers and told one, "Shoot your arrow to the north."
Klickitat shot his arrow to the north of Nch'i-wána. As far as that arrow went
was the Klickitat Tribe's. Great Spirit told the other brother, "Shoot your
arrow to the south." Wy'east shot his arrow south to the Willamette River
Valley. As far as that arrow went was the Multnomah Tribe's. The Great
Spirit said, "I'll build this sign of peace for you over Nch'i-wána." The Great
Spirit built a large land bridge with tall trees and river rocks on it. It was
called Bridge of the Gods. Multnomahs took trips across the bridge and
traded in fish, for a long, long time. But they began to quarrel and fight. The
Great Spirit got angry because the people shouldn't quarrel and fight. Great
Spirit took away the sun. The people pleaded, "Please give us the sun, or
we'll die from the cold!" The Great Spirit went to an old woman way up
in the mountain. An old gray-haired woman. Her name was Loo-wit. She
had fire. The Great Spirit said, "So what do you want if you share your fire
with the people?" Loo-wit thought. She thought long. She thought hard. She
thought long and hard. She said, "I want to become young and beautiful."
The Great Spirit said, "Tomorrow that will be. Take your fire to the bridge."
The Great Spirit returned the sun to the people. As the sun was rising over
Nch'i-wána, on the Bridge of the Gods was a young, beautiful woman watching fire. And the people rejoiced because they knew it was a gift from the
Great Spirit. Wy'east and Klickitat wanted to marry the young woman. One
would bring a gift. One would bring another gift. One would bring a bigger
gift. One would bring a bigger and better gift. And they started fighting,
and the people were hurt. The Great Spirit got angry, and he caused the
earth to shake. And the Bridge of the Gods fell into the river. As punishment
he changed the people into mountains. Wy'east changed into Mount Hood.
Klickitat, Mount Adams. Loo-wit into Mount St. Helens. And that's how the
mountains came to be.[24]

Like Wy'east and Klickitat, the chiefs in the Bridge of the Gods story, Grand
Ronde and Warm Springs leaders continue to want a better life for themselves
and their people. However, after generations of encroachment from colonizing
settler societies; mass land dispossession; destruction of habitats and traditional economies that supported tribal people; and assimilationist/civilization

projects that undermined, ruptured, or completely destroyed social and political systems and other Indigenous ways of knowing, there are now a wide range of perspectives on what constitutes and fosters a better life for Native nations. This appears to have led to some of the divisiveness within and between Native nations. Today tribal leaders have multiple pressures, including the membership expectation that tribal leaders will meet the economic, educational, social, and cultural needs of the tribe, both on and off the reservation; a lack of consensus over what issues and values to prioritize; issues of nepotism and family politics; and at times the desire of leaders to advance themselves for personal gain.

Grand Ronde's opposition to the Bridge of the Gods Casino proposal was not the only barrier to the Warm Springs efforts to locate a new casino in Cascade Locks, but it severely tested intertribal relations. Leaders from both Grand Ronde and Warm Springs stated that they felt they were doing what they had to do to support the needs of their own tribal members. Although each nation at times acknowledged that the other was doing the same to protect its community, commentary from the tribe members illuminated the fact that conflict arose from more than just competition over business. Rather, the conflict was about kinship, identity, political alliances, and shared and divergent histories. A number of Grand Ronde and Warm Springs members have expressed that it creates a problem for all Native nations when tribes "quarrel and fight" publicly in the casino era and that these public conflicts can severely damage the relationship and camaraderie of contemporary Native nations. In the following pages I explore three areas most often discussed by tribal members and their employees when explaining factors they saw as contributing to intertribal conflict: termination and restoration, racialized identities, and claims to ceded land and political space.

Termination and Restoration

When Grand Ronde members began to articulate their objections to a casino in the Columbia River Gorge, Warm Springs leaders expressed their surprise that Grand Ronde would oppose them publicly and actively lobby against them. In response to Grand Ronde's vocal opposition, Warm Springs people often stated that this was particularly offensive in light of the fact that Warm Springs had been a key advocate for Grand Ronde when the latter fought to be restored in the 1980s. Warm Springs members and representatives commonly expressed the sentiment that if the Grand Ronde people remembered this history, they wouldn't have lobbied against the Warm Springs casino proposal.

Others noted that if Warm Springs hadn't helped Grand Ronde, the latter's federal recognition might not have been restored, and by extension the Grand Ronde tribe would not have a casino and so would be unable to fund a campaign against the proposed Warm Springs casino.

Recalling the historical moment when Warm Springs supported Grand Ronde's restoration efforts, Calica explains that Warm Springs leaders were compelled to help terminated Native nations in part because they felt that these nations had been deeply wronged by the policy of termination.[25] Calica notes that when the terminated Native nations had sought reinstatement as federally recognized Native nations, there had been a "fairly significant reliance" on the non-terminated Native nations, Warm Springs and Umatilla. Suppah (Warm Springs) describes how Warm Springs donated time and resources to restoration efforts: "At the time, the people really needed help to get restored, so they asked Warm Springs to help them out. We knew United States Representative Al Ullman well, we knew United States Senator Mark Hatfield well, and we utilized those connections to leverage assisting them in getting restored."[26]

As a tribe that had never been terminated and that had a stable economy and strong leaders, Warm Springs had had thirty years to build relationships with federal and state agencies, and it enjoyed a certain level of political clout in the 1980s. Warm Springs attorney Dennis Karnopp explains, "There was a time before gaming when Warm Springs was the most politically active tribe in Oregon on both a national and a statewide scale. And [they] had very, very good relationships—as we continue to have—with senators and representatives in Congress. Warm Springs [leaders'] view of these issues at that time was very valuable to congressional leadership."[27]

Warm Springs used their political connections and resources to support Grand Ronde during this period, and some Warm Springs people remembered helping organize meetings with terminated nations before and after restoration to provide information about how to function as a federally recognized Native nation and provide cultural and spiritual support to Grand Ronde.[28] "The reason that there is conflict right now really comes down to oral tradition," says Warm Springs member Brent Florendo. "I think that the Indian people do not remember the story of the relationship between Warm Springs and Grand Ronde. All these tribes up and down the valley were terminated, and when they went for restoration, Warm Springs stepped forward and used our political clout and supported them as best we could. So that they could get restored, and they got restored.[29]

When Warm Springs people remembered this history, many strongly expressed that supporting terminated Native nations in Oregon was the right thing to have done. Wendell Jim, however, perceives that helping Grand Ronde and other terminated nations in their work to get reinstated came at a price for Warm Springs: "The federal government earmarks money for federally recognized tribes for Indian health, housing, or education. But as we continue to add a restored tribe or a new tribe gets federally recognized, that pie is still the same amount, but you have more tribes trying to divvy that pie up now."[30] When Warm Springs people chose to advocate for Grand Ronde and other terminated Native nations, they did so with full knowledge that federal support of Native nations might not increase and that the funds available would need to be shared with newly restored tribal nations.

Particularly difficult for many Warm Spring people during the conflict over the proposed casino was a perceived departure from usual intertribal interactions, in which Native nations in Oregon had tended to either support each other's endeavors or stay clear of one another's business when they chose not to be supportive. Chief Heath (Warm Springs) shares his frustrations with this change in intertribal relations between Grand Ronde and Warm Springs: "We should still be Indians, in our heart, and try to help other tribes. Not try to tear tribes down. We don't appreciate Grand Ronde coming against our people. We're trying to do something to help our people. You have done something to help your people. Now that you've got it, why are you against us?"[31] Many Warm Springs people say that it made them sad or angry to know that another tribe with whom they'd had such close relations, who knew about their economic hardships, would use casino profits to lobby against what many saw as their best chance for economic stability. A common sentiment in Warm Springs was that Grand Ronde had forgotten this historical relationship of friendship and support between the two communities.

Several Warm Springs members believe that Grand Ronde's public opposition came from their leaders but did not necessarily reflect the point of view held by all Grand Ronde people. A few Warm Springs members describe instances in which Grand Ronde members sought them out and expressed their displeasure with their own leaders' choice to oppose the Warm Springs casino. Former Warm Springs Tribal Council member Aurolyn Stwyer recalls, "I did have individual Grand Ronde people approaching me and telling me that there was a silent majority that did not agree with the leadership and would offer me some information about who to talk to. There were a few individuals that approached me when I went to Salem. They knew we were in town, and they would find us and talk."[32]

In addition, many Warm Springs members suggest that there was a difference between the way the perceived this relationship and the views of younger, newly emergent leaders who did not have the same emotional ties or feelings of obligation to Warm Springs. Grand Ronde elder Kathryn Harrison, who was central to the Siletz and Grand Ronde restoration efforts, provides a number of examples in which Warm Springs advocated for Grand Ronde restoration and culturally and politically supported them after restoration. Harrison specifically notes the efforts of one Warm Springs tribal member, Rudy Clements: "He would tell us what to expect as a recognized tribe and he was great teacher, just a great teacher. Of course there was always food, and the council would come in now and then, and some of the elders would come and tell us stories. It was a great relationship. I think most of all because we were being accepted again. We were taking our rightful place in the family of Indian nations."[33]

Harrison's comment reflects the sense of justice Grand Ronde members felt at being recognized as Indian peoples. She also recalls that Clements invited newly restored Native nations to Kah-Nee-Ta for classes on how to function as a federally recognized tribe: "After we got restored, Grand Rondes were invited to Kah-Nee-Tah—of course we thought we were all big because that was the place to go in those days. It was Rudy and some of his people that came in and taught us what the laws were—some of it we knew already, but it was a good refresher course. He did a good job, and at the end we all got certificates. Then Rudy would come down to Grand Ronde to talk to our people, and he taught dancing, singing and drumming. He was a good friend."[34]

Harrison says that some Grand Ronde members don't have a historical memory that goes back far enough to recognize all that went into the restoration process or the relationships that it built between tribal communities. She also explains that while Warm Springs was a great help to Grand Ronde, it was by no means the only community that supported Grand Ronde's restoration efforts. According to Harrison, other Northwest tribes, tribal organizations, public officials, and individuals from the non-Indian communities also supported Grand Ronde.[35]

Like many Grand Ronde people interviewed, John Mercier is happy to acknowledge that Warm Springs played a role in Grand Ronde restoration efforts: "I do know that Indian people in general have a tradition of supporting each other. Warm Springs maintained that tradition, and they supported the Grand Rondes in the Grand Rondes' restoration efforts."[36] Although the majority of Grand Ronde people I interviewed had positive things to say about this historical relationship between the two tribes, several said that hey wished they knew more about the history of the relationship during the restoration period.

While Grand Ronde people often agree that Warm Springs helped Grand Ronde during and after restoration, not everyone concurs on the scope of that assistance or its relevance to Grand Ronde's opposition to a Bridge of the Gods Casino. Tribal Council chair Chris Mercier notes that some Grand Rondes thought Warm Springs had been very helpful to restoration while others felt that Warm Springs hadn't done that much.[37] Grand Ronde member Wesley "Buddy" West says, "I have been told that Warm Springs did support us, and I applaud them for that. I am sure that we would have supported them if they were in the same situation. I just personally cannot support a Warm Springs casino at Cascade Locks, when it actually hurts our tribe and the tribal members if that were to come to pass."[38] Tribal Council vice-chair Angela Blackwell echoes the complex reactions of Grand Ronde members and leaders regarding this issue: "All of the people that were actually a part of trying to get us restored have been really sorry to see us at odds with Warm Springs, because Warm Springs, in their eyes, were the ones that were there and helpful to us in gaining restoration. Current council members and current tribal members don't know it, and they don't remember it, so they don't feel the same kind of obligation to Warm Springs that some of the old timers do. There's a difference in how Warm Springs is perceived, and [that] depends on who you talk to."[39]

Blackwell expresses a common perception among Grand Ronde people that those most distressed by Grand Ronde's opposition to the proposed Warm Springs casino were Grand Ronde members who had been involved with the restoration process. In addition, she notes that this had led to internal disagreements within Grand Ronde over the decision to formally oppose the Bridge of the Gods Casino project through avenues such as joining the Coalition for Oregon's Future and allocating funds to oppose off-reservation gaming in the state. Other Grand Ronde members confirm that this was not an easy decision for the leaders and say that the community had mixed reactions after learning the outcome of the vote. In many cases, individuals can understand the decision but are sad that it seemed to create a rupture between the tribes. Some express their dislike for the decision but understand the difficult predicament of their leaders in their desire to protect the well-being of Grand Ronde members.

A few Grand Ronde members express concern that the history between Warm Springs and Grand Ronde during restoration was used to argue that

Grand Ronde shouldn't object to the gorge casino, even though it could have hurt their community. Several, including individuals who say that Warm Springs was an important ally, express frustration at hearing what they believe is a Warm Springs claim that Grand Ronde's restoration was achieved solely because of Warm Springs support. Reynold Leno expresses a concern shared by other Grand Rondes that the narrative of Warm Springs assistance worked to obscure their own efforts in the restoration process: "We got restored because we're Indians, not because some other tribe says we were Indians. So whether it would have been Warm Springs, Yakama, or anybody else, restoration was done by us, and we were restored because we are Indians. We never quit being Indians. I was terminated when I was four years old, but it didn't make me quit being an Indian."[40]

The more that Warm Springs people articulated their disappointment with Grand Ronde for opposing their casino plans, citing the relationship of support during restoration, the more Grand Ronde people expressed their frustration with the narrative that Warm Springs support was the primary reason they got restored. Although almost all the people interviewed feel that it was unfortunate that there were such hard feelings between the two tribes, many feel that the restoration narrative has worked to obscure the tremendous efforts of the Grand Ronde people and called into question their authenticity as Indians.

"Real" Indians: Racialized Identities

While Grand Ronde and Warm Springs experienced a number of parallel events as Indian people, including being subjected to removals, reservation conditions, and federal laws and policies, the two tribes' experiences were nonetheless quite different. Termination and restoration created disparities in the experiences of Native nations in Oregon that had previously not existed. Some maintained their status as recognized Native nations, while others saw this status severed unilaterally by Congress. Even after several of Oregon's terminated Native nations were restored, many tribal people, even some Grand Ronde members, viewed these restored nations as "new tribes," lagging behind non-terminated Native nations in culture, resources, and political clout. Blackwell explains her view of this phenomenon as it affects Grand Ronde and Warm Springs: "There is a really big difference between the terminated tribes of Oregon and the non-terminated tribes of Oregon. Warm Springs and Umatilla are the only two tribes that were never terminated. For some tribal people it seems as though Grand Ronde people are less Indian. We are not seen as real because we are not isolated to a reservation. We are not full-blood, most of us aren't, because our parents married people outside of the tribe. So we don't look like Indians to them."[41]

Blackwell further notes that restored Native nations are often accused of being too assimilated, acculturated to the dominant society, and perhaps even less racially Native as a result of intermarrying more often with non-Natives. Grand Ronde elder Chips Tom and Tribal Council member Kathleen Tom discuss their memories of this:

> Kathleen: Non-terminated Indians used to make fun of us. They'd call us the hamburger Indians.
> Chips: "Ground round," like the hamburger.
> Kathleen: Yeah, and they'd make fun of us. When we were terminated, they kind of went, "You're not Indian, because you don't have your roll numbers." So, you know, there was some of that before.[42]

The Toms discerned that the term "hamburger Indians" was used to imply that Grand Ronde people were all mixed, not fully Native people in the way non-terminated Native people were.

Several Grand Ronde members assert that termination legislation, as it applied to their Native nation, needs to be understood as an illegal action on the part of the federal government. As David Lewis argues, "There are many actions taken by Indian agents and the tribes that together suggest the conclusion that the Grand Ronde Tribe did not consent to termination."[43] Lewis adds that he thinks the non-terminated Native nations in Oregon believe that Grand Ronde members voluntarily gave up their rights to be Native people: "They think that we voted or chose to be terminated. So while we know the truth— while elders here know the truth, that we didn't choose to be terminated, that we were just terminated without our vote—it's been difficult re-educating tribal folks out there that we didn't agree to termination."[44]

Even though some Grand Ronde people considered the idea of consenting to termination legislation, Lewis notes that Grand Ronde leaders were under the impression that termination would free the tribe from federal ward status and that they would be unencumbered by federal guardianship. The rhetoric in support of termination legislation relied on ideals of emancipation, which may have appealed to some tribal people who were frustrated with the management (or mismanagement) of tribal affairs by the BIA. Ultimately Congress voted to unilaterally sever the government-to-government relationship with Grand Ronde without clear tribal consent.[45]

Termination, relocation, and restoration are central to the tribal identity and historical narrative of Grand Ronde, just as continuity in traditions and an unbroken treaty have been central features of the Warm Springs core identity as a tribe. Thorsgard (Grand Ronde) explains that, in his view, the impact of termination on tribal identity is neither well understood nor accepted by non-terminated tribes:

> It has a lot to do with the self-identification of Grand Ronde. I don't think Warm Springs has the same understanding of it because they didn't undergo the process of termination. I think they feel sorry for us, and they helped with restoration, but they don't understand the pain that is sometimes associated with being a terminated tribe. When your whole life is dictated by federal policy—which is something that Warm Springs is aware of to a certain degree—your sense of identity, of self, and community is completely raked and destroyed. This can lead to post-traumatic stress disorder even for tribal members who didn't go through the process of termination because they have to reestablish their connection to a value of self. That's really what Grand Ronde has been going through.[46]

Thorsgard's statement illuminates the problems that can exist between Native nations as a result of not understanding each other's histories or contemporary realities. While racial, cultural, and physical markers of difference are often identified as contributing factors in intertribal conflicts, the diversity of Indian Country is also the outcome of intergenerational conditions, institutionalized through law and policy that affected tribal communities in diverse and sometimes inequitable ways.

Ceded Lands and Political Space

As anthropologist Ella Clark wrote in her collection of Indian legends, "Tribes from central Oregon to northeastern Washington related traditions about a legendary rock 'bridge' that spanned the Columbia River 'one sleep' below the site of The Dalles. When it fell, old Indians said to early travelers, its rocks formed the Cascades in the river."[47] The Cascade Falls serve as a geographical boundary in two 1855 Oregon treaties. Grand Ronde's Treaty with the Confederated Tribes of the Willamette Valley (also known as the Treaty with the Kalapuya) names Cascade Falls in the Columbia River as its northeastern boundary, while the Warm Springs Treaty with the Tribes of Middle Oregon identifies the same location as its northwestern boundary.

When Warm Springs asserted their intention to build a new casino in Cascade Locks, a new dimension was added to the conflict developing between the two communities. Both tribes made cultural and legal claims to the region of Cascade Locks. Warm Springs maintained that it had long-term and uninterrupted exercise of sovereign authority in the Cascade Locks region, while Grand Ronde representatives observed that, depending on how the boundaries were drawn, some parts of Cascade Locks were within the lands ceded by one of their treaties. They therefore argued that they should have a seat at the table to discuss tribal economic development in that region, particularly when it could directly affect their tribe.

Grand Ronde's articulation of legal claim to the Cascade Locks region came as a shock to Warm Springs tribal members, and many note that it appeared to be another tactic to block the Warm Springs casino plans. Aurolyn Stwyer remembers how she first became aware that Grand Ronde was making a political claim to Cascade Locks:

> As vice-chairwoman of the Tribal Council I took a trip to Washington, DC, to meet with the assistant secretary of the interior and our state senators. On one of our visits we saw some brochures that the Grand Ronde tribe was passing out on the Hill. It was a map of their territory, and on the map was Cascade Locks. After that we were constantly cleaning up misconceptions about our connection to Cascade Locks. I was raised on the river in Cascade Locks during the fishing season. My father was the ceremonial fisherman for our tribe. My brother graduated at Cascade Locks High School. My mother named a downtown street, Wanapa ("By the River"), in Cascade Locks. I have a personal history of our people exercising our treaty rights fishing at Cascade Locks. My son does today in our family arena. So you can imagine the shock to see Grand Ronde put in a map showing Cascade Locks as their territory.[48]

Many at Warm Springs took these claims by another tribe as an unwelcome intrusion into their ceded lands. Among other evidence for establishing Cascade Locks as Warm Springs territory, they pointed to their 1855 treaty and an Indian Claims Commission (ICC) case decided on December 18, 1972.[49] Warm Springs attorney Karnopp argues that even if Grand Ronde had historically retained treaty rights in the Cascade Locks region, their legal and political rights were severed when Grand Ronde was terminated.[50] While there are a number of Grand Ronde people who strongly dispute this conclusion,

Karnopp's contention highlights the complicated legal arguments that have been developed by tribes struggling to defend their claims to culturally and economically significant places.

Many Warm Springs people have stated that their relationship to the land at Cascade Locks and the adjacent Columbia River is deeply meaningful. Indeed, it is foundational to their tribal identity. In Karnopp's words, "One thing that really is important in the Warm Springs tribal perspective is that they are river people. They lived along the Columbia River and the tributaries and were a salmon people. That is central to their whole history as a people, not just as individuals. The people on the reservation don't think of just the reservation as their homeland. They've got reserved rights to other places—rights they exercise—and so they think of the Cascade Locks area [as] part of their home."[51] Karnopp remarks that there were many people who had ideas about where Warm Springs could and should build a new casino, but for Warm Springs people, building a casino along the Columbia River was important beyond the potential fiscal benefit from the great location. It would mean reestablishing a tribally controlled land base along the river.

A number of Grand Ronde people acknowledge that they are aware that Warm Springs disputed their tribe's claims to the Cascade Locks area. Blackwell explains this by again citing the termination of Grand Ronde as the reason that there is a difference of opinion over land claims: "There's a lot of disagreement about the Cascade Locks land, as far as whether Grand Ronde has any cultural links or ties to it. Because we were terminated, some people just don't see us as being really Indians and discount our cultural ties to that land. Our treaties actually go right through Cascade Locks and over to the Coast Range."[52]

While Grand Ronde people who speak out about their relationship to the Cascade Locks region do not deny Warm Springs claims to the area, they argue that they had concurrent historical, cultural, and political claims. In response to the ICC case that Warm Springs uses as evidence that Cascade Locks is their ceded land, Leno (Grand Ronde) explains that "when that commission made its determination, it was in '72. We weren't restored, so we had no input into it."[53] Many Grand Ronde members disclose that, for their members, it was a challenge just to survive during the thirty years the tribe was terminated, leaving few with the time or resources to advocate for their tribe's claims and relationships to land and resources.

A number of individuals at Grand Ronde comment that their tribe was in the process of reestablishing a political presence in their aboriginal territories, their usual and accustomed land use areas, and the ceded lands defined in their treaties—a relationship that many Grand Rondes argue was severed during the termination era. Reestablishing cultural and political relationships to the land has been a complicated process. As Lewis explains, Grand Ronde's attempts to do so directly inform the conflict over the proposed Cascade Locks casino site:

> The assumption is, if we chose to be terminated, chose to stop being Indian and start basically being white or assimilated Indians, that we're not being responsible towards our ancestors and to the spiritual needs of the land. The fact is we still want to be responsible for that kind of stuff, and in fact we still feel that responsibility. That plays into our relationship with Warm Springs. I think in a sense they moved into various areas that were within our ceded lands and started taking those responsibilities upon themselves because they have also ancestral connections with various areas. We feel at times that the oversight of Warm Springs comes into or overlaps with our area. That relates to the casino issue. They're placing the casino on what we call the line in Cascade Locks. We know that there is a boundary line that went down through Cascade Locks that was decided by two different treaties. It's written into the Willamette Valley Treaty and right next to it the Middle Oregon Treaty. So the question is, are they trying to place their new casino on the Willamette Valley side or on their side? What we've come to in our investigation [is that] it looks like they're placing it on the line, with part of it on their side, and part may be on our side. So we're saying that while that may be the best piece of land in the area, it's still on a line, and over the line, we think.[54]

There are people from both tribes who are adamant that Cascade Locks is part of their ceded lands, but some members also acknowledge that ambiguities in treaty-defined boundaries make it difficult to determine with certainty where one treaty boundary ended and the other began. Oregon tribes rely heavily on treaties to protect claims and to position themselves politically in relation to the state and other tribes. Treaties are important documents that have been used successfully to defend rights and land, yet they are far from perfect in many ways, and at times they add to the confusion and disagreement between tribes.

Multifaceted circumstances bring these two communities into conflict over a political space that overlaps. Since the treaty-making period in the mid-nineteenth century, Warm Springs has fought, often successfully, to have their political space recognized by federal and state agencies, so it is not surprising that many Warm Springs people feel that their long-standing primacy and legal claim to the Cascade Locks region has been wrongly challenged. Conversely, many Grand Rondes explain that Congress unilaterally and illegitimately severed their claims to political space through termination legislation. Today Grand Ronde members are actively reestablishing themselves in an area in which they believe they have cultural and political claims and rights, but members often express that they are treated as though they don't deserve a place at the table due to the fact that Grand Ronde is a restored tribe.

Discussing tribal conflicts over ceded lands and political space, some narrators state that Native nations in many ways became their own greatest enemy—at times adopting colonial mentalities and logics to impose even stricter boundaries and divisions on themselves than those imposed upon them by the settler society via federal Indian laws and policies. The intricacies of these disputes are complicated and even painful, but for both communities the struggles over ceded lands and political space are about much more than competition for casino markets. They are about tribal relationships to land, the recognition of rights, and the continuance of healthy tribal communities.

BEYOND SYMPTOMS TO AN "INDIAN FIRST" MENTALITY

When it comes to decisions about tribally important cultural and political spaces, both Grand Ronde and Warm Springs desire a seat at the table. They don't always agree, however, about who has a right to be at the table, particularly when they are at odds over overlapping boundaries and claims. Nonetheless, almost all of the Grand Ronde and Warm Springs members I interviewed say that they would have liked to have seen their two tribes interacting differently in order to avoid the conflict between the communities over the Bridge of the Gods Casino. Suppah (Warm Springs) made a connection between strong tribal unity and the long-term health of tribal communities: "The interactions that I appreciate the most are when tribal people band together, unite, and help each other. That always works better. It has a way of dissolving fences—and we have a bad tendency of building fences. For us to evolve as a nation these [fences] are going to have to come down. I hope that the interaction [will] be one of acceptance that the tribes have the abilities to take care of themselves."[55]

Several individuals state that they thought the tribes' leaders should have had more conversations about mutually beneficial solutions instead of quickly taking oppositional standpoints. Others feel that mediation between the tribes would have helped them work together to build a statewide tribal casino economy. While many narrators have ideas about how tribes might work together, several express doubt that the tribal leaders will employ these cooperative strategies, particularly given that they want to get the best deal for their own members.

Reflecting on the strained relationship between Grand Ronde and Warm Springs, Grand Ronde elder Bob Tom says that he felt many of the comments made and positions argued by tribal leaders were really symptoms that resulted from colonization, perpetuated through federal laws and policies and often obscured from view:

> Sometimes tribes are talking about symptoms, and you can talk about symptoms all day and kind of be complaining, but identifying symptoms helps you identify need. Rarely do tribes go beyond talking about the symptoms and talk about the real problems. A symptom is a tribe isolated in central Oregon without a nearby population to support a casino economy. If one tribe isn't as far along culturally, that is a symptom of termination. So you hear two tribes talking about symptoms, but they don't ever get right down and talk about the problem and start dealing with the problem.[56]

Tom further says that he thinks the issues most often addressed reflect what he called a "government mentality," in which tribes argue their position with only their own people's interests in mind. Tom points out that tribal representatives have spent a lot of time debating symptoms, such as which tribe was more disadvantaged as a result of their reservation and their proximity to the broader settler society, the differences created as a result of federal termination, and cultural or racial differences. Instead, Tom argues, tribes should be talking with each other with an "Indian first" mentality, one in which the tribal leaders consider each other in decision-making and embrace an approach that works for the best interests of all tribal people.[57] Tom is not alone in his assessment. Several other tribal members note that tribes had more strength when they worked alongside each other, not by ignoring the differences between tribes, not by claiming the same Indian experiences, but by learning about the other's experiences and collaborating to make power for all.

In the case of the intertribal conflict that emerged between Grand Ronde and Warm Springs, several areas of commonality become apparent through interviews and conversations with tribal members and their employees. Narrators from both communities talk at length about how important it is for them to find ways to support their respective tribes as healthy, self-determined nations that provide good governance, services, and resources to their membership. Blackwell points out that revenues from Grand Ronde's Spirit Mountain Casino support tribal autonomy, including freedom from restrictive federal oversight: "Gaming revenues have really allowed us to examine the needs of our own people and decide for ourselves where the greatest needs are instead of the federal government deciding for us."[58]

Blackwell further explains that gaming dollars made it possible for Grand Ronde to provide for their members in ways that had previously been impossible, with leaders directing profits to vital services and resources, such as housing, health care, and educational programs. Warm Springs members also want their fellow citizens to thrive, to determine their own futures, and to be provided for by the tribe. Suppah says that he hopes one day Warm Springs will be able to build and operate their own school system: "We would divorce ourselves from the state and the counties and simply build our own school, pay for it ourselves, administer it ourselves, create our own curriculum, and hire our own teachers. We already have the early childhood center. That would be all the way from [kindergarten to twelfth grade], and then potentially, down the road, we would look at some sort of vocational school or a small Indian college."[59]

Other Warm Springs members also share their goals for their tribe's future. Gerald Danzuka Jr. desires an effective archival system that would help protect and preserve the culture and heritage of the three Warm Springs peoples (Wasco, Warm Springs, and Northern Paiute).[60] Wendell Jim wants to see any tribally owned business operated by highly skilled tribal members trained to fill key roles.[61]

Both Grand Ronde and Warm Springs tribes want to correct misconceptions among the general non-Native public about the tribes and ensure that accurate information is available. Florendo (Warm Springs) argues that the circumstances that contribute to intertribal conflict will continue to exist until the broader public is reeducated about tribal histories, contemporary concerns, and concepts such as sovereignty: "Until we establish Native Studies programs, until we establish across-the-board teaching of Native America in our elementary, junior high, and high schools, making a level playing field, it's going to stay the same."[62]

Other Grand Ronde and Warm Springs members also note that as long as tribes' economic opportunities and the recognition of tribal rights are beholden to public opinion and the whims of public officials (who often have minimal or distorted knowledge of Native nations), tribes will continue to struggle in a system that is inequitable and discriminatory.

Despite the tensions between Grand Ronde and Warm Springs as a result of the casino economy and the proposed Bridge of the Gods Casino, interviewees made it very clear that the two tribes continue to be deeply intertwined. Blackwell shares her view on current relations between the tribes: "There are definitely issues where there's a common concern that we will work together on. And we still see each other at conferences, like the Affiliated Tribes of Northwest Indians or the National Congress of the American Indian. So the relationship isn't all bad—it's definitely a disagreement in this one area—but not everybody in Warm Springs agrees with the position that Warm Springs has taken, and not everybody in Grand Ronde agrees with the position Grand Ronde has taken."[63]

Members from the two tribes continue to share political goals and participate in federal and regional organizations (although in at least one case Native nations withdrew from an Oregon intertribal gaming coalition in what appears to be the fallout of this disagreement over the gorge casino). Many tell stories of Warm Springs members working for Grand Ronde and vice versa, families intermarrying, and friendships between the tribes, or they remark that the tribes in Oregon continue to attend shared cultural and social events, such as powwows throughout the state, or the Canoe Journey, an intertribal event hosted each year by one of the tribal nations located along the Pacific Northwest Coast.

Intertribal conflicts in the tribal casino era are often contentious, painful, and complex. Brought into sharp focus are both real and imagined differences between Native nations. These include the many ways that tribes have transformed over time into their current legal and political forms and the rights they have been reserved, retained, or restored. Additionally, casino conflicts bring up conversations about lands and resources, distance and interaction with the broader settler society, cultural ruptures each tribe has experienced, and revitalization projects they have initiated. As this chapter demonstrates, Native nations are active participants in critical contemporary discussions that shape political, economic, and social outcomes. When intertribal conflicts in the casino era are historically and experientially contextualized, it can become easier to understand the variations in tribal perspectives on the issue as well as to identify areas where tribes might find common ground. As a result of shared as well as divergent legal, economic, political, and tribal experiences, the Grand Ronde and Warm Springs communities form unique perspectives on and responses to economic development opportunities available through the casino economy. By placing their relationship at the center of inquiry, this investigation contextualizes the formation of Grand Ronde and Warm Springs in the particular sociopolitical climate of Oregon and illustrates distinct tribal perspectives and interpretations of historical and contemporary concerns in the casino era.

CHAPTER 7

At the Kitchen Table

Gathering across Difference

The biggest problem is around the question of unity. Our people are not used to success, so not . . . in a position where their voice counts, and they don't have a concept of how to work together. People might get upset to hear me say this, but sometimes you have a meeting, you see how people's pride gets hurt so easy. They're sensitive, they're distrustful. We're very paranoid. All of these things make it very difficult to get to a comfortable level of consensus on any issue. It's almost like going into a dysfunctional family; they're probably going to fight each other for the rest of their lives. Part of what we have to do is just get people to believe in each other and help support each other.

—Ray Halbritter (Oneida), in Taiaiake Alfred,
Wasáse: Indigenous Pathways of Action and Freedom

If tribes could become more organized, there are a lot of potential partnerships out there the tribes could enter into with one another. If the tribes could look past their differences and realize that they have a lot of resources that would be even greater if they were willing to share and pool them.

—Chris Mercier (Grand Ronde)

THIS BOOK ENDS WITH POSSIBILITIES FOR NEW BEGINNINGS FOR intertribal relations in the casino era. As the above quote from Ray Halbritter illustrates, Native people, like Native nations, at times find it difficult to negotiate their relationships with one another and have to confront feelings of disempowerment, distrust, and dysfunction. Tribal relations are framed and reframed every few decades as Native nations react and respond to changing political, legal, and social landscapes in the United States. For example, the experience of colonialism, dovetailed with ongoing projects of coloniality (systemic violence, marginalization, and oppression on which the United States is built and maintained), have taken a toll on Native nations, and the circumstances that lead to intertribal conflict are directly influenced by complex social events and systems that are sustained by external governments, laws and policies, public opinion, and the media. However, as the comments of Chris Mercier above emphasize, Native nations today have an incredible opportunity to pool resources and work in coalition with one another if they are willing to move beyond their colonially imposed differences and find ways to partner in mutually beneficial ways.

Like other Native nations across the United States, the Confederated Tribes of Grand Ronde and the Confederated Tribes of Warm Springs each have stories that tell of their existence, survival, resistance, and continuance. With both parallel and divergent experiences, the two nations respond in distinctive ways to economic opportunities, and these experiences influence how they perceive, participate in, and interact with others in the tribal casino economy. Tribal members and non-member employees from both Grand Ronde and Warm Springs often say that reconciliation between the two tribes may not be easy to achieve after the conflict over the proposed Warm Springs Bridge of the Gods Casino in Cascade Locks, Oregon. However, some comment on the need for unity between Oregon tribes, particularly due to the fact that Grand Ronde and Warm Springs share tribal and colonial history as well as many contemporary concerns, such as cultural resource protection, tribal sovereignty, and the education of the broader, dominant society.

In the beautifully written afterword to *American Indian Literary Nationalism*, Lisa Brooks (Abenaki) introduces a "kitchen table" methodology that draws on the observation by Greg Sarris (Federated Indians of Graton Rancheria) that the gathering of Native communities to dialogue about contentious issues is "never idealistic or easy" and the assertion by Simon Ortiz (Acoma Pueblo) that, as Native peoples, "we must take great care with each other."[1] Anxiety over intertribal conflict in the tribal casino economy is quite pervasive across Native communities, particularly when Native nations become involved in actions such as opposing competing tribal casinos, disenrolling tribal members, and blocking unrecognized tribes' applications to gain federal recognition. Native people are invited—metaphorically but also sometimes literally—to come together at the kitchen table and discuss difficult issues that affect relations within and between Native nations, to meet across difference and rebuild tribal relations. Native nations are explicitly asked to rethink and reframe their own perceptions of themselves through a decolonized lens (as sovereign peoples), encourage tribal leaders to honestly examine events and experiences of coloniality that shape and affect their contemporary lives, invite each other to understand how intertribal relations have been reordered through colonial logics, and advance decolonized policies (economic and otherwise) that align with each Native nation's distinct worldview and goals. Conversation around the kitchen table does not guarantee that everyone will agree; lively debate and occasional strains in the relationships are to be expected. But even within difficult moments there exists the potential for nourishment and sustenance, as a fuller and more complex picture of issues at hand comes into sharper focus—as long as those participating remain at the table.

As I have discussed in this book, Native people often express alarm over some of the new, unexpected, and not always positive consequences of the tribal casino economy, such as the apparent increase in intertribal conflict that stems from intense debates between Native nations over gaming markets. In this final chapter I discuss the tendency of critics of intertribal conflict in the casino era to analyze these social phenomena without fully contextualizing the constituent historical and contemporary conditions. Additionally, I argue that engaging Native peoples in a discussion about intertribal conflict in the casino era simultaneously reveals ongoing internal and external challenges to tribal sovereignty and the great tenacity of Native nations that struggle daily to determine their own future. I propose that Indigenous approaches to conflict resolution may offer an applicable approach to promote engagement between tribal communities that works to empower all Native nations.

A "LETTER FROM BIRMINGHAM JAIL": EXAMINE THE CONDITIONS

I have often been asked why Native nations "fight so much" over casinos and the potential wealth the casino economy signifies. For example, casinos have been linked to the current trend of disenrolling tribal members, which has been covered heavily by the mainstream media. In response to Grand Ronde's decision to disenroll some of their members, a 2013 article in *Indian Country Today* made the connection between this practice and the casino economy, noting, "As has been the case with many tribes, enrollment questions seem to be related to [the] creation of a tribal casino."[2] In these conversations, as in the national tribal casino discourse, intertribal conflict is often framed as a consequence of tribal "corruption" and "greed."

Tribal relations and the long history of struggle give way to sound bites about tribes with casinos being "money hungry," "inauthentic," "assimilated," or having "crooked" leaders. Over the years, many individuals, including some who believed themselves to be progressive and antiracist, have told me that Native nations contending among themselves for casino markets does not align with their expectations of Native people. In these conversations I sometimes find myself feeling a degree of annoyance before I resign myself to the task of contextualizing the issue for whomever I am talking with and demonstrating how the previous messages they have received are problematic. To do this I usually start by introducing the conflicts that arose from the proposed Bridge of the Gods Casino in Cascade Locks, Oregon, and explaining the historical conditions that produced the varied perspectives on the issue held by Grand Ronde and Warm Springs people.

As my work writing this book neared completion, my thoughts often turned to the famous letter written by Martin Luther King Jr. on April 16, 1963, from a jail cell in Birmingham, Alabama. King's letter responds to so-called progressive white clergy, who had publicly criticized the nonviolent direct action tactics employed by the civil rights movement and King's endorsement of those tactics. King points out that white people in the US South, even those who thought themselves progressive and anti-segregationist, often viewed the protesters involved in direct nonviolent actions such as lunch counter sit-ins as the *cause* of the violence that ensued. In his letter, King chides the clergy who "deplore the demonstrations taking place in Birmingham" but fail "to express a similar concern for the conditions that brought about the demonstrations." He further notes, "I am sure that none of you would want to rest content with the superficial kind of social analysis that deals merely with effects and does not grapple with underlying causes."[3] King argues that any analysis of the demonstrations must also include an analysis of the conditions that led people to protest in the first place, including the long history of violence against black people and the ideology of white supremacy that denies people of color civil rights and equal opportunity.

Although the civil rights movement and the dispute over the Bridge of the Gods Casino represent different sets of circumstances in separate historical moments, I found King's words helpful for understanding the problems of analysis in both situations. In both cases critics were quick to judge effects, the actions or behaviors of marginalized communities, condemning them as inappropriate and the cause of the trouble. King asks his critics to examine the conditions that led to the circumstances at hand. Similarly, an analysis of the effect of the tribal casino economy on intertribal relations must include an analysis of the historical, social, and political conditions that produced this economy.

Tribes' actions within the tribal casino economy and tribal perspectives on intertribal conflict in the casino era are expressions of autonomy and sovereignty. They illuminate the fact that Native nations are distinct, with differing standpoints within the broader casino discourse. Though the conflicts within and between tribes can be brutal and the outcomes troubling, the very fact that tribes continue to struggle over issues of identity, political boundaries, and intertribal relations should perhaps be understood as a form of "survivance," a concept from Gerald Vizenor that conjoins survival and resistance.[4] As a didactic panel at the National Museum of the American Indian stated,

> Native societies that survived the firestorm of Contact faced unique challenges. No two situations were the same, even for Native groups in the same area at the same time. But in nearly every case, Native people faced a contest for power and possessions that involved three forces—guns, churches, and governments. These forces shaped the lives of Native peoples who survived the massive rupture of the first century of Contact. By adopting the very tools that were used to change, control, and dispossess them, Native nations reshaped their cultures and societies to keep them alive. This strategy is called survivance.[5]

In the case of intertribal conflict over the Bridge of the Gods Casino, Grand Ronde and Warm Springs likewise used the "tools that were used to change, control, and dispossess them" in their struggles to determine their own future, survive as distinct communities, and stay connected to culturally significant geographies. Their stories, as shared in public discourse, legal proceedings, and official documentation, accentuate powerful histories of survival and highlight the multifaceted connections the tribes have to each other and to the Cascade Falls.

When Grand Ronde and Warm Springs entered the gaming economy in 1995, it was not an easy decision for tribal leaders to make, and tribal members had diverse responses and concerns about the ethics and morality of tribal casinos. Further, these two tribes entered the gaming economy from very different socioeconomic and historical circumstances. Grand Ronde was attempting to recover after thirty years of termination, while Warm Springs was facing a severe economic downturn after enjoying many years of stability. Beyond Grand Ronde's public opposition to the proposed Warm Springs gorge casino, Warm Springs encountered a number of other barriers, including regional opposition from citizen groups such as Friends of the Columbia Gorge. At the state level in Oregon, Governor Kitzhaber's policy of one casino per tribe, on reservation, served to frustrate Warm Springs efforts, and subsequent governor Ted Kulongoski's unclear policy toward off-reservation gaming created additional challenges for Warm Springs. Warm Springs encountered threats to their project at the federal level as well. Changes in presidential administrations, congressional calls for Indian Gaming Regulatory Act (IGRA) reform, and Supreme Court cases addressing the tribal casino economy all worked to destabilize an economic landscape that was already difficult to predict. Many tribes, like Warm Springs, have found themselves engaged in a long, arduous, expensive, and ultimately unsuccessful process to situate a casino off their reservation in accordance with the IGRA.

Enacted in 1988, the IGRA has now been in effect for nearly thirty years. During that time a tribal casino discourse emerged nationally in the press, films, and television, which promulgated the image, narrative, and rhetoric of the "rich Indian" or "casino Indian." As with other socially constructed representations of Indians in public discourse, the discourse on tribally owned casinos has often obscured the complexities of tribal experiences and the ongoing projects of coloniality that regularly impact Native communities. In this way, policy makers and the broader non-Native public continue to use the public discourse on the tribal casino economy to deny Indigenous peoples their rights, which thereby affects intertribal relationships and tribes' ability to fulfill their caretaking responsibilities to the land. Regionally, the *Oregonian's* coverage of the conflict between Grand Ronde and Warm Springs over the Bridge of the Gods Casino provides an example of popularly consumed text that framed tribal relations in the casino era in terms of conflict, without presenting the tribes' own nuanced interpretations of their historical, cultural, and contemporary connections to one another or to the Cascade Locks region.

Tribal members can be their own nation's harshest critics and often scrutinize other Native nations carefully. Members from both Grand Ronde and Warm Springs express concern that intertribal conflict over the tribal casino economy created a situation in which Native nations were actively working to delegitimize one another's histories and claims to land, resources, and political clout. Many believe that intertribal conflict leads to negative public perceptions, which may encourage undesirable changes to laws and policies. Others articulate the fear that Native nations are engaged in a process of "self-termination," limiting their own sovereignty and right to determine their futures. In addition, some tribal members explain that while Grand Ronde and Warm Springs both experienced tremendous violence as a result of colonial projects and logics, both have continually asserted their agency when making decisions that affect their members. As Native nations have done in the past, Grand Ronde and Warm Springs must make wise choices about how to interact in the casino era as a matter of survival, resistance, and continuance since intertribal relations can significantly affect the political power available to Native people.

Reframing tribal relations in the casino era to highlight difference as a deficit (a tactic that works to delegitimize and undermine each Native nation's sovereign rights and stories of survival, resistance, and continuation) has led some Native nations to engage in divisive lawsuits, overheated rhetoric, and short-term political alliances to oppose competing tribal casinos and block other nations' applications to gain federal recognition. In addition, the choices tribal leaders make on behalf of their communities can foster the recognition of tribes' rights, responsibilities, and relationship to certain land, or they can work to limit them. Examining intertribal tensions in the casino era brings into sharp focus deeply normalized systems of inequality that continue to permeate both Native and non-Native people's thinking on Indian gaming and intertribal conflict. While I affirm that each Native nation involved in the casino economy must be free to determine how it participates, I propose that intertribal conflict, seemingly a result of the short-term protection of economic resources, can actually work against long-term goals of decolonization for all Native peoples, which require the return to them of land, resources, rights, and power. Native nations are distinct sovereign entities with the inherent right to make their own political decisions, yet the future of Native nations across the United States is linked by shared experiences with colonialism and its ongoing projects.

CONFLICT RESOLUTION AND CONFLICT TRANSFORMATION

Native nations are engaged in a day-to-day struggle to endure. To do so, they spend much of their time and resources mediating their relationships with federal and state politicians and agencies. While these relationships are certainly important to attend to, it is arguably as important (if not more so) that Native nations spend a significant amount of time talking to one another and building alliances that might better protect the interests of all Indigenous peoples, as Vine Deloria Jr. has proposed.[6] Colonial invasion, treaties, and federal Indian laws and policies have radically reordered Native nations' relationships to one another and severely limited Native people's ability to resolve their own conflicts.

When comparing Eurocentric models of conflict resolution to Indigenous models, peace studies scholar Polly O. Walker explains, "Although problem-solving methods are considered to be more beneficial to relationships than the more adversarial court-based processes of adjudication and arbitration, reaching an agreement is prioritized over healing relationships."[7] Walker writes, "Indigenous approaches to addressing conflict are more accurately described as conflict transformation in that they seek to address the conflict in ways that heal relationships and restore harmony to the group. In contrast, Western conflict resolution methods prioritize reaching an agreement between individual parties over mending relationships that have been damaged by the conflict."[8] As such, intertribal conflict in the casino era is usually mediated by federal or state entities (for example, the office of the secretary of the interior, the Bureau of Indian Affairs, or a state governor's office) or else through lawyers and lobbyists that benefit directly from (but rarely feel the repercussions of) intertribal conflict.

Conversely, Indigenous conflict resolution approaches tend to have several aims. They promote discussion while recognizing that words hold power, in hopes of restoring harmony, reason, and balance while avoiding more serious conflicts in the future. These models are employed as a means to reach consensus, so that participants feel reconciled with one another and the agreements that are reached. The goal of each party is to restore relationships so that they can continue in a healthy way or build new relationships if previous ones have been too badly damaged.

There are several well-known Indigenous models for conflict resolution, including Cherokee talking circles, Native Hawaiian Ho'oponopono, the Haudenosaunee Great Law of Peace, and the Navajo Justice and Harmony Ceremony.[9] These models, free from federal and state regulation, might be applied to support intertribal reconciliation and restoration for Native nations in conflict over the tribal casino economy. Reflecting on these, I have wondered what conflict resolution model would support intertribal values and promote cooperation while leaving room for Native nations, in all their diversity, to exist as recognized (and respected) independent nations. In a political economy where tribal histories and stories of survival are used as artillery to undermine and stymie competition and delegitimize claims to land, resources, and rights, how do Native nations that share so many similarities and connections meet across the vast differences in experience and identity to strengthen rather than tear down these relations?

Dian Million (Tanana Athabascan) contends in her book *Therapeutic Nations: Healing in an Age of Indigeneous Human Rights* that there are endless possibilities for alliance between those who have as their goal generative life and who are willing to engage one another with respect. Million shows that there are Indigenous concepts that support inclusion of a diversity of views, similar to the conceptual framework of the "Truth of the Pumpkin," introduced in chapter 1. In an interview with Millon, Jeannette Armstrong (Okanogan) explains that the Okanogan word *naw'qinwixw* can be applied in cases where people see issues in different ways, with different eyes, and from different perspectives (for example, in a conflict or disagreement), yet she also advocates for dialogue between those with different views:

> I'll try and tell you how I see it, what I know about it, how I think about it, how I feel about it, how I feel it might affect me, or affect things that I know about, and that will help inform you. But I'm requesting the same things from you. I want you to tell me how you feel about it, how it affects you, the things you know about how it affects you. Then we'll have a better understanding; we'll have a chance at a better understanding of what it is we need to do. We can only do that by giving as much clarity from our diverse points of view. So to seek the most diverse view is what *naw'qinwixw* asks for.[10]

Okanogan culture is not alone in this regard. Native nations have a long history of reframing tribal relations through processes such as condolence (asking what is hurting a community and what it needs to be healthy), reconciliation (sharing stories, highlighting ways each tribe deals with colonialism, and listening to grievances, with healing as the goal), and commitment to collaboration, building alliances and working together across differences to better understand the roots of intertribal conflict and to fully appreciate the choreographies of power that Native peoples struggle against.

In the words of clinical psychologist Eduardo Duran, "Liberation discourse involves taking a critical eye to the processes of colonization that have had a deep impact on the identity of Original Peoples; as a result a new narrative of healing will emerge."[11] Equipped with tools for intertribal understanding such as Duran's liberation discourse, Grand Ronde and Warm Springs peoples and their allies perhaps can critically engage with colonization and coloniality within the tribal casino discourse and develop a Native-centered analysis of the tribal casino economy that offers a "new narrative of healing." For example, one Warm Springs member suggests that Grand Ronde and Warm Springs communities engage in a tribe-to-tribe conversation at Willamette Falls (a place important to both nations), free from oppressive federal and state oversight, and honestly assess the tensions between the tribes. This might open up a new space in which to share tribal histories and possibilities for resurgence.

I realize that there is not a simple solution to intertribal conflict in the casino era. The process will not be easy. Colonization has been in action for more than five hundred years, and like Native nations throughout the continent, those in Oregon have actively resisted, accommodated, and adapted. As Patricia Monture-Angus (Mohawk) maintains, "It is not just the colonial relations that must be undone but all of the consequences (addictions, loss of language, loss of parenting skills, loss of self-respect, abuse and violence, and so on). Colonialism is no longer a linear, vertical relationship—colonizer does to colonized—it is a horizontal and entangled relationship (like a spider web). Now, sometimes the colonized turn the colonial skills and images they learned against others who are less powerful in their communities, thus mimicking their oppressors."[12]

This is particularly important to keep in mind when discussing how tribes make claims of independence, self-determination, and sovereignty while simultaneously relying heavily on colonial logics and documentation to support their positions and forward their goals. It is certain that tribal relations will continue to transform in the future. Still, there are many reasons to be hopeful and countless examples of Native people in Oregon, the Northwest, and nationally who work tirelessly to cultivate balance, Indigenous values, and community health within Native nations.

Over the past ten years, I have often thought about the characteristics of intertribal conflict in the casino era and wondered about how Native nations might negotiate these relationships within a framework of decolonization. As Monture-Angus asserts, "Colonialism breeds negative expectations in the hearts of the colonized," and as such Native nations fail to establish adequate long-term strategic plans, work in isolation, and act can selfishly and in undignified manners.[13] While it is true that the actions of Native nations are easier to understand once contextualized and historicized, intertribal conflict has at times done immeasurable damage to the long-term goals of tribal sovereignty, cultural revitalization, and land restoration. I ask that Native peoples consider, as Monture-Angus suggests, that "the hope for the future does not lie in institutions because institutions are artificial creations," but instead "the solution lies with the people. . . . Being self-determined is simply about the way you choose to live your life every day."[14] Then Native nations must ask whose agenda is really promoted by intertribal conflicts pertaining to the casino economy.

My intentions in this book have been to highlight the complexities of tribal experiences, examine ruptures in tribal lives caused by projects of colonialism, celebrate the perseverance of Native peoples, and promote understanding between Native nations in the casino era. As a Native studies scholar, I walk humbly in the immense (and hard to fill) footsteps of Native studies scholars, activists, and authors who have forged inroads into academia to claim space for Native peoples' voices and perspectives. Like them, I write for multiple audiences. In part, when I write (like when I teach) I seek to inform a non-Native public of Native peoples' histories and experiences from Indigenous perspectives and plainly demonstrate to non-Native people that colonialism continues to be endemic in US institutions that subjugate and oppress Native peoples, limiting their rights and opportunities. I also propose that when non-Native people have the opportunity to become more aware of their own participation and collusion with projects of coloniality, they are capable of changing this behavior, hence becoming allies and accomplices of Native nations. Simultaneously, I write directly to Native people. It is my hope that Native people actively recognize the presence and pernicious nature of colonialism within our communities, our educational systems, and our decision-making practices. In this book, I illustrate that Native nations become vulnerable when they are engaged in public and political intertribal conflict, and conversely I suggest that they are stronger and more effective advocates for their citizens when they collaborate and partner with other Native nations. As much as this book is a critique of the projects of domination that have created and compounded many of the current problems in Indian Country, it is a call to action to Native nations across the United States to engage in community reflection, clear-minded decision-making, and positive social transformation as we engage in economic planning.

NOTES

PREFACE

1 I use the term "elder" whenever narrators use this term to describe themselves or they are described in this way by others in their community.

2 When narrators were not active public figures or employees of the tribe, a third party would obtain consent from the potential narrator for me to contact them. On these two occasions I did not have access to a third party to make the introduction.

3 Eva M. Garroutte, *Real Indians: Identity and the Survival of Native America* (Berkeley: University of California Press, 2003).

4 Eva M. Garroutte and Kathleen D. Westcott, "'The Stories Are Very Powerful': A Native American Perspective on Health, Illness and Narrative," in *Religion and Healing in Native America*, ed. Suzanne Crawford (Westport, CT: Praeger, 2008), 163–84.

5 Charles E. Trimble, Barbara W. Sommer, and Mary Kay Quinlan, *The American Indian Oral History Manual: Making Many Voices Heard* (Walnut Creek, CA: Left Coast Press, 2008), 21.

6 Events that might be discussed in the interviews included the termination of Grand Ronde, the proposal to build the Bridge of the Gods Casino, and the Draft Environmental Impact Statement public hearings; general themes included treaties, ceded lands, trust lands, what treaties and land mean to Grand Ronde or Warm Springs, what challenges each community faces, decolonization, and economic sovereignty.

7 Editorial staff, "Letters to the Editor," *Indian Country Today*, November 20, 2013.

8 Linda Tuhiwai Smith, *Decolonizing Methodologies: Research and Indigenous Peoples*, (New York: Zed Books; Dunedin, NZ: University of Otago Press, 1999), 7.

9 Smith, *Decolonizing Methodologies: Research and Indigenous Peoples*, 5.

CHAPTER I

1 For a version of the Bridge of the Gods story, see Ella Elizabeth Clark, *Indian Legends of the Pacific Northwest* (Berkeley: University of California Press, 1953), 20–22.

2 For more on the topic of fishing economies along the Columbia River, see Katrine Barber, *Death of Celilo Falls* (Seattle: University of Washington Press, 2005).

3 In this context, trust land is that which belongs to individual Native people or tribes but where legal title is held "in trust" by the US government for the benefit of that individual or tribe.

4 State-tribal compacts are legal agreements negotiated between tribes and state governments to regulate class III gambling operations.

5 The Indian Gaming Regulatory Act separates gaming operations into three classifications. Class I games consist of social and traditional games with limited prizes. Bingo and card games not explicitly prohibited by the state in which the tribe resides constitute Class II games. Class III games are the most contentious and most regulated forms of gambling and include blackjack, slot machines and table games such as roulette and craps. See US Congress, Indian Gaming Regulatory Act, Pub. L. 100-497 (1988).

6   See "The Hand Oregon Was Dealt," *Oregonian*, April 6, 2005; "Blurring the Gorge Casino
    Issue," *Oregonian*, June 5, 2005; Janie Har and Jeff Mapes, "Tribal Rift Deepens over
    Casino," *Oregonian*, June 24, 2005; Janie Har, "Casino Choices Go before Public," *Orego-
    nian*, September 15, 2005; Janie Har, "Oregon Tribes Testify on Casino Proposal," *Ore-
    gonian*, November 10, 2005; Jeff Mapes, "Grand Ronde Rolls into Governor's Race over
    Casino," *Oregonian*, March 25, 2006; "Basic Fairness Matters, Even in Casino Debates,"
    Oregonian, March 27, 2006; Jeff Mapes, "Tribe's Ads Stir Governor's Race," *Oregonian*,
    April 4, 2006; "Down and Dirty in the Primary Election," *Oregonian*, April 24, 2006;
    Harry Esteve, "Tribe Tries New Idea to Stop Casino in the Gorge," *Oregonian*, June 9,
    2006.

7   Walter D. Mignolo, *Local Histories/Global Designs: Coloniality, Subaltern Knowledges,
    and Border Thinking*, Princeton Studies in Culture/Power/History (Princeton, NJ:
    Princeton University Press, 2012), ix.

8   Elisabeth Middleton, "A Political Ecology of Healing," *Journal of Political Ecology* 17
    (2010): 2; italics in original.

9   Ibid., 11.

10 For example, members from both Native nations went to Chemawa Indian School, a
    boarding school in Salem, Oregon.

11 David G. Lewis, "Confederated Tribes of Grand Ronde," *Oregon Encyclopedia*, https://
    oregonencyclopedia.org/articles/confederated_tribes_of_grand_ronde/#.WYizl
    SMrJz8.

12 There are variations in the spelling of each of these tribal names, and some Native
    communities have had more than one name ascribed to them. This is a common phe-
    nomenon in Indian Country due to explorers, Indian agents, and academics recording
    variations on tribal names or recording incorrectly.

13 For more on termination legislation, see Donald L. Fixico, *Termination and Relocation,
    Federal Indian Policy, 1945–1960* (Albuquerque: University of New Mexico Press, 1986);
    Roberta Ulrich, *American Indian Nations from Termination to Restoration, 1953–2006*
    (Lincoln: University of Nebraska Press, 2010).

14 I place "autonomous" before "self-sufficiency" in order to differentiate tribes' rights to
    determine their own route to and definitions of self-sufficiency. Too often rhetoric of
    self-sufficiency is embedded in the arguments that inform racist and paternalistic laws
    and policies that actually undermine tribal autonomy—for example, the Dawes Act
    (1887) and the Indian Reorganization Act (1934).

15 Richard White, *The Roots of Dependency: Subsistence, Environment, and Social Change
    among the Choctaws, Pawnees, and Navajos* (Lincoln: University of Nebraska Press,
    1983), xix.

16 Ibid.

17 As a personal example, one of my relatives harvested huckleberries, Indian carrots,
    camas bulbs, and bitterroot each year, selling a portion of his harvest to other com-
    munity members in the tribe.

18 Fishing rights in the Pacific Northwest provide a complex and multifaceted example
    entailing harassment of Native peoples, treaty violations, and resource exploitation.
    For more on the histories of Native American struggles to retain fishing rights, including
    "fish-ins" and important court cases, see Joseph C. Dupris, Kathleen S. Hill, and William
    H. Rodgers, *The Si'lailo Way: Indians, Salmon, and Law on the Columbia River* (Durham,
    NC: Carolina Academic Press, 2006).

19 Duane Champagne, Karen Jo Torjesen, and Susan Steiner, *Indigenous People and the*

Modern State. Contemporary Native American Communities (Walnut Creek, CA: AltaMira Press, 2005), 3–23.

20 Vine Deloria Jr. and Clifford M. Lytle, *American Indians, American Justice* (Austin: University of Texas Press, 1983), xi.

21 Donald L. Fixico, *The Invasion of Indian Country in the Twentieth Century: American Capitalism and Tribal Natural Resources* (Niwot: University Press of Colorado, 1998), ix–x.

22 Dean Howard Smith, *Modern Tribal Development: Paths to Self-Sufficiency and Cultural Integrity in Indian Country*, Contemporary Native American Communities (Walnut Creek, CA: AltaMira Press, 2000), 13–22.

23 Colleen M. O'Neill, introduction to Brian C. Hosmer and Colleen M. O'Neill, *Native Pathways: American Indian Culture and Economic Development in the Twentieth Century* (Boulder: University Press of Colorado, 2004), 1–20.

24 John M. Broder, "More Slot Machines for Tribes, $1 Billion For California," *New York Times*, June 22, 2004.

25 Eric C. Henson, *The State of the Native Nations: Conditions under U.S. Policies of Self-Determination: The Harvard Project on American Indian Economic Development* (New York: Oxford University Press, 2008), 2.

26 Robert Whelan and Carsten Jensen, *The Contributions of Indian Gaming to Oregon's Economy in 2011 and 2010: A Market and Economic Impact Analysis for the Oregon Tribal Gaming Alliance* (Portland, OR: ECONorthwest, 2012), www.otga.net/wp-content/up loads/2010-2011-Final-OTGA-Report.pdf.

27 The Burns Paiute Tribe closed their casino in 2012.

28 Jeff Mapes, "Tribe Plans New Casino Home next to U.S. 26," *Oregonian*, February 11, 2011.

29 Public Law 280 (1953) itself transferred jurisdiction to the state over criminal and civil offenses on reservations in California, Minnesota, Nebraska, Oregon (with the exception of the Confederated Tribes of Warm Springs), and Wisconsin. See US Congress, Pub. L. 83-280, 18 U.S.C. § 1162, 28 U.S.C. § 1360 (1953).

30 The Organized Crime Control Act of 1970 (Pub. L. 91–452, 84 Stat. 922) made violation of state gambling laws also a violation of federal law.

31 Kathryn R. L. Rand and Steven A. Light, *Indian Gaming Law: Cases and Materials* (Durham, NC: Carolina Academic Press, 2008), 77–79.

32 For instance, monies from annual dividends might contribute to road maintenance, policing, schools, fire departments, and other community services for the counties and states.

33 Steven A. Light and Kathryn R. L. Rand, *Indian Gaming and Tribal Sovereignty: The Casino Compromise* (Lawrence: University Press of Kansas, 2005), 3–4. The work of the Institute for the Study of Tribal Gaming focuses on public administration, law, and political science. See Northern Plains Indian Law Center, Institute for the Study of Tribal Gaming, University of North Dakota School of Law, http://law.und.edu/npilc /gaming.

34 For a discussion of the meaning and scope of tribal sovereignty, see Vine Deloria Jr. and Clifford M. Lytle, *The Nations Within: The Past and Future of American Indian Sovereignty* (Austin: University of Texas Press, 1984). Regarding self-determination and autonomy: Article 3 of the United Nations Declaration of the Rights of Indigenous Peoples states that Indigenous peoples have the right to self-determination to freely pursue economic development. Article 4 states the right of Indigenous peoples to self-determination and autonomy in governing and financing their autonomous functions. *United Nations*

Declaration on the Rights of Indigenous Peoples (United Nations, 2008), un.org/esa
/socdev/unpfii/documents/DRIPS_en.pdf. For an analysis of the impact of Indian
gaming on public perception and the federal acknowledgment process, see Renée Ann
Cramer, *Cash, Color, and Colonialism: The Politics of Tribal Acknowledgment* (Norman:
University of Oklahoma Press, 2005). For a discussion of the extent of federal power
over Native nations, see Russel Lawrence Barsh and James Youngblood Henderson, *The
Road: Indian Tribes and Political Liberty* (Berkeley: University of California Press, 1980).

35   Gambling is not a new phenomenon for Native American communities. Ethnographer
Stewart Culin demonstrated in the early 1900s that hundreds of games were played in
Native North America, and he noted that most tribes' games were central to cultural
and religious traditions. Culin, *Games of the North American Indians*, 2 vols. (Lincoln:
University of Nebraska Press, 1992). In *Gambler Way: Indian Gaming in Mythology, History, and Archaeology in North America* (Boulder, CO: Johnson Books, 1996), Kathryn
Gabriel explores the historical importance of gaming and gambling for Native cultures.
Games and gambling were intertwined with daily life as a way to understand the world,
to teach, and to pray. Festivals were common times when gaming occurred, and games
were used in religious rites, providing a context for understanding the natural world,
such as the four directions or the seasons. Gambling was also a way to informally redistribute resources such as food and wealth within a Native nation or between neighboring Native communities. Native myths are full of stories about the Gambler,
sometimes as a sinister force and other times as a trickster or a cultural hero. Gamblers
often preside over the world of the dead, and Gambler stories are often about an individual or community facing fear of annihilation.

36   The term "Indian gaming," as in the language of the Indian Gaming Regulatory Act
(1988), denotes all the forms of gaming operations that tribes have the right to conduct,
whereas "tribal casino economy" refers specifically to Class III casino-style gaming
establishments. Because the right to open and operate gaming operations or casinos is
held only by federally recognized tribes, the terms "tribal casino economy" or "tribal
gaming economy" are most accurate.

37   The Eastern Band also broke ground on a second casino, the Harrah's Murphy Casino
& Hotel, on October 16, 2013. "Eastern Band of Cherokee Indians Breaks Ground on New
$110M Harrah's Casino," *Indian Country Today*, October 18, 2013.

38   For more information about the Red Power movement, see Paul Chaat Smith and Robert
Allen Warrior, *Like a Hurricane: The Indian Movement from Alcatraz to Wounded Knee*
(New York: New Press, 1996).

39   See "Gaming Tribe Report," National Indian Gaming Commission, updated June 21,
2017, https://www.nigc.gov/images/uploads/state.pdf.

40   Walter R. Echo-Hawk, *In the Courts of the Conqueror: The Ten Worst Indian Law Cases
Ever Decided* (Golden, CO: Fulcrum, 2010), 425.

41   See Light and Rand, *Indian Gaming and Tribal Sovereignty*; Kathryn R. L. Rand and
Steven A. Light, *Indian Gaming Law and Policy* (Durham: Carolina Academic Press,
2006); Rand and Light, *Indian Gaming Law: Cases and Materials*; W. Dale Mason, *Indian
Gaming: Tribal Sovereignty and American Politics* (Norman: University of Oklahoma
Press, 2000); and Jeff Corntassel and Richard C. Witmer II, *Forced Federalism: Contem-
porary Challenges to Indigenous Nationhood*, American Indian Law and Policy (Norman:
University of Oklahoma Press, 2008).

42   See Jessica R. Cattelino, *High Stakes: Florida Seminole Gaming and Sovereignty* (Durham, NC: Duke University Press, 2008).

43	Regarding federal recognition, see Cramer, *Cash, Color, and Colonialism*; and Mark E. Miller, *Forgotten Tribes: Unrecognized Indians and the Federal Acknowledgment Process* (Lincoln: University of Nebraska Press, 2004). Regarding stereotypes, see Alexandra Harmon, *Rich Indians: Native People and the Problem of Wealth in American History* (Chapel Hill: University of North Carolina Press, 2010).

44	Deborah A. Miranda, *Bad Indians: A Tribal Memoir* (Berkeley: Heyday, 2012), 2.

45	Lawrence W. Gross, "Cultural Sovereignty and Native American Hermeneutics in the Interpretation of Sacred Stories of the Anishinaabe," *Wicazo Sa Review* 18, no. 2 (2003), 127–34.

46	Dina Gilio-Whitaker (Colville), research associate for the Center for World Indigenous Studies, writes about Indian-on-Indian racism: "When Indians exhibit intracultural racism it is an exercise of internalized oppression, i.e. self-hatred, outwardly directed. It is the manifestation of the colonized mind." Dina Gilio-Whitaker, "Racism in Our Ranks," *Indian Country Today*, February 26, 2014.

47	Echo-Hawk, *In the Courts of the Conqueror*, 15.

48	Jonathan Lear, *Radical Hope: Ethics in the Face of Cultural Devastation* (Cambridge: MA: Harvard University Press, 2006), 52.

49	Jennifer Nez Denetdale, *Reclaiming Diné History: The Legacies of Navajo Chief Manuelito and Juanita* (Tucson: University of Arizona Press, 2007), 11.

50	Duane H. Yazzie, Clarence Chee, Steve A. Darden, Irving Gleason, and Jennifer Nez Denetdale, *The Impact of the Navajo-Hopi Land Settlement Act of 1974 P.L. 93-531 et al.*, Public Hearing Report (Navajo Nation Human Rights Commission, 2012), 16.

51	Ibid., 2–3.

52	For more about the Red Power movement and intertribal coalitions, see Chaat Smith and Warrior, *Like a Hurricane*; and Joane Nagel, *American Indian Ethnic Renewal: Red Power and the Resurgence of Identity and Culture* (New York: Oxford University Press, 1996).

53	The Warm Springs Tribal Council decided in 2013 to end its bid to build a casino along the Columbia River Gorge due to concern over the high costs of the project (including economic, political, and social costs). There is some disagreement among Warm Springs members as to whether or not the Tribal Council had the right to make this decision without a referendum put to the membership.

54	Norman Jewison, director, *Fiddler on the Roof* (United States: United Artists CBS/Fox Video, 1971), DVD.

55	The source of this quotation is unknown to me. I found it in this form in my mother's teaching materials after she passed away.

CHAPTER 2

1	Native people in Oregon at times identify with one another in a general way as "Indian people" who have commonality forged from their shared experience of colonization, while *Native nations* refers to tribes that maintain a distinct political and cultural identity that separates them governmentally from one another.

2	George W. Aguilar Sr., *When the River Ran Wild! Indian Traditions on the Mid-Columbia and the Warm Springs Reservation* (Portland: Oregon Historical Society Press, in association with University of Washington Press, 2005), 101.

3	See Dorothy O. Johansen and Charles M. Gates, *Empire of the Columbia: A History of the Pacific Northwest* (New York: Harper & Row, 1957), 3.

4	For more about the Doctrine of Discovery, see Robert J. Miller, Jacinta Ruru, Larissa

Behrendt, and Tracey Lindberg, *Discovering Indigenous Lands: The Doctrine of Discovery in the English Colonies* (Oxford: Oxford University Press, 2010).

5   See Jeff Zucker, Kay Hummel, Bob Høgfoss, Faun Rae Hosey, and Jay Forest Penniman, *Oregon Indians: Culture, History and Current Affairs: An Atlas and Introduction* (Portland: Oregon Historical Society, 1983); Robert H. Ruby and John A. Brown, *A Guide to the Indian Tribes of the Pacific Northwest*, Civilization of the American Indian Series (Norman: University of Oklahoma Press, 1986); Carolyn M. Buan, Richard Lewis, and Oregon Council for the Humanities, *The First Oregonians: An Illustrated Collection of Essays on Traditional Lifeways, Federal-Indian Relations, and the State's Native People Today* (Portland: Oregon Council for the Humanities, 1991).

6   For more information about early social interactions between Oregon tribes (trade and intermarriage), see Robert H. Ruby, John A. Brown, and Cary C. Collins, *A Guide to the Indian Tribes of the Pacific Northwest*, 3rd ed., Civilization of the American Indian Series (Norman: University of Oklahoma Press, 2010); Stephen Dow Beckham, *Oregon Indians: Voices from Two Centuries*, Northwest Readers (Corvallis: Oregon State University Press, 2006); Buan, Lewis, and Oregon Council for the Humanities, *First Oregonians*.

7   US Continental Congress, Ordinance for the Government of the Territory of the United States Northwest of the River Ohio (1787), Library of Congress, https://www.loc.gov/item/90898154.

8   Stephen Dow Beckham, *The Indians of Western Oregon: This Land Was Theirs* (Coos Bay, OR: Arago Books, 1977), 113.

9   Ibid., 116–17.

10   Aguilar, *When the River Ran Wild!*, 5–13.

11   US Congress, Act to Establish the Territorial Government of Oregon (1848).

12   Williams G. Robbins, "Oregon Donation Land Act," *Oregon Encyclopedia*, https://oregonencyclopedia.org/articles/oregon_donation_land_act.

13   Joseph C. Dupris, Kathleen S. Hill, and William H. Rodgers, *The Si'lailo Way: Indians, Salmon, and Law on the Columbia River* (Durham, NC: Carolina Academic Press, 2006), 43.

14   Beckham, *Indians of Western Oregon*, 118.

15   Ibid., 123–26.

16   The land east of the Cascades was dry, rocky, high desert that was less desirable to white settlers but already inhabited by the Klamath, Tenino, Northern Paiute, and other eastern Oregon tribes.

17   Beckham, *Indians of Western Oregon*, 123.

18   Ibid., 130.

19   Ibid., 131.

20   For more about the violence in the southern Oregon region between Native peoples and settlers, see John Beeson, *A Plea for the Indians: With Facts and Features of the Late War in Oregon* (New York: J. Beeson, 1857); Stephen Dow Beckham, *Requiem for a People: The Rogue Indians and the Frontiersmen*, Northwest Reprints (Corvallis: Oregon State University Press, 1996); E. A. Schwartz, *The Rogue River Indian War and Its Aftermath, 1850–1980* (Norman: University of Oklahoma Press, 1997).

21   For information about the Palmer treaties, see Clark Hanson, "Oregon Voices: Indian Views of the Stevens-Palmer Treaties," *Oregon Historical Quarterly* 106, no. 3 (2005): 475–89; Robert J. Miller, *Native Americans Discovered and Conquered: Thomas Jefferson, Lewis and Clark, and Manifest Destiny*, Native America Yesterday and Today

(Westport, CT: Praeger, 2006); Charles F. Wilkinson, *The People Are Dancing Again: The History of the Siletz Tribe of Western Oregon* (Seattle: University of Washington Press, 2010).

22 Bryan McKinley Jones Brayboy, "Toward a Tribal Critical Race Theory in Education" *Urban Review* 37, no. 5 (December 2005): 425–46.

23 See Stephanie Woodard, "Native Americans Expose the Adoption Era and Repair Its Devastation," *Indian Country Today*, December 6, 2011.

24 On "vanishing Indian" ideology: Philip J. Deloria, *Playing Indian*, Yale Historical Publications (New Haven: Yale University Press, 1998), 64–65. The vanishing Indian has been a pervasive theme in American history, perpetuated through a variety of mechanisms including federal policy, scholarship, photography, art, and film. Joanna Hearne argues, "This 'vanishing' is not a single trope or image but rather a series of distinct types of discourse that are collectively informed by a tenacious narrative." Joanna Hearne, *Smoke Signals: Native Cinema Rising*, Indigenous Films (Lincoln: University of Nebraska Press, 2012), 5.

25 Though these separate and distinct peoples were politically, culturally, and legally organized as Grand Ronde, there was never any Native nation that went by this name prior to the reservation years. For more regarding Oregon tribes, see Beckham, *The Indians of Western Oregon*.

26 David G. Lewis, "Termination of the Confederated Tribes of the Grand Ronde Community of Oregon: Politics, Community, Identity" (PhD diss., University of Oregon 2009), 70.

27 Eirik Thorsgard, interview by the author, Grand Ronde, Oregon, August 9, 2010.

28 For more information about Chinuk Wawa, see Chinuk Wawa Dictionary Project, *Chinuk Wawa: Kakwa nsayka ulman-tilixam łaska munk kəmtəks nsayka / As our elders teach us to speak it* (Seattle: University of Washington Press, 2012).

29 Thorsgard interview.

30 While no other languages are taught at Grand Ronde, several other tribal languages continue to be spoken to various degrees by Grand Ronde members.

31 Thorsgard interview.

32 For more on this process of resettlement, see Lewis, "Termination of the Confederated Tribes of the Grand Ronde Community of Oregon," 93–97.

33 William "Wink" J. Soderberg, interview by the author, Grand Ronde, Oregon, August 10, 2010.

34 Lewis, "Termination of the Confederated Tribes of the Grand Ronde Community of Oregon: Politics, Community, Identity," 95.

35 Beckham, *Oregon Indians*, 225–33.

36 Soderberg interview. This experience is also described in Beckham, *Oregon Indians*, 226, the source of "self-styled executioner."

37 Soderberg interview.

38 Lewis, "Termination of the Confederated Tribes of the Grand Ronde Community of Oregon: Politics, Community, Identity," 105–28.

39 Ibid., 107.

40 Ibid., 143–46.

41 US Congress, Committee on Interior and Insular Affairs, *Termination of Federal Supervision over Certain Tribes of Indians: Joint Hearing before the Subcommittees of the Committees on Interior and Insular Affairs*, pt. 3, *Western Oregon* (Washington, DC: Government Printing Office, 1954), 154–58, 160–62.

42 Ibid., 162.

43 Ibid., 160.

44 Ibid., 161.

45 Lewis, "Termination of the Confederated Tribes of the Grand Ronde Community of Oregon," 197.

46 US Congress, State Jurisdiction Over Offenses Committed by or against Indians in the Indian Country, Pub. L. 280 (1953).

47 US Congress, Committee on Interior and Insular Affairs, *Termination of Federal Supervision over Certain Tribes of Indians*, 183.

48 Ibid.

49 US Congress, Western Oregon Termination Act, Pub. L. 588 (1954).

50 Robert "Bob" P. Tom, interview by the author, Ashland, Oregon, April 30, 2007.

51 Soderberg interview.

52 David G. Lewis, interview by the author, Grand Ronde, Oregon, August 10, 2010.

53 Some interviewees gave a figure of 2.5 acres, others 7 acres. Cultural Protections Coordinator Eirik Thorsgard said that he thought that the acreage was closer to 2.5 and explained that it was important to understand that while it was a small parcel of land, it still became the site of a tremendous restoration effort by the Grand Ronde people.

54 On destruction of tribal economy, see Cheryle Kennedy, *Testimony before the United States Senate Committee on Indian Affairs Oversight Hearing on Indian Gaming* (US Senate Committee on Indian Affairs, 2006); and Beckham, *Indians of Western Oregon*, 191.

55 Lewis interview.

56 Leon "Chips" Tom and Kathleen Tom, interview by the author, Grand Ronde, Oregon, July 10, 2007.

57 Thorsgard interview.

58 I was unable to determine the number of people who attended this meeting. According to David G. Lewis, the story widely told is that there were so many people they had to hold the meeting outside.

59 Kathryn M. Harrison, interview by the author, Grand Ronde, Oregon, July 10, 2007, and August 26, 2010.

60 Ibid.

61 Ibid.

62 Information for this paragraph was gained through interviews and informal conversations with several Grand Ronde Tribal Council members in 2007.

63 The Chachalu story was shared by the Grand Ronde Cultural Resources Department.

64 The Eugene office has since closed.

65 For more information about Wasco, Warm Springs, and Northern Paiute ancestral territory, see Zucker et al., *Oregon Indians*; Ruby and Brown, *A Guide to the Indian Tribes of the Pacific Northwest*; Buan, Lewis, and Oregon Council for the Humanities, *First Oregonians*.

66 For histories of tribal life on the Columbia River, see Eugene S. Hunn, *Nch'i-wána, "The Big River": Mid-Columbia Indians and Their Land* (Seattle: University of Washington Press, 1990); Robert Boyd, *People of the Dalles: The Indians of Wascopam Mission: A Historical Ethnography Based on the Papers of the Methodist Missionaries*, Studies in the Anthropology of North American Indians (Lincoln: University of Nebraska Press, in cooperation with the American Indian Studies Research Institute, Indiana University, Bloomington, 1996); and Andrew H. Fisher, *Shadow Tribe: The Making of Columbia River Indian*

Identity, Emil and Kathleen Sick Lecture-Book Series in Western History and Biography (Seattle: Center for the Study of the Pacific Northwest, in association with University of Washington Press, 2010).

67 "Treaty with the Tribes of Middle Oregon, 1855," Oregon State Library Digital Collections, https://digital.osl.state.or.us/islandora/object/osl:33435.

68 Aguilar, *When the River Ran Wild!*, 15–20.

69 Roberta Ulrich, *Empty Nets: Indians, Dams, and the Columbia River*, Culture and Environment in the Pacific West (Corvallis: Oregon State University Press, 1999), 25.

70 One example of such behavior was the case of the Taylor family in the late nineteenth century. The Taylors purchased land near the river and completely enclosed it so that Native people could not fish there. See Dupris, Hill, and Rodgers, *The Si'lailo Way*, 61.

71 Ibid., 58.

72 Ibid., 45.

73 Aguilar, *When the River Ran Wild!*, 126–27.

74 Dupris, Hill, and Rodgers, *The Si'lailo Way*, 49.

75 Chinook would speak about his firsthand knowledge of what was said between Warm Springs leaders and Huntington, and his recollections were widely known in his community. For more information about the fraudulent treaty and Warm Spring resistance see ibid., 41–53.

76 Ruby, Brown, Collins, Kinkade, and O'Neill, *Guide to the Indian Tribes of the Pacific Northwest*, 3rd ed., 88–89.

77 This was a perspective of several Northern Paiute people interviewed for this book.

78 "The McQuinn Strip Boundary Dispute: 1871-1972," Confederated Tribes of Warm Springs, https://warmsprings-nsn.gov/treaty-documents/the-mcquinn-strip-boundary -dispute.

79 Melinda Jette, "Warm Springs Agency Boarding School, 1890," Oregon History Project, https://oregonhistoryproject.org/articles/historical-records/warm-springs-agency- boarding-school-1890/#.WYPOoiMrLJw.

80 Ulrich, *Empty Nets*, 24.

81 Aguilar, *When the River Ran Wild!*, 118.

82 Lewis "Louie" E. Pitt Jr., interview by the author, Portland, Oregon, March 28, 2009.

83 Delvis Heath Sr., interview by the author, Portland, Oregon, March 28, 2009.

84 Columbia River Inter-Tribal Fish Commission, *Empty Promises, Empty Nets*, Chinook Trilogy 2 (Portland: Columbia River Inter-Tribal Fish Commission, 1994), videocassette (VHS).

85 *United States v. Oregon*, 302 F. Supp. 899 (1969).

86 *United States v. Washington*, 384 F. Supp. 312 (1974).

87 One example of this can be seen in the years after 1855, during which the Warm Springs and Wasco peoples maintained the memory of their treaty rights through their oral traditions. The unique system of confederation of the Wasco, Warm Springs, and Northern Paiute under a new IRA government also constituted a form of resistance.

88 The other Native nation in Oregon that avoided termination was the Confederated Tribes of the Umatilla Indians.

89 Heath interview.

90 Pitt interview.

91 Wendell Jim, interview by the author, Warm Springs, Oregon, March 22, 2012.

92 Ron Suppah Sr., interview by the author, Warm Springs, Oregon, March 11, 2008.

93 For example, my late great-uncle Russell was Warm Springs and my late aunt Ruthie was Wasco and Japanese, yet they were entirely Warm Spring Indians.

94 Pitt interview.

CHAPTER 3

1   Paul Pasquaretta, *Gambling and Survival in Native North America* (Tucson: University of Arizona Press, 2003), 123.

2   Katherine A. Spilde, "Rich Indian Racism: The Uses of Indian Imagery in the Political Process," paper presented at the 11th International Conference on Gambling and Risk Taking, Las Vegas, Nevada, 2000.

3   Ray Halbritter and Steven P. McSloy, "Empowerment or Dependence? The Practical Value and Meaning of Native American Sovereignty," *New York University Journal of International Law and Policy* 26, no. 3 (1994): 567–68.

4   Thomas D. Peacock, Priscilla A. Day, and Robert B. Peacock, "At What Cost? The Social Impact of American Indian Gaming," *Journal of Health and Social Policy* 10, no. 4 (1999): 23–34.

5   Spilde, "Rich Indian Racism."

6   The "one casino per tribe, on reservation" policy was discussed widely in newspaper articles that covered Warm Springs efforts to build the Bridge of the Gods Casino in Cascade Locks, Oregon, and was both supported and contested by individuals giving public testimony at casino hearings.

7   *Carcieri v. Salazar*, 555 U.S. 379 (2009).

8   Gale Courey Toensing, "Feinstein Insists Carcieri Fix Address Her Opposition to Tribal Gaming," *Indian Country Today*, December 2, 2013.

9   For information on this issue from a Grand Ronde source, "Proposed Cowlitz Casino Receives Legal Setback," *Smoke Signals* (Grand Ronde, OR), March 18, 2013.

10 "Tribal Economy," *Oregonian*, June 23, 1991.

11 Don Hamilton, "Oregon Indian Tribes Seek Economic Vitality," *Oregonian*, June 23, 1991.

12 Soderberg interview.

13 John Mercier, interview by the author, Grand Ronde, Oregon, August 11, 2008.

14 Foster Church, "Tribe Adds Testimony at Land Bill Hearing," *Oregonian*, April 13, 1988.

15 US Congress, Grand Ronde Restoration Act, Pub. L. 98-165, 97 Stat. 1064 (1983).

16 Confederated Tribes of the Grand Ronde Community of Oregon, *Proposed Grand Ronde Reservation Plan* (Grand Ronde, OR: Confederated Tribes, 1985).

17 Ibid.

18 Grand Ronde Reservation Act, Pub. L. 100-425, 102 Stat. 1594 (1988).

19 For articles that use the language of compromise, see Church, "Tribe Adds Testimony at Land Bill Hearing"; Alan R. Hayakawa, "House Bill Creates Reservation Area for Grand Rondes," *Oregonian*, May 12, 1988.

20 Reynold L. Leno, interview by the author, Grand Ronde, Oregon, July 9, 2007, and March 17, 2008.

21 John Mercier interview.

22 Kathryn M. Harrison, interview by the author, Grand Ronde, Oregon, July 10, 2007, and August 26, 2010.

23 Leno interviews.

24 Soderberg interview.

25 Chips and Kathleen Tom interview.

26 Ibid.
27 Soderberg interview.
28 Roberta Ulrich, "Most Agree, Tribal Casino Should Be a Good Gamble," *Oregonian*, September 28, 1993.
29 Roberta Ulrich, "Grand Ronde Tribe Gets Go-Ahead on Gambling Hall," *Oregonian*, June 14, 1994.
30 An Act to Make Certain Technical Corrections, Pub. L. 103-263, 108 Stat. 707 (1994).
31 Lewis interview.
32 Soderberg interview.
33 According to *Oregon Blue Book*, Grand Ronde has 5,306 members. "Confederated Tribes of the Grand Ronde Community," *Oregon Blue Book*, http://bluebook.state.or.us /national/tribal/grandronde.htm.
34 Spirit Mountain Community Fund, https://thecommunityfund.com/about-us.
35 Jim interview.
36 Don Hamilton, "Oregon Indian Tribes Seek Economic Vitality," *Oregonian*, June 23, 1991.
37 Faye C. Wahenika, interview by the author, Warm Springs, Oregon, March 14, 2008.
38 Gerald J. Danzuka Jr., interview by the author, Warm Springs, Oregon, March 12, 2008.
39 Ibid.
40 Pitt interview.
41 Suppah interview.
42 Roberta Ulrich, "Tribe May Try Hand at Casino Gambling," *Oregonian*, December 19, 1994.
43 Charles "Jody" Calica, interview by the author, Warm Springs, Oregon, July 12, 2007.
44 Heath interview.
45 Ulrich, "Tribe May Try Hand at Casino Gambling."
46 Suppah interview.
47 Pitt interview.
48 Ibid.
49 Dennis C. Karnopp, interview by the author, Portland, Oregon, March 28, 2009.
50 Confederated Tribes of Warm Springs, "Constitution and By-Laws of the Confederated Tribes of Warm Springs Reservation of Oregon," Article VI ("Initiative and Referendum"), https://warmsprings-nsn.gov/treaty-documents/constitution-and-bylaws.
51 Suppa interview.
52 Rudy Clements and Nat Shaw, "Warm Springs Votes to Build a Casino on the Columbia River Gorge," *Bend (OR) Bugle*, May 22, 2002.
53 Karnopp interview.
54 Ulrich, "Tribe May Try Hand at Casino Gambling."
55 Karnopp interview.
56 Wahenika interview.
57 Aurolyn Stwyer, interview by the author, Warm Springs, Oregon March 4, 2014.
58 Oregon, Office of the Governor, *Tribal-State Government-to-Government Compact for Regulation of Class III Gaming between the Confederated Tribes of the Warm Springs Reservation of Oregon and the State of Oregon* (Salem: Oregon, Office of the Governor, 1995), 13.
59 Karnopp interview.
60 Jim interview.
61 Suppah interview.
62 Karnopp interview.

63 The tribes acquired this acreage, originally allotted to Thomas Jim (Wasco), in 1974. For more information, see Dave McMechan, "The Interesting Case of Thomas Jim," *Spilyay Tymoo*, August 22, 2002.

64 "Riverbank Gambling," *Oregonian*, September 18, 1998.

65 "Gambling in the Gorge: Sound Principles Are about to Collide in the Columbia Gorge as the Warm Springs Tribes Consider Locations for a New Casino," *Oregonian*, November 22, 1998.

66 US Congress, Columbia River Gorge National Scenic Area Act, 16 U.S.C. §§ 544–544p (1986, amended 2003).

67 These arguments were articulated by organizations such as People Against a Casino Town and Friends of the Columbia Gorge, published in a number of *Oregonian* articles, and expressed by Hood River community members at public meetings.

68 While this was the official position taken by Warm Springs tribal leaders, other interested parties, such as Friends of the Gorge and Grand Ronde, dispute this claim. Over the years Warm Springs people also articulated concern over building on the environmentally sensitive Hood River site.

69 Karnopp interview.

70 For more information about fishing disputes of the 1960s and 1970s, see Trova Heffernan, *Where the Salmon Run: The Life and Legacy of Billy Frank Jr.* (Olympia: Washington State Heritage Center Legacy Project, in association with University of Washington Press, 2012); Dupris, Hill, and Rodgers, *The Si'lailo Way*; Lawney L. Reyes, *Bernie Whitebear: An Urban Indian's Quest for Justice* (Tucson: University of Arizona Press, 2006).

71 Karnopp interview.

CHAPTER 4

1   The term "tribal casino discourse" in this chapter refers to all spoken, written, or otherwise recorded discussion, debate, and communication that contributes to a social dialogue about the tribal casino economy in the United States.

2   In this regard, there is not a clear dichotomy between Native and non-Native people in Oregon; both are consumers of this discourse.

3   Corntassel and Witmer, *Forced Federalism*, 27.

4   Echo-Hawk, *In the Courts of the Conqueror*, 13.

5   "Indianness" in this case does not refer to real expressions or experiences of Native people but invented or imagined qualities of the "Indian" in the popular imagination. For more information on the concept of Indianness, see P. J. Deloria, *Playing Indian*.

6   Hulleah J. Tsinhnahjinnie and Veronica Passalacqua, *Our People, Our Land, Our Images: International Indigenous Photographers* (Davis: C. N. Gorman Museum, University of California; Berkeley: Heyday Books, 2006), xi.

7   See Rennard Strickland, *Tonto's Revenge: Reflections on American Indian Culture and Policy*, Calvin P. Horn Lectures in Western History and Culture (Albuquerque: University of New Mexico Press, 1997).

8   See Robert Brent Toplin, *Hollywood as Mirror: Changing Views of "Outsiders" and "Enemies" in American Movies*, Contributions to the Study of Popular Culture (Westport, CT: Greenwood Press, 1993); and Cattelino, *High Stakes*.

9   Cattelino, *High Stakes*, 7.

10 For a discussion of unresolved legacies of colonialism and settler anxieties manifest, see Shari M. Huhndorf, *Going Native: Indians in the American Cultural Imagination* (New York: Cornell University Press, 2001); and P. J. Deloria, *Playing Indian*.

11   Alexandra Harmon writes that "as the twenty-first century approached and then got underway, the press documented and contributed to a new round of national discourse about Indians' economic status and aims." Harmon, *Rich Indians*, 249.

12   For more information about how etched images were employed by European colonial powers to create an image of Indian peoples as "savages," see Michael Gaudio, *Engraving the Savage: The New World and Techniques of Civilization* (Minneapolis: University of Minnesota Press, 2008). For examples of painted images of Native peoples drawn by English colonist John White, see John White, P. H. Hulton, and British Museum, *America, 1585: The Complete Drawings of John White* (Chapel Hill: University of North Carolina Press; London: British Museum Publications, 1984).

13   As one example, Spanish theories concerning the degree to which Indigenous peoples were human beings led to the development of the Requerimiento. This 1513 legal declaration was read aloud by Spanish conquistadors to Indigenous communities (most of whom, of course, did not speak Spanish), informing them that if they chose they could convert to Catholicism and become subjects to the crown. If Native people did not surrender and convert immediately, the Spanish could engage in a "just war" against them. The mass murders that resulted from this proclamation were religiously and legally sanctioned acts of genocide.

14   Robert A. Williams, *Like a Loaded Weapon: The Rehnquist Court, Indian Rights, and the Legal History of Racism in America*, Indigenous Americas (Minneapolis: University of Minnesota Press, 2005); Echo-Hawk, *In the Courts of the Conqueror*.

15   James J. Rawls, *Indians of California: The Changing Image* (Norman: University of Oklahoma Press, 1984), xiv.

16   Corntassel and Witmer, *Forced Federalism*, 8. See also Stephen Cornell, *The Return of the Native: American Indian Political Resurgence* (New York: Oxford University Press, 1988); and Robert F. Berkhofer Jr., *The White Man's Indian: Images of the American Indian, from Columbus to the Present* (New York: Vintage Books, 1979).

17   Corntassel and Witmer, *Forced Federalism*, 8.

18   Echo-Hawk, *In the Courts of the Conqueror*, 57, 73.

19   Corntassel and Witmer, *Forced Federalism*, 16, 9. "Previously conducted studies": Cornell, *The Return of the Native: American Indian Political Resurgence*; John M. Coward, *The Newspaper Indian: Native American Identity in the Press, 1820–90*, the History of Communication (Urbana: University of Illinois Press, 1999); Sharon O'Brien, *American Indian Tribal Governments*, Civilization of the American Indian Series (Norman: University of Oklahoma Press, 1989); Mary Ann Weston, *Native Americans in the News: Images of Indians in the Twentieth Century Press*, Contributions to the Study of Mass Media and Communications (Westport, CT: Greenwood Press, 1996); and David E. Wilkins, *American Indian Politics and the American Political System*, 2nd ed., Spectrum Series, Race and Ethnicity in National and Global Politics (Lanham, MD: Rowman & Littlefield, 2007).

20   Weston, *Native Americans in the News*, 49–50, 99–122.

21   Corntassel and Witmer, *Forced Federalism*, 10.

22   Ibid., 8.

23   Cramer, *Cash, Color, and Colonialism*, 56.

24   Michael Marcantel, director, "Bart to the Future," *The Simpsons* (television series), Fox, March 19, 2000.

25   In a conversation I had with Dr. Cutcha Risling Baldy (Hupa), Native studies scholar and blogger (cutcharislingbaldy.com/blog) about this scene with Homer Simpson dancing

through the casino going "Hi-How-Are-Ya," Risling Baldy pointed out that *Simpsons* writers may have been reproducing a famous Charlie Hill (Oneida) joke, told in one of his stand-up comedy segments on *The Richard Pryor Show in* 1977. She notes, "There's something about this moment then, because it's pulling from what Charlie Hill is doing (a subversive moment of being an Indian in front of an audience that expects a certain kind of Indian who is playing with that kind of Indian image) to make a joke at Indians' expense done by Homer."

26   Philip J. Deloria, *Indians in Unexpected Places* (Lawrence: University Press of Kansas, 2004), 2.

27   Trey Parker, "Red Man's Greed," *South Park* (television series), Comedy Central, April 30, 2003.

28   Cattelino, *High Stakes*, 211.

29   Colin Bucksey, director, "Honey," *The Glades* (television series), A&E Network, September 5, 2010.

30   Veena Sud, producer, *The Killing* (television series), AMC, season 1, 2011.

31   Dina Gilio-Whitaker, "The Indians in Netflix's 'House of Cards,'" *Indian Country Today*, February 28, 2014.

32   Harmon, *Rich Indians*, 3.

33   Spilde, "Rich Indian Racism."

34   Katherine A. Spilde, "Educating Local Non-Indian Communities about Indian Nation Governmental Gaming: Messages and Methods," in *Indian Gaming: Who Wins?*, ed. Angela Mullis and David Kamper (Los Angeles: UCLA Indian Studies Center, 2000), 83.

35   Spilde, "Rich Indian Racism."

36   Justin Martin, interview by the author, Salem, Oregon, March 16, 2008.

37   The *Oregonian* was founded in 1850, nine years before Oregon became a state. The newspaper is a daily available both in print and online.

38   It should not be surprising that the story of a proposed casino in the Columbia River Gorge, close to Portland, would be of interest to the newspaper's audience. It is notable that coverage of opposition to a casino in the gorge (whether in Hood River or Cascade Locks) often came from individuals and organizations in the Portland metro area.

39   Danzuka interview.

40   Harmon, *Rich Indians*, 3.

41   Don Hamilton, "Oregon Indian Tribes Seek Economic Vitality," *Oregonian*, June 23, 1991.

42   Roberta Ulrich, "Grand Ronde Tribe Gets Go-Ahead on Gambling Hall," *Oregonian*, June 14, 1994.

43   For examples of scholarship that focus on the damaging use of discourse and imagery to affect colonial-Indian policies and laws, see Rawls, *Indians of California*; Weston, *Native Americans in the News*; Coward, *Newspaper Indian*; Cramer, *Cash, Color, and Colonialism*; Corntassel and Witmer, *Forced Federalism*; and Echo-Hawk, *In the Courts of the Conqueror*.

44   Roberta Ulrich and Carmel Finley, "Siletz Plan Lincoln City Gaming Hall," *Oregonian*, November 16, 1994.

45   Courtenay Thompson, "Indian Gaming Betting on Image," *Oregonian*, November 4, 1996.

46   Ibid.

47   Corntassel and Witmer, *Forced Federalism*, 4–5.

48   Harmon, *Rich Indians*, 3, 2.

49 Roberta Ulrich, "Tribe First: Institutional Financing for Casino," *Oregonian*, March 23, 1995.

50 Roberta Ulrich, "Indians Do Better Jobs than Feds," *Oregonian*, July 19, 1995.

51 Roberta Ulrich, "Gambling on Their Own," *Oregonian*, May 2, 1995.

52 James Long and Steve Mayes, "Indian Casino Raising the Bet," *Oregonian*, October 22, 1995.

53 Courtenay Thompson, "Kitzhaber Signs Gaming Pact with Tribe," *Oregonian*, January 11, 1997.

54 Ibid.

55 Courtenay Thompson, "Tribe Gives Public a Piece of the Action," *Oregonian*, January 10, 1997.

56 Thompson, "Kitzhaber Signs Gaming Pact with Tribe."

57 Ibid.

58 Ibid.

59 See "Oregon: The Little Reno," *Oregonian*, January 19, 1997.

60 Courtenay Thompson, "Indians Turn from Feds to State to Bolster Clout," *Oregonian*, January 24, 1997.

61 Kenneth N. Hansen and Tracy A. Skopek, *The New Politics of Indian Gaming: The Rise of Reservation Interest Groups* (Reno: University of Nevada Press, 2011), 135.

62 Greg Leo, interview by the author, Salem, Oregon, March 16, 2008.

63 For an example, see, "Roberts' Fight Pays Off," *Oregonian*, December 27, 1992.

64 Chris Mercier, interview by the author, Grand Ronde, Oregon, April 23, 2007, and August 9, 2010.

65 Courtenay Thompson, "Casino's High Profits Mean More Aid to Tribal Members," *Oregonian*, December 23, 2000.

66 See Courtenay Thompson, "PSU Native American Center Gets," *Oregonian*, May 11, 1999; Courtenay Thompson, "Museum Names New Center after Grand Ronde," *Oregonian*, June 30, 2000; Vince Kohler, "Spirit Mountain Grant Will Let Museum Grow," *Oregonian*, July 20, 2000; Osker Spicer, "Community Helpers Builders Donate Camp Bridge," *Oregonian*, October 22, 2000; Osker Spicer, "Community Helpers Clinic Gets Pacificare Grant," *Oregonian*, August 6, 2000; Angie Chuang, "Dream Catchers Tribal Casino Profits Will Benefit Forest Grove Students," *Oregonian*, August 18, 2000; Cheryl Martinis, "Death Bypasses Section of Highway," *Oregonian*, January 21, 2001; and Cheryl Martinis, "One-Third of Education Center Funds Collected," *Oregonian*, June 18, 2001.

67 "Spirit Mountain Community Fund," https://thecommunityfund.com/about-us.

68 Thompson, "Casino's High Profits Mean More Aid to Tribal Members"; Martinis, "Death Bypasses Section of Highway."

69 Many Grand Ronde leaders explained this perspective to me during informal conversations and formal interviews.

70 Spirit Mountain Community Fund.

71 "Senate race": see Jeff Mapes, "Tribes Aim to Unravel Gorton's Candidacy," *Oregonian*, July 31, 2000. "Attack ad": Jim Lynch, "Tribes Invest Record Cash in State Politics," *Oregonian*, January 15, 2003.

72 There are countless historical examples of Native nations as activists and political players, and many of these political fights did include states and their citizens. Therefore, a framing that depicts Native nations as previously apolitical entities is clearly erroneous.

The real difference is that Native nations had generally (though not always) been poorer than they are now.

73   Jeff Mapes, "Grand Ronde Endorses Candidates," *Oregonian*, January 16, 2002; Jim Lynch, "Kulongoski Silence Adds Fuel to Fight over Casino," *Oregonian*, November 21, 2002; Steve Duin, "Is It Time to Go All-In on Casinos?," *Oregonian*, June 15, 2006; Harry Lonsdale, "Get Big Money out of Oregon's Politics," *Oregonian*, May 31, 2006; Jeff Mapes, "Tribe's Ads Stir Governor's Race," *Oregonian*, April 4, 2006.

74   "The Deal Is Not in the Cards," *Oregonian*, December 6, 2003; Eric Mortenson and Jeff Mapes, "A Casino at Racetrack?" *Oregonian*, March 10, 2005.

75   James Mayer, "Coalition Opposing Casino Puts Ads on TV," *Oregonian*, May 25, 2005; "Blurring the Gorge Casino Issue," *Oregonian*, June 5, 2005; Janie Har and Jeff Mapes, "Tribal Rift Deepens over Casino," *Oregonian*, June 24, 2005; Lonsdale, "Get Big Money Out of Oregon's Politics"; Dave Hogan, "$6 Million Spent in Governor's Race," *Oregonian*, May 13, 2006; and Jeff Mapes, "Grand Ronde Rolls into Governor's Race over Casino," *Oregonian*, March 25, 2006.

76   See Spilde, "Rich Indian Racism."

77   See Harry Esteve, "Tribes Don't Leave Casino Measure to Chance," *Oregonian*, October 28, 2012; Jeff Mapes, "Tribe Plans New Casino Home Next to U.S. 26," *Oregonian*, February 11, 2011; "Clock Ticks Down on Warm Springs Tribes," *Oregonian*, December 30, 2010; "Light Flashes Green for Gorge Casino," *Oregonian*, August 7, 2010; Harry Esteve, "Odds Grow Long on Gorge Casino," *Oregonian*, December 24, 2007; Harry Esteve, "Tribes Take Gamble in Turf War," *Oregonian*, June 25, 2006; Duin, "Is It Time to Go All-In on Casinos"; "Down and Dirty in the Primary Election," *Oregonian*, April 24, 2006; "The Hand Oregon Was Dealt," *Oregonian*, April 6, 2005.

78   See Richard Read, "Little to Live on but Hope"; Steve Duin, "Up Next, the Scenic Casino," *Oregonian*, September 17, 1998; Michael Taylor, "Casino Not Only Money-Maker," *Oregonian*, August 24, 2001.

79   Duin, "Up Next, the Scenic Casino."

80   "Riverbank Gambling," *Oregonian*, September 18, 1998.

81   Lynch, "Kulongoski Silence Adds Fuel to Fight over Casino"; Jim Maass, "Don't Build It: They Won't Come," *Oregonian*, February 20, 2008; David Wu, "Don't Detract from Our National Treasure," *Oregonian*, March 17, 2008; Bill Perry, Nick Graham, and Kevin Gorman, "Casino at Cascade Locks Off-Reservation Site a Terrible Precedent," *Oregonian*, April 14, 2008.

82   Taylor, "Casino Not Only Money-Maker."

83   Lewis L. McArthur, "Don't Permit Casino in Hood River," *Oregonian*, August 31, 2001.

84   "Others in the conversation": Randy Gragg, "Design of Gorge Casino Remains at Risk," *Oregonian*, April 14, 2005; Janie Har, "Casino Hearing Weighs Gambling Jobs against Gorge's Natural Beauty," *Oregonian*, September 20, 2005; Douglas O'Hearn and Madonna O'Hearn, letter to editor, *Oregonian*, February 20, 2008; Wu, "Don't Detract from Our National Treasure." According to the Environmental Protection Agency, contaminants in the Columbia River from past and current human activities include mercury, DDT, PCBs, and polybrominated diphenyl ether (PBDE) flame retardants. Industrial, agricultural, and pharmaceutical practices have contributed these and many other contaminants to the river over the past 150 years. These toxins build up over time and can be found in plants and animals, including salmon, a fish central to the cultural and economic life of many Oregon tribes. Environmental Protection Agency, *Columbia River Basin: State of the River Report for Toxics, January 2009* (Seattle: US Environmental

Protection Agency, Region 10, 2009), www.epa.gov/sites/production/files/documents
/columbia_state_of_the_river_report_jan2009.pdf.

85 Warm Springs director of governmental affairs Louie Pitt Jr. explains, "There's nobody
that's fought more [for the salmon] than the Warm Springs tribes. We work with our
neighbors to try to help them to understand that it's a good investment to take care of
the lands and the waters, because then you don't have to go in again and fix it because
you didn't do it right in the first place, and so take the time to do it right. And usually
these guys are young folks who just don't have a clue about who is really the champions
of the state of Oregon, and our ten million acres—we're the ones, the old guard in the
effort, and the intergenerational job that [we] need to do is teach these punks a few
things about who's who around here." Pitt interview.

86 See Stu Watson, "Odds Favor Alternative Plan for Gorge Casino," *Oregonian*, October 28,
2001.

87 Duin, "Up Next, the Scenic Casino."

88 The Columbia River Gorge Scenic Area Act was passed by Congress in 1986 to protect
certain natural, cultural, and recreational resources in the gorge and to encourage
growth only in urban areas.

89 Steve Lundgren, "Tribes Look for Casino Architect," *Oregonian*, August 8, 2002.

90 Michael Lang, "In My Opinion Tribes Have No Right to a Casino in Columbia Gorge,"
Oregonian, January 12 2003.

91 Janie Har, "Casino Choices Go before Public," *Oregonian*, September 15, 2005.

92 See Courtenay Thompson, "Tribes Turn to Casino in Madras," *Oregonian*, February 5,
2000; Courtenay Thompson, "Tribes Won't Bet on Madras," *Oregonian*, May 25, 2000;
Steve Lundgren, "Tribes Face Vote on Casino Site," *Oregonian*, March 15, 2002; Michael
Lang, "Article on Gorge Casino Based on False Premises," *Oregonian*, January 12, 2003;
Janie Har, "Tribe Pushes Gorge Casino Talks," *Oregonian*, March 30, 2004; and Perry,
Gorman, and Graham, "Casino at Cascade Locks Off-Reservation Site a Terrible
Precedent."

93 "The Best Bet in the Columbia Gorge," *Oregonian*, December 10, 2004.

94 "The Hand Oregon Was Dealt," *Oregonian*, April 6, 2005; "The Big Gamble in the Gorge,"
Oregonian, September 12, 2005.

95 See "The Hand Oregon Was Dealt," *Oregonian*, April 6, 2005; "Blurring the Gorge Casino
Issue," *Oregonian*, June 5, 2005; Mapes, "Tribal Rift Deepens over Casino"; Har, "Casino
Choices Go before Public"; Janie Har, "Oregon Tribes Testify on Casino Proposal," *Orego-
nian*, November 10, 2005; Mapes, "Grand Ronde Rolls into Governor's Race over Casino";
"Basic Fairness Matters, Even in Casino Debates," *Oregonian*, March 27, 2006; Mapes,
"Tribe's Ads Stir Governor's Race"; "Down and Dirty in the Primary Election," *Orego-
nian*, April 24, 2006; Harry Esteve, "Tribe Tries New Idea to Stop Casino in the Gorge,"
Oregonian, June 9, 2006.

96 Leno interviews.

97 Lynch, "Tribes Invest Record Cash in State Politics"; "The Big Gamble in the Gorge,"
Oregonian, September 12, 2005; "Basic Fairness Matters, Even in Casino Debates," *Oregonian*, March 27, 2006.

98 Esteve, "Tribes Take Gamble in Turf War"; Courtenay Thompson and Jeanie Senior,
"Decision on Casino Site Will Deal New Hand," *Oregonian*, October 24, 1999; Mapes,
"Tribal Rift Deepens over Casino"; Mapes, "Grand Ronde Rolls into Governor's Race
over Casino."

99 Pitt interview.

100 Wahenika interview.

101 There are tribally owned newspapers and radio stations—for example, Grand Ronde owns the *Smoke Signals* newspaper, and Warm Springs owns the *Spilyay Tymoo* paper and KWSO Radio—but these reach a mainly Native audience.

102 See, for example, Cheryle Kennedy, "Oregon Will Lose with Off-Reservation Casino," *Oregonian*, July 3, 2006.

103 Steve Lundgren, "Tribes Square Off over Casino," *Oregonian*, March 24, 2002. Grand Ronde's arguments also served to oversimplify the off-reservation issue by implying both directly and indirectly that Warm Springs would despoil the Columbia River Gorge with its casino.

104 Thompson and Senior, "Decision on Casino Site Will Deal New Hand"; Lundgren, "Tribes Square Off over Casino."

105 See "Light Flashes Green for Gorge Casino," *Oregonian*, August 7, 2010; "Clock Ticks Down on Warm Springs Tribes," December 30, 2010; and Esteve, "Tribes Don't Leave Casino Measure to Chance."

106 Lobbyist Justin Martin (Grand Ronde) notes that "Warm Springs [is] trying to provide for their members, but they're also knowingly taking from Grand Ronde's market. And we've heard people talk—'Well, isn't enough enough' or 'Why can't we all get along; can't we all share?' Well, that's a nice thought, but no, we really can't. Did Warm Springs share timber revenues with all the tribes throughout the state for all those years? No. It's just an impossibility of the situation. Our governments aren't socialist governments either, so we can't just distribute profits amongst all nine tribes." Justin Martin, interview by the author, Salem, Oregon, March 16, 2008.

107 See "Light Flashes Green for Gorge Casino," *Oregonian*, August 7, 2010.

108 See "Clock Ticks Down on Warm Springs Tribes," *Oregonian*, December 30, 2010; Jeff Mapes, "Odds Improve for Cascade Locks Casino," *Oregonian*, August 8, 2010; "Light Flashes Green for Gorge Casino," August 7, 2010; and Jeff Mapes, "Odds Get Longer for Tribal Casino in Cascade Locks," *Oregonian*, May 5, 2010.

109 Miranda, *Bad Indians*, xvi.

110 Leo interview.

CHAPTER 5

1 See Light and Rand, *Indian Gaming and Tribal Sovereignty*; *Seminole Tribe of Florida v. Butterworth*, 658 F. 2nd 310 (1981); and *California v. Cabazon Band of Mission Indians*, 480 U.S. 202 (1987).

2 Karnopp interview. The Friends of the Columbia Gorge eventually came out in opposition to a Cascade Locks casino. As the size and scope of the project grew, the organization became concerned with the possible long-term adverse effects of the proposed Warm Springs casino project.

3 US Congress, Columbia River Gorge National Scenic Area Act.

4 Karnopp interview.

5 Courtenay Thompson, "Oregonians Rank as High-Rollers," *Oregonian*, May 7, 1999.

6 Courtenay Thompson and Jeanie Senior, "Decision on Casino Site Will Deal New Hand," *Oregonian*, October 24, 1999.

7 Courtenay Thompson, "Kitzhaber Signs Gaming Pact with Tribe," *Oregonian*, January 11, 1997.

8   See Courtenay Thompson, "Warm Springs Tribes Will Pause, Reassess New Casino Sites," *Oregonian*, November 6, 1999.

9   Ibid.

10   Courtenay Thompson, "Tribes Won't Bet on Madras," *Oregonian*, May 25, 2000.

11   Heath interview.

12   Karnopp interview.

13   Thompson, "Tribes Won't Bet on Madras."

14   Stu Watson, "Tribe Revives Casino Plan," *Oregonian*, February 15, 2001.

15   Brent Florendo, interview by the author, Ashland, Oregon, April 25, 2007.

16   Bobby Eagleheart, "Alternative to Building a Casino," *Spilyay Tymoo*, October 4, 2001.

17   Dave McMechan, "Tribes Face Challenges in Gaming Expansion," *Spilyay Tymoo*, October 4, 2001.

18   Ibid.

19   Dave McMechan, "Gaming Will Likely Be a Key Issue of New Year," *Spilyay Tymoo*, December 27, 2001.

20   "Gaming Discussion Enters Critical Phase," *Spilyay Tymoo*, February 7, 2002.

21   "Survey Supports Gorge Casino," *Spilyay Tymoo*, April 4, 2002.

22   Dave McMechan, "Other Tribes Concerned about Gorge Casino," *Spilyay Tymoo*, March 7, 2002.

23   Martin interview.

24   Courtenay Thompson, "Casino's High Profits Mean More Aid to Tribal Members," *Oregonian*, December 23, 2000.

25   "Tribal Leaders Express Dismay and Disappointment with Warm Springs' Casino Approach," *Smoke Signals*, May 15, 2002.

26   Ibid.

27   Ibid.

28   Steve Lundgren, "Tribes Square Off Over Casino," *Oregonian*, March 24, 2002.

29   Rudy Clements and Nat Shaw, "Warm Springs Votes to Build a Casino on the Columbia River Gorge," *Bend (OR) Bugle*, May 22, 2002.

30   Suppah interview.

31   Steve Lundgren, "Tribes Vote May 21 on Building Casino," *Oregonian*, May 6, 2002.

32   Stu Watson, "Odds Favor Alternative Plan for Gorge Casino," *Oregonian*, October 28, 2001.

33   Dave McMechan, "Candidate Visits Tribal Council," *Spilyay Tymoo*, December 13, 2001.

34   Jeff Mapes, "Grand Ronde Endorses Candidates," *Oregonian*, January 16, 2002.

35   Janie Har, "Kitzhaber Says He Won't Block Casino," *Oregonian*, November 8, 2002.

36   Alex Pulaski, "Oregon's Stance on Casinos Undefined," *Oregonian*, March 16, 2003.

37   Ibid.

38   In addition to the Warm Springs proposal to build a casino in the gorge, the Cowlitz Tribe of Washington had announced plans to open a casino in La Center, only sixteen miles north of Portland.

39   Martin interview.

40   "Chairman Discusses Grand Ronde Plan," *Spilyay Tymoo*, March 6, 2003.

41   Janie Har and Henry Stern, "Governor Rejects Tribe's Ballpark Idea," *Oregonian*, March 13, 2003.

42   Associated Press, "Tribes Begin Casino Talks," *Spilyay Tymoo*, April 1, 2004.

43   Michael Lang, "In My Opinion Tribes Have No Right to a Casino in Columbia Gorge," *Oregonian*, April 3, 2004.

44   Vic Atiyeh, "Cascade Locks Is Best Solution for Casino," *Spilyay Tymoo*, April 1, 2004.

45   Associated Press, "State Ballot Measure Proposes Casino in Portland," *Spilyay Tymoo*, January 20, 2004.

46   Around that time, brothers Mark and Dean McKay also proposed to build a nontribal casino on their family land in St. Paul, Oregon. In a letter to Sterling Anderson, the Marion Country planning manager, Mark McKay wrote, "We should have the same rights as tribes." Ron Soble, "Farmland Owners Claim Right to Build Casino," *Oregonian*, January 26, 2005.

47   Joseph Spector, "New York Voters OK Private Casinos," *USA Today*, November 6, 2013.

48   Oregon, Office of the Governor, *Tribal-State Government-to-Government Compact for Regulation of Class III Gaming between the Confederated Tribes of the Warm Springs Reservation of Oregon and the State of Oregon* (Salem: Oregon, Office of the Governor, 2005), http://archivedwebsites.sos.state.or.us/Governor_Kitzhaber_2003/governor/com pacts/WarmSprings/compact.pdf.

49   Dave McMechan, "Giant Step toward Prosperity," *Spilyay Tymoo*, April 14, 2005.

50   Siobhán Taylor, interview by the author, Grand Ronde, Oregon, April 23, 2007, and Portland, Oregon, March 18, 2008.

51   Ibid.

52   Grand Ronde Tribal Council, "Special Tribal Council Meeting Minutes," Confederated Tribes of Grand Ronde, May 20, 2005, available on website of City of Locks, Oregon, http://clbb.net/leftmenus/Casino/SPECIAL%20TRIBAL%20COUNCIL%20MEETING %20MINUTES%20052005.pdf.

53   Angela Blackwell, interview by the author, Grand Ronde, Oregon, April 23, 2007.

54   James E. Cason, letter to Ron Suppah, chairman, Confederated Tribes of Warm Springs Reservation of Oregon, May 20, 2005, US Department of the Interior, Indian Affairs. http://bia.gov/sites/bia_prod.opengov.ibmcloud.com/files/assets/as-ia/oig/oig/pdf /idc1-025217.pdf.

55   "Governor Supports Casino Fee to Trust," *Spilyay Tymoo*, August 4, 2005.

56   Pitt interview.

57   US Congress, Indian Gaming Regulatory Act. As defined in the act, "Indian lands" means—"(a) all land within the limits of any Indian reservation; (b) any lands title to which is either held in trust by the United States for the benefit of any Indian tribe or individual or held by any Indian tribe or individual subject to restriction by the United States against alienation and over which an Indian tribe exercises governmental power."

58   American Gaming Association, "Off-Reservation Gaming," http://web.archive.org /web/20150911030230/http://www.americangaming.org:80/government-affairs/key -issues/reservation-gaming.

59   US Congress, Indian Gaming Regulatory Act.

60   Web Ruble, "Chamber Urges Troutdale Study Casino Proposal," *Oregonian*, May 6, 1992.

61   "Roberts' Fight Pays Off," *Oregonian*, December 27, 1992.

62   For more information on Siletz's bid to obtain trust land for gaming and their challenge to the constitutionality of the governor's concurrence requirement, see *Confederated Tribes of Siletz Indians of Oregon v. United States*, 841 F. Supp. 1479 (D. Or. 1994).

63   McMechan, "Candidate Visits Tribal Council."

64   Dennis C. Karnopp, "Casino Would Be Seventh 'Off-Reservation' Casino," *Spilyay Tymoo*, July 21, 2005.

65   Ibid.

66   Taylor interviews.

67   An Act to Make Certain Technical Corrections, Pub. L. 103-263, 108 Stat. 707 (1994).

68   Roberta Ulrich, "Grand Ronde Tribe Gets Go-Ahead on Gambling Hall," *Oregonian*, June 14, 1994.

69   James Long, "Indian Casinos: What's in the Cards?" *Oregonian*, October 23, 1995.

70   At times such critics can include other Native nations concerned about how off-reservation gaming will affect their own economic circumstances. See Damian Mann, "'Reservation Shopping' at Center of Tribal Tiff," *Mail Tribune* (Medford, OR), April 8, 2013; Michael Waterson, "Sen. Lois Wolk Accuses Wappo Tribe of 'Reservation Shopping,'" *Napa Valley Register*, October 2, 2013; Judy Keen, "Tribe, City at Odds over Casino," *USA Today*, October 4, 2010.

71   Ron Suppah, "House Committee Testimony of Tribal Council Chairman Ron Suppah," *Spilyay Tymoo*, November 24, 2005.

72   Jerry Reynolds, "House Majority Votes with Pombo on Gaming Bill Setback," *Indian Country Today*, September 20, 2006.

73   Associated Press, "Grand Ronde to Run More Casino Ads," *Spilyay Tymoo*, June 8, 2006.

74   Wesley "Buddy" West, interview by the author, Grand Ronde, Oregon, April 23, 2007.

75   Chris Mercier interviews.

76   Danzuka interview.

77   Karnopp interview; Suppah interview; and Ronald Suppah, "Chairman Comments on Article," *Spilyay Tymoo*, February 1, 2007.

78   Suppah, "Chairman Comments on Article."

79   Suppah interview.

80   Pitt interview.

81   For articles that include aspects of this part of the public debate between Grand Ronde and Warm Springs, see Siobhán Taylor, "Grand Ronde Continues Outreach to Warm Springs," *Smoke Signals*, January 15, 2007; and Suppah, "Chairman Comments on Article."

82   Wendell Jim interview.

83   Associated Press, "Kempthorne's Opposition May Keep Casino Stalled," *Register-Guard* (Eugene, OR), December 25, 2007.

84   Gale Courey Toensing, "Bush-Era Commutable-Distance Gaming Rule Nixed," *Indian Country Today*, July 19, 2011.

85   It is a drive of a little over seventy miles from the northwest corner of the Warm Springs Reservation to Cascade Locks. Although it was not helpful to the Warm Springs cause, the rule was rescinded by Assistant Secretary of Indian Affairs Larry Echo-Hawk in 2011 after consultations with Native nations, who recommended that it be overturned because Kempthorne had failed to consult with Native nations about the rule or involve them in the review process.

86   The National Environmental Policy Act mandates that any federal decision maker must prepare an environmental impact statement for any proposed federal action that may have a significant impact on the human or natural environment. See US Congress, National Environmental Policy Act, 42 U.S.C. § 4321 et seq. (1969).

87   Bureau of Indian Affairs, US Department of the Interior, Northwest Regional Office, *Draft Environmental Impact Statement* (Portland, OR: Bureau of Indian Affairs, Northwest Regional Office, 2008).

88   Suppah, "House Committee Testimony of Tribal Council Chairman Ron Suppah."

89   Associated Press, "Tribes Frustrated by Casino Delays," *Spilyay Tymoo*, November 8, 2007.

90 Bureau of Indian Affairs, US Department of the Interior, Northwest Regional Office, *Draft Environmental Impact Statement*.

91 Ibid.

92 Leo interview.

CHAPTER 6

1 The Treaty with the Tribes of Middle Oregon is also known as the "Treaty of Wasco, Columbia River, Oregon Territory with the Taih, Wyam, Tenino, & Dock-Spus Band of the Walla-Walla, and the Dalles, Ki-Gal-Twai-La, and the Dog River Bands of the Wasco." Confederated Tribes of Warm Springs, https://warmsprings-nsn.gov/treaty-docu ments/treaty-of-1855.

2 Ian Lovett, "Tribes Clash as Casinos Move away from Home," *New York Times*, March 3, 2014.

3 See Norimitsu Onishi, "Lucrative Gambling Pits Tribe against Tribe," *New York Times*, August 4, 2012; and Lovett, "Tribes Clash as Casinos Move away from Home."

4 Lovett, "Tribes Clash as Casinos Move away from Home."

5 Ibid.; Onishi, "Lucrative Gambling Pits Tribe against Tribe."

6 Lovett, "Tribes Clash as Casinos Move away from Home."

7 "California Proposition 48, Referendum on Indian Gaming Compacts (2014)," Ballotpedia,https://ballotpedia.org/California_Proposition_48,_Referendum _on_Indian_Gaming_Compacts_(2014).

8 "Proposition 5 Tribal-State Compacts. Tribal Casinos," SmartVoter (League of Women Voters of California Education Fund), http://smartvoter.org/1998nov/ca/state/prop/5.

9 Maura Dolan and Tom Gorman, "State High Court Overturns Indian Gaming Initiative," *Los Angeles Times*, August 24, 1999; "Proposition 1a: Gambling on Tribal Lands." Smart-Voter (League of Women Voters of California Education Fund), 2000, http://smartvoter .org/2000/03/07/ca/state/prop/1A

10 Lovett, "Tribes Clash as Casinos Move away from Home."

11 Monica Alonzo, "Proposed West Valley Casino Is Pitting Valley Indian Tribes against One Another," *Phoenix New Times*, February 6, 2014.

12 Lovett, "Tribes Clash as Casinos Move away from Home."

13 Alonzo, "Proposed West Valley Casino Is Pitting Valley Indian Tribes against One Another."

14 Lovett, "Tribes Clash as Casinos Move away from Home."

15 Peter d'Errico, "Casino Wars: Friends, Enemies, and States," *Indian Country Today*, April 7, 2014.

16 Suppah interview.

17 For a map depicting the vast trade network that operated along the Columbia River, see "Celilo Falls and Places Nearby" at Warm Springs artist Lillian Pitt's website, lillianpitt .com/culture/celilo_trade.html.

18 Robert "Bob" P. Tom, interview by the author, Ashland, Oregon, April 30, 2007.

19 This was the case on both the Grand Ronde and Warm Springs reservations.

20 Thorsgard interview.

21 Wahenika interview.

22 Leno interviews.

23 Calica interview.

24 Ed Edmo, "Bridge of the Gods," adapted for the Tears of Joy Puppet Theater, Native American Family Days, Mt. Scott Community Center, November 16, 2013.
25 Calica interview.
26 Suppah interview.
27 Karnopp interview.
28 Ron Suppah Sr. remembers that the Wasco chief would go to Grand Ronde for name-giving ceremonies and to share Wasco culture. Suppah interview.
29 Florendo interview.
30 Jim interview.
31 Heath interview.
32 Stwyer interview.
33 Harrison interviews.
34 Ibid.
35 Ibid.
36 John Mercier interview.
37 Chris Mercier interviews.
38 West interview.
39 Blackwell interview.
40 Leno interview.
41 Blackwell interview.
42 Chips and Kathleen Tom interview.
43 Lewis, "Termination of the Confederated Tribes of the Grand Ronde Community of Oregon," 205.
44 Lewis interview.
45 Lewis, "Termination of the Confederated Tribes of the Grand Ronde Community of Oregon," 205.
46 Thorsgard interview.
47 Ella Elizabeth Clark, *Indian Legends of the Pacific Northwest* (Berkeley: University of California Press, 1953), 20.
48 Stwyer interview.
49 *Confederated Tribes of the Warm Springs Reservation of Oregon v. United States*, 29 Ind. Cl. Comm. 324 (1972).
50 Karnopp interview.
51 Ibid.
52 Blackwell interview.
53 Leno interview.
54 Lewis interview.
55 Suppah interview.
56 Tom interview.
57 Ibid.
58 Blackwell interview.
59 Suppah interview.
60 Danzuka interview.
61 Jim interview.
62 Florendo interview.
63 Blackwell interview.

CHAPTER 7

1   Jace Weaver, Craig S. Womack, and Robert Allen Warrior, *American Indian Literary Nationalism* (Albuquerque: University of New Mexico Press, 2006), 230–31.

2   Kevin Taylor, "Disenrollment Tragedy: Family of 1855 Treaty-Signer Getting Booted," *Indian Country Today*, December 9, 2013.

3   Martin Luther King Jr., "Letter from Birmingham Jail," Stanford University, Martin Luther King, Jr. Research and Education Institute, Online King Records Access (OKRA). http://okra.stanford.edu/transcription/document_images/undecided/630416-019 .pdf.

4   See Gerald Vizenor, *Survivance: Narratives of Native Presence* (Lincoln: University of Nebraska Press, 2008); Gerald Vizenor, *Manifest Manners: Narratives on Post-Indian Survivance* (Lincoln: University of Nebraska Press, 1999).

5   "Our People: Giving Voices to Our Histories," Washington, DC, National Museum of the American Indian, September 21, 2004–January 5, 2014, curated by Paul Chaat Smith (Comanche).

6   See Vine Deloria Jr., *Custer Died for Your Sins: An Indian Manifesto* (New York: Macmillan, 1969); Vine Deloria Jr., *Behind the Trail of Broken Treaties: An Indian Declaration of Independence* (New York: Delacorte Press, 1974); Vine Deloria Jr., *God Is Red* (New York: Grosset & Dunlap, 1973); Vine Deloria Jr., *Red Earth, White Lies: Native Americans and the Myth of Scientific Fact* (New York: Scribner, 1995); and Vine Deloria Jr., *We Talk, You Listen: New Tribes, New Turf* (Lincoln: University of Nebraska Press, 2007).

7   Polly O. Walker, "Decolonizing Conflict Resolution: Addressing the Ontological Violence of Westernization," *American Indian Quarterly* 28, nos. 3–4 (2004): 536.

8   Ibid., 528.

9   Walker, "Decolonizing Conflict Resolution: Addressing the Ontological Violence of Westernization."

10 Dian Million, *Therapeutic Nations: Healing in an Age of Indigenous Human Rights* (Tucson: University of Arizona Press, 2013), 27.

11 Eduardo Duran, *Healing the Soul Wound: Counseling with American Indians and Other Native Peoples*, Multicultural Foundations of Psychology and Counseling (New York: Teachers College Press, 2006), 1.

12 Patricia Monture-Angus, *Journeying Forward: Dreaming First Nations' Independence* (Halifax, NS: Fernwood, 1999), 11.

13 Ibid., 74.

14 Ibid., 159.

BIBLIOGRAPHY

Aguilar, George W., Sr. *When the River Ran Wild! Indian Traditions on the Mid-Columbia and the Warm Springs Reservation*. Portland: Oregon Historical Society Press, in association with University of Washington Press, 2005.

Alfred, Taiaiake. *Wasáse: Indigenous Pathways of Action and Freedom*. Peterborough, ON: Broadview Press, 2005.

Alonzo, Monica. "Proposed West Valley Casino Is Pitting Valley Indian Tribes against One Another." *Phoenix New Times*, February 6, 2014.

American Gaming Association. "Off-Reservation Gaming." http://web.archive.org/web /20150911030230/http://www.americangaming.org:80/government-affairs/key -issues/reservation-gaming.

Associated Press. "Grand Ronde to Run More Casino Ads." *Spilyay Tymoo*, June 8, 2006.

———. "Kempthorne's Opposition May Keep Casino Stalled." *Register-Guard* (Eugene, OR), December 25, 2007.

———. "State Ballot Measure Proposes Casino in Portland." *Spilyay Tymoo*, January 20, 2004.

———. "Tribes Begin Casino Talks." *Spilyay Tymoo*, April 1, 2004.

———. "Tribes Frustrated by Casino Delays." *Spilyay Tymoo*, November 8, 2007.

Atiyeh, Vic. "Cascade Locks Is Best Solution for Casino." *Spilyay Tymoo*, April 1, 2004.

Barber, Katrine. *Death of Celilo Falls*. Seattle: University of Washington Press, 2005.

Barsh, Russel Lawrence, and James Youngblood Henderson. *The Road: Indian Tribes and Political Liberty*. Berkeley: University of California Press, 1980.

Beckham, Stephen Dow. *The Indians of Western Oregon: This Land Was Theirs*. Coos Bay, OR: Arago Books, 1977.

———, ed. *Oregon Indians: Voices from Two Centuries*. Northwest Readers. Corvallis: Oregon State University Press, 2006.

———. *Requiem for a People: The Rogue Indians and the Frontiersmen*. Northwest Reprints. Corvallis: Oregon State University Press, 1996.

Beeson, John. *A Plea for the Indians, with Facts and Features of the Late War in Oregon*. 2nd ed. New York: J. Beeson, 1857.

Berkhofer, Robert F., Jr. *The White Man's Indian: Images of the American Indian, from Columbus to the Present*. New York: Vintage Books, 1979.

Blackwell, Angela. Interview by the author. Grand Ronde, Oregon, April 23, 2007.

Boyd, Robert. *People of the Dalles: The Indians of Wascopam Mission: A Historical Ethnography Based on the Papers of the Methodist Missionaries*. Studies in the Anthropology of North American Indians. Lincoln: University of Nebraska Press in cooperation with the American Indian Studies Research Institute, Indiana University, Bloomington, 1996.

Brayboy, Bryan McKinley Jones. "Toward a Tribal Critical Race Theory in Education." *Urban Review* 37, no. 5 (December 2005): 425–46.

Broder, John M. "More Slot Machines for Tribes, $1 Billion for California." *New York Times*, June 22, 2004.

Bryan v. Itasca County, 426 U.S. 373 (1976).

Buan, Carolyn M., Richard Lewis, and Oregon Council for the Humanities. *The First Oregonians: An Illustrated Collection of Essays on Traditional Lifeways, Federal-Indian Relations, and the State's Native People Today*. Portland: Oregon Council for the Humanities, 1991.

Bucksey, Colin, director. "Honey." *The Glades* (television series), A&E Network, September 5, 2010.

Bureau of Indian Affairs, US Department of the Interior, Northwest Regional Office. *Draft Environmental Impact Statement*. Portland, OR: Bureau of Indian Affairs, Northwest Regional Office, 2008.

Calica, Charles "Jody." Interview by the author. Warm Springs, Oregon, July 12, 2007.

"California Proposition 48, Referendum on Indian Gaming Compacts (2014)." Ballotpedia. https://ballotpedia.org/California_Proposition_48,_Referendum_on_Indian_Gaming _Compacts_(2014).

California v. Cabazon Band of Mission Indians. 480 U.S. 202 (1987).

Carcieri v. Salazar, 555 U.S. 379 (2009).

Cason, James E. Letter to Ron Suppah, chairman, Confederated Tribes of Warm Springs Reservation of Oregon, May 20, 2005. U.S. Department of the Interior, Indian Affairs. http:// bia.gov/sites/bia_prod.opengov.ibmcloud.com/files/assets/as-ia/oig/oig/pdf/idc1 -025217.pdf.

Cattelino, Jessica R. *High Stakes: Florida Seminole Gaming and Sovereignty*. Durham, NC: Duke University Press, 2008.

Chaat Smith, Paul, and Robert Allen Warrior. *Like a Hurricane: The Indian Movement from Alcatraz to Wounded Knee*. New York: New Press, 1996.

Champagne, Duane, Karen Jo Torjesen, and Susan Steiner. *Indigenous People and the Modern State*. Contemporary Native American Communities. Walnut Creek, CA: AltaMira Press, 2005.

Chinuk Wawa Dictionary Project. *Chinuk Wawa: Kakwa nsayka ulman-tilixam łaska munk kəmtəks nsayka / As our elders teach us to speak it*. Seattle: University of Washington Press, 2012.

Chuang, Angie. "Dream Catchers Tribal Casino Profits Will Benefit Forest Grove Students." *Oregonian*, August 18, 2000.

Church, Foster. "Tribe Adds Testimony at Land Bill Hearing." *Oregonian*, April 13, 1988.

Clark, Ella E. *Indian Legends of the Pacific Northwest*. Berkeley: University of California Press, 1953.

Clements, Rudy, and Nat Shaw. "Warm Springs Votes to Build a Casino on the Columbia River Gorge." *Bend (OR) Bugle*, May 22, 2002.

Columbia River Inter-Tribal Fish Commission. *Empty Promises, Empty Nets*. Chinook Trilogy 2. Portland: Columbia River Inter-Tribal Fish Commission, 1994. Videocassette (VHS), 29 min.

"Confederated Tribes of the Grand Ronde Community." *Oregon Blue Book*. http://bluebook. state.or.us/national/tribal/grandronde.htm.

Confederated Tribes of the Grand Ronde Community of Oregon. *Proposed Grand Ronde Reservation Plan*. Grand Ronde, OR: Confederated Tribes, 1985.

Confederated Tribes of Siletz Indians of Oregon v. United States, 841 F.Supp. 1479 (D. Or. 1994).

Confederated Tribes of the Warm Springs Reservation of Oregon v. United States, 29 Ind. Cl. Comm. 324 (1972).

Confederated Tribes of Warm Springs. "Constitution and By-Laws of the Confederated Tribes of Warm Springs Reservation of Oregon as Amended." Confederated Tribes of Warm Springs. https://warmsprings-nsn.gov/treaty-documents/constitution-and-bylaws.

Cornell, Stephen. *The Return of the Native: American Indian Political Resurgence*. New York: Oxford University Press, 1988.

Corntassel, Jeff, and Richard C. Witmer II. *Forced Federalism: Contemporary Challenges to Indigenous Nationhood*. American Indian Law and Policy Series. Norman: University of Oklahoma Press, 2008.

Coward, John M. *The Newspaper Indian: Native American Identity in the Press, 1820–90*. The History of Communication. Urbana: University of Illinois Press, 1999.

Cramer, Renée Ann. *Cash, Color, and Colonialism: The Politics of Tribal Acknowledgment*. Norman. University of Oklahoma Press, 2005.

Culin, Stewart. *Games of the North American Indians*. 2 vols. Lincoln: University of Nebraska Press, 1992.

Danzuka, Gerald J., Jr. Interview by the author. Warm Springs, Oregon, March 12, 2008.

Deloria, Philip J. *Indians in Unexpected Places*. Cultureamerica. Lawrence: University Press of Kansas, 2004.

———. *Playing Indian*. Yale Historical Publications. New Haven: Yale University Press, 1998.

Deloria, Vine, Jr. *Behind the Trail of Broken Treaties: An Indian Declaration of Independence*. New York: Delacorte Press, 1974.

———. *Custer Died for Your Sins: An Indian Manifesto*. New York: Macmillan, 1969.

———. *God Is Red*. New York: Grosset & Dunlap, 1973.

———. *Red Earth, White Lies: Native Americans and the Myth of Scientific Fact*. New York: Scribner, 1995.

———. *We Talk, You Listen: New Tribes, New Turf*. Lincoln: University of Nebraska Press, 2007.

Deloria., Vine, Jr., and Clifford M. Lytle. *American Indians, American Justice*. Austin: University of Texas Press, 1983.

———. *The Nations Within: The Past and Future of American Indian Sovereignty*. Austin: University of Texas Press, 1984.

Denetdale, Jennifer Nez. *Reclaiming Diné History: The Legacies of Navajo Chief Manuelito and Juanita*. Tucson: University of Arizona Press, 2007.

d'Errico, Peter. "Casino Wars: Friends, Enemies, and States." *Indian Country Today*, April 7, 2014.

Dolan, Maura, and Tom Gorman. "State High Court Overturns Indian Gaming Inititive." *Los Angeles Times*, August 24, 1999.

Duin, Steve. "Is It Time to Go All-in on Casinos?" *Oregonian*, June 15, 2006.

———. "Up Next, the Scenic Casino." *Oregonian*, September 17, 1998.

Dupris, Joseph C., Kathleen S. Hill, and William H. Rodgers. *The Si'lailo Way: Indians, Salmon, and Law on the Columbia River*. Durham, NC: Carolina Academic Press, 2006.

Duran, Eduardo. *Healing the Soul Wound: Counseling with American Indians and Other Native Peoples*. Multicultural Foundations of Psychology and Counseling. New York: Teachers College Press, 2006.

Eagleheart, Bobby. "Alternative to Building a Casino." *Spilyay Tymoo*, October 4, 2001.

Echo-Hawk, Walter R. *In the Courts of the Conqueror: The Ten Worst Indian Law Cases Ever Decided*. Golden, CO: Fulcrum, 2010.

Edmo, Ed. "Bridge of the Gods." Adapted for the Tears of Joy Puppet Theater, told at Native American Family Days, Mt. Scott Community Center, Portland, Oregon, November 16, 2013.

Environmental Protection Agency. *Columbia River Basin: State of the River Report for Toxics, January 2009*. Seattle: US Environmental Protection Agency, Region 10, 2009. www.epa .gov/sites/production/files/documents/columbia_state_of_the_river_report_jan2009 .pdf.

Esteve, Harry. "Odds Grow Long on Gorge Casino." *Oregonian*, December 24, 2007.

———. "Tribes Don't Leave Casino Measure to Chance." *Oregonian*, October 28, 2012.

———. "Tribes Take Gamble in Turf War." *Oregonian*, June 25, 2006.

———. "Tribe Tries New Idea to Stop Casino in the Gorge." *Oregonian*, June 9, 2006.

Fisher, Andrew H. *Shadow Tribe: The Making of Columbia River Indian Identity.* Emil and Kathleen Sick Lecture-Book Series in Western History and Biography. Seattle: Center for the Study of the Pacific Northwest in association with University of Washington Press, 2010.

Fixico, Donald L. *The Invasion of Indian Country in the Twentieth Century: American Capitalism and Tribal Natural Resources.* Niwot: University Press of Colorado, 1998.

———. *Termination and Relocation, Federal Indian Policy, 1945–1960.* Albuquerque: University of New Mexico Press, 1986.

Florendo, Brent. Interview by the author. Ashland, Oregon, April 25, 2007.

Gabriel, Kathryn. *Gambler Way: Indian Gaming in Mythology, History, and Archaeology in North America.* Boulder, CO: Johnson Books, 1996.

"Gaming Tribe Report." National Indian Gaming Commission. https://www.nigc.gov/images /uploads/state.pdf.

Garroutte, Eva M., *Real Indians: Identity and the Survival of Native America.* Berkeley: University of California Press, 2003.

Garroutte, Eva M., and Kathleen D. Westcott. "'The Stories Are Very Powerful': A Native American Perspective on Health, Illness and Narrative." In *Religion and Healing in Native America*, edited by Suzanne Crawford, 163–84. Westport, CT: Praeger Press, 2008.

Gaudio, Michael. *Engraving the Savage: The New World and Techniques of Civilization.* Minneapolis: University of Minnesota Press, 2008.

Gilio-Whitaker, Dina. "The Indians in Netflix's 'House of Cards.'" *Indian Country Today*, February 28, 2014.

———. "Racism in Our Ranks." *Indian Country Today*, February 26, 2014.

Gragg, Randy. "Sight Lines: Design of Gorge Casino Remains at Risk." *Oregonian*, April 14, 2005.

Grand Ronde Tribal Council. "Special Tribal Council Meeting Minutes." May 20, 2005. Confederated Tribes of Grand Ronde.

Gross, Lawrence W. "Cultural Sovereignty and Native American Hermeneutics in the Interpretation of Sacred Stories of the Anishinaabe." *Wicazo Sa Review* 18, no. 2 (Spring 2003): 127–34.

Halbritter, Ray, and Steven P. McSloy. "Empowerment or Dependence? The Practical Value and Meaning of Native American Sovereignty." *New York University Journal of International Law and Policy* 26, no. 3 (1994): 531–72.

Hamilton, Don. "Oregon Indian Tribes Seek Economic Vitality." *Oregonian*, June 23, 1991.

Hansen, Kenneth N., and Tracy A. Skopek. *The New Politics of Indian Gaming: The Rise of Reservation Interest Groups.* Reno: University of Nevada Press, 2011.

Hanson, Clark. "Oregon Voices: Indian Views of the Stevens-Palmer Treaties." *Oregon Historical Quarterly* 106, no. 3 (2005): 475–89.

Har, Janie. "Casino Choices Go before Public." *Oregonian*, September 15, 2005.

———. "Casino Hearing Weighs Gambling Jobs against Gorge's Natural Beauty." *Oregonian*, September 20, 2005.

———. "Kitzhaber Says He Won't Block Casino." *Oregonian*, November 8, 2002.

———. "Oregon Tribes Testify on Casino Proposal." *Oregonian*, November 10, 2005.

———. "Tribe Pushes Gorge Casino Talks." *Oregonian*, March 30, 2004.

Har, Janie, and Jeff Mapes. "Tribal Rift Deepens over Casino." *Oregonian*, June 24, 2005.

Har, Janie, and Henry Stern. "Governor Rejects Tribe's Ballpark Idea." *Oregonian*, March 13, 2003.

Harmon, Alexandra. *Rich Indians: Native People and the Problem of Wealth in American History*. Chapel Hill: University of North Carolina Press, 2010.

Harrison, Kathryn M. Interview by the author. Grand Ronde, Oregon, July 10, 2007, and August 26, 2010.

Hayakawa, Alan R. "House Bill Creates Reservation Area for Grand Rondes." *Oregonian*, May 12, 1988.

Hearne, Joanna. *Smoke Signals: Native Cinema Rising*. Indigenous Films. Lincoln: University of Nebraska Press, 2012.

Heath, Delvis, Sr. Interview by the author. Portland, Oregon, March 28, 2009.

Heffernan, Trova. *Where the Salmon Run: The Life and Legacy of Billy Frank Jr*. Olympia: Washington State Heritage Center Legacy Project, in association with University of Washington Press, 2012.

Henson, Eric C. *The State of the Native Nations: Conditions under U.S. Policies of Self-Determination: The Harvard Project on American Indian Economic Development*. New York: Oxford University Press, 2008.

Hines, Donald M. *Celilo Tales: Wasco Myths, Legends, Tales of Magic and the Marvelous*. Issaquah, WA: Great Eagle, 1996.

Hogan, Dave. "$6 Million Spent in Governor's Race." *Oregonian*, May 13, 2006.

Hosmer, Brian C., and Colleen M. O'Neill. *Native Pathways: American Indian Culture and Economic Development in the Twentieth Century*. Boulder: University Press of Colorado, 2004.

Huhndorf, Shari M. *Going Native: Indians in the American Cultural Imagination*. Ithaca, NY: Cornell University Press, 2001.

Hunn, Eugene S. *Nch'i-wána, "The Big River": Mid-Columbia Indians and Their Land*. Seattle: University of Washington Press, 1990.

Indian Country Today. "Eastern Band of Cherokee Indians Breaks Ground on New $110M Harrah's Casino." October 18, 2013.

———. "Letters to the Editor." November 20, 2013.

Jette, Melinda. "Warm Springs Agency Boarding School, 1890." Oregon History Project. 2004. https://oregonhistoryproject.org/articles/historical-records/warm-springs-agency -boarding-school-1890/#.WYPOoiMrLJw

Jewison, Norman. *Fiddler on the Roof*. DVD. 1971; Beverly Hills, CA: MGM Home Entertainment, 2007.

Jim, Wendell. Interview by the author. Warm Springs, Oregon, March 22, 2012.

Johansen, Dorothy O., and Charles M. Gates. *Empire of the Columbia: A History of the Pacific Northwest*. 2nd ed. New York: Harper & Row, 1967.

Johnson v. M'Intosh, 21 U.S. 543 (1823).

Karnopp, Dennis C. "Casino Would Be Seventh 'Off-Reservation' Casino." *Spilyay Tymoo*, July 21, 2005.

———. Interview by the author. Portland, Oregon, March 28, 2009.

Keen, Judy. "Tribe, City at Odds over Casino." *USA Today*, October 4, 2010.

Kennedy, Cheryle. "Oregon Will Lose with Off-Reservation Casino." *Oregonian*, July 3, 2006.

———. *Testimony before the United States Senate Committee on Indian Affairs Oversight Hearing on Indian Gaming*. US Senate Committee on Indian Affairs, 2006. https://www.indian senate.gov/sites/default/files/upload/files/Kennedy.pdf.

King, Martin Luther, Jr. "Letter from a Birmingham Jail." Stanford University, Martin Luther King, Jr. Research and Education Institute, Online King Records Access (OKRA). http:// okra.stanford.edu/transcription/document_images/undecided/630416-019.pdf.

Kohler, Vince. "Spirit Mountain Grant Will Let Museum Grow." *Oregonian*, July 20, 2000.

Lang, Michael. "Article on Gorge Casino Based on False Premises." *Oregonian*, January 12 2003.
———. "In My Opinion Tribes Have No Right to a Casino in Columbia Gorge." *Oregonian*, April 3, 2004.
Lear, Jonathan. *Radical Hope: Ethics in the Face of Cultural Devastation*. Cambridge, MA: Harvard University Press, 2006.
Leno, Reynold L. Interviews by the author. Grand Ronde, Oregon, July 9, 2007, and March 17, 2008.
Leo, Greg. Interview by the author. Salem, Oregon, March 16, 2008.
Lewis, David G. "Termination of the Confederated Tribes of the Grand Ronde Community of Oregon: Politics, Community, Identity." PhD diss., University of Oregon, 2009.
———. Interview by the author. Grand Ronde, Oregon, August 10, 2010.
Light, Steven A., and Kathryn R. L. Rand. *Indian Gaming and Tribal Sovereignty: The Casino Compromise*. Lawrence: University Press of Kansas, 2005.
Long, James. "Indian Casinos: What's in the Cards?" *Oregonian*, October 23, 1995.
Long, James, and Steve Mayes. "Indian Casino Raising the Bet." *Oregonian*, October 22, 1995.
Lonsdale, Harry. "Get Big Money out of Oregon's Politics." *Oregonian*, May 31, 2006.
Lovett, Ian. "Tribes Clash as Casinos Move away from Home." *New York Times*, March 3, 2014.
Lundgren, Steve. "Tribes Face Vote on Casino Site." *Oregonian*, March 15, 2002.
———. "Tribes Look for Casino Architect." *Oregonian*, August 8, 2002.
———. "Tribes Square Off over Casino." *Oregonian*, March 24, 2002.
———. "Tribes Vote May 21 on Building Casino." *Oregonian*, May 6, 2002.
Lynch, Jim. "Kulongoski Silence Adds Fuel to Fight over Casino." *Oregonian*, November 21, 2002.
———. "Tribes Invest Record Cash in State Politics." *Oregonian*, January 15, 2003.
Maass, Jim. "Don't Build It: They Won't Come." *Oregonian*, February 20, 2008.
Mann, Damian. "'Reservation Shopping' at Center of Tribal Tiff." *Mail Tribune* (Medford, OR), April 8, 2013.
Mapes, Jeff. "Grand Ronde Endorses Candidates." *Oregonian*, January 16, 2002.
———. "Grand Ronde Rolls into Governor's Race over Casino." *Oregonian*, March 25, 2006.
———. "Odds Get Longer for Tribal Casino in Cascade Locks." *Oregonian*, May 5, 2010.
———. "Odds Improve for Cascade Locks Casino." *Oregonian*, August 8, 2010.
———. "Tribe Plans New Casino Home Next to U.S. 26." *Oregonian*, February 11, 2011.
———. "Tribe's Ads Stir Governor's Race." *Oregonian*, April 4, 2006.
———. "Tribes Aim to Unravel Gorton's Candidacy." *Oregonian*, July 31, 2000.
Marcantel, Michael, director. "Bart to the Future." *The Simpsons* (television series), Fox, March 19, 2000.
Martin, Justin. Interview by the author. Salem, Oregon, March 16, 2008.
Martinis, Cheryl. "Death Bypasses Section of Highway." *Oregonian*, January 21, 2001.
———. "One-Third of Education Center Funds Collected." *Oregonian*, June 18, 2001.
Mason, W. Dale. *Indian Gaming: Tribal Sovereignty and American Politics*. Norman: University of Oklahoma Press, 2000.
Mayer, James. "Coalition Opposing Casino Puts Ads on TV." *Oregonian*, May 25, 2005.
McArthur, Lewis L. "Don't Permit Casino in Hood River." *Oregonian*, August 31, 2001.
McMechan, Dave. "Candidate Visits Tribal Council." *Spilyay Tymoo*, December 13, 2001.
———. "Gaming Will Likely Be a Key Issue of New Year." *Spilyay Tymoo*, December 27, 2001.
———. "Giant Step toward Prosperity." *Spilyay Tymoo*, April 14, 2005.
———. "The Interesting Case of Thomas Jim." *Spilyay Tymoo*, August 22, 2002.

———. "Other Tribes Concerned about Gorge Casino." *Spilyay Tymoo*, March 7, 2002.

———. "Tribes Face Challenges in Gaming Expansion." *Spilyay Tymoo*, October 4, 2001.

"The McQuinn Strip Boundary Dispute: 1871–1972." Confederated Tribes of Warm Springs. https://warmsprings-nsn.gov/treaty-documents/the-mcquinn-strip-boundary-dispute.

Mercier, Chris. Interview by the author. Grand Ronde, Oregon, April 23, 2007, and August 9, 2010.

Mercier, John. Interview by the author. Grand Ronde, Oregon, August 11, 2008.

Middleton, Elisabeth. "A Political Ecology of Healing." *Journal of Political Ecology* 17 (2010): 1–28.

Mignolo, Walter D. *Local Histories/Global Designs: Coloniality, Subaltern Knowledges, and Border Thinking*. Princeton Studies in Culture/Power/History. Princeton, NJ: Princeton University Press, 2012.

Miller, Mark E. *Forgotten Tribes: Unrecognized Indians and the Federal Acknowledgment Process*. Lincoln: University of Nebraska Press, 2004.

Miller, Robert J. *Native Americans Discovered and Conquered: Thomas Jefferson, Lewis and Clark, and Manifest Destiny*. Native America Yesterday and Today. Westport, CT: Praeger, 2006.

Miller, Robert J., Jacinta Ruru, Larissa Behrendt, and Tracey Lindberg. *Discovering Indigenous Lands: The Doctrine of Discovery in the English Colonies*. Oxford: Oxford University Press, 2010.

Million, Dian. *Therapeutic Nations: Healing in an Age of Indigenous Human Rights*. Tucson: University of Arizona Press, 2013.

Miranda, Deborah A. *Bad Indians: A Tribal Memoir*. Berkeley, CA: Heyday, 2012.

Monture-Angus, Patricia. *Journeying Forward: Dreaming First Nations' Independence*. Halifax, NS: Fernwood, 1999.

Mortenson, Eric, and Jeff Mapes. "A Casino at Racetrack?" *Oregonian*, March 10, 2005.

Nagel, Joane. *American Indian Ethnic Renewal: Red Power and the Resurgence of Identity and Culture*. New York: Oxford University Press, 1996.

O'Brien, Sharon. *American Indian Tribal Governments*. Civilization of the American Indian Series. Norman: University of Oklahoma Press, 1989.

O'Hearn, Douglas, and Madonna O'Hearn. Letter to editor. *Oregonian*, February 20, 2008.

Onishi, Norimitsu. "Lucrative Gambling Pits Tribe against Tribe." *New York Times*, August 4, 2012.

Oregon, Office of the Governor. *Tribal-State Government-to-Government Compact for Regulation of Class III Gaming between the Confederated Tribes of the Warm Springs Reservation of Oregon and the State of Oregon*. Salem: Oregon, Office of the Governor, 1995. http://archivedwebsites.sos.state.or.us/Governor_Kitzhaber_2003/governor/compacts/Warm Springs/compact.pdf.

Oregonian. "Basic Fairness Matters, Even in Casino Debates." March 27, 2006.

———. "The Best Bet in The Columbia Gorge." December 10, 2004.

———. "The Big Gamble in The Gorge." September 12, 2005.

———. "Clock Ticks Down on Warm Springs Tribes." December 30, 2010.

———. "The Deal Is Not in the Cards." December 6, 2003.

———. "Down and Dirty in the Primary Election." April 24, 2006.

———. "Gambling in the Gorge: Sound Principles Are about to Collide in the Columbia Gorge as the Warm Springs Tribes Consider Locations for a New Casino." November 22, 1998.

———. "The Hand Oregon Was Dealt." April 6, 2005.

———. "Light Flashes Green for Gorge Casino." August 7, 2010.

————. "Oregon: The Little Reno." January 19, 1997.

————. "Riverbank Gambling." September 18, 1998.

————. "Roberts' Fight Pays Off." December 27, 1992.

————. "Tribal Economy." June 23, 1991.

————. "Tribal Rift Deepens Over Casino." June 5, 2005.

————. "Tribes Rush to the Betting Window." May 10, 2006.

Parker, Trey. "Red Man's Greed." *South Park* (television series), Comedy Central, April 30, 2003.

Pasquaretta, Paul. *Gambling and Survival in Native North America*. Tucson: University of Arizona Press, 2003.

Peacock, Thomas D., Priscilla A. Day, and Robert B. Peacock "At What Cost? The Social Impact of American Indian Gaming." *Journal of Health and Social Policy* 10, no. 4 (February 1999): 23–34.

Perry, Bill, Kevin Gorman, and Nick Graham. "Casino at Cascade Locks Off-Reservation Site a Terrible Precedent." *Oregonian*, April 14, 2008.

Pitt, Lewis "Louie" E., Jr. Interview by the author. Portland, Oregon, March 28, 2009.

"Proposition 5: Tribal-State Compacts. Tribal Casinos." SmartVoter (League of Women Voters of California Education Fund), 1998. http://smartvoter.org/1998nov/ca/state/prop/5.

"Proposition 1a: Gambling on Tribal Lands." SmartVoter (League of Women Voters of California Education Fund), 2000. http://smartvoter.org/2000/03/07/ca/state/prop/1A.

Pulaski, Alex. "Oregon's Stance on Casinos Undefined." *Oregonian*, March 16, 2003.

Rand, Kathryn R. L., and Steven A. Light. *Indian Gaming Law and Policy*. Durham, NC: Carolina Academic Press, 2006.

————. *Indian Gaming Law: Cases and Materials*. Durham, NC: Carolina Academic Press, 2008.

Rawls, James J. *Indians of California: The Changing Image*. Norman: University of Oklahoma Press, 1984.

Read, Richard. "Little to Live on but Hope." *Oreognian*, December 6, 2009.

Reyes, Lawney L. *Bernie Whitebear: An Urban Indian's Quest for Justice*. Tucson: University of Arizona Press, 2006.

Reynolds, Jerry. "House Majority Votes with Pombo on Gaming Bill Setback." *Indian Country Today*, September 20, 2006.

Robbins, Williams G. "Oregon Donation Land Act." *Oregon Encyclopedia*. https://oregonencyclopedia.org/articles/oregon_donation_land_act.

Ruble, Web. "Chamber Urges Troutdale Study Casino Proposal." *Oregonian*, May 6, 1992.

Ruby, Robert H., and John A. Brown. *A Guide to the Indian Tribes of the Pacific Northwest*. Civilization of the American Indian Series. Norman: University of Oklahoma Press, 1986.

Ruby, Robert H., John A. Brown, and Cary C. Collins. *A Guide to the Indian Tribes of the Pacific Northwest*. 3rd ed. Civilization of the American Indian Series. Norman: University of Oklahoma Press, 2010.

Schwartz, E. A. *The Rogue River Indian War and Its Aftermath, 1850–1980*. Norman: University of Oklahoma Press, 1997.

Seminole Tribe of Florida v. Butterworth. 658 F. 2nd 310 (1981).

Smith, Dean Howard. *Modern Tribal Development: Paths to Self-Sufficiency and Cultural Integrity in Indian Country*. Contemporary Native American Communities. Walnut Creek, CA: AltaMira Press, 2000.

Smith, Linda Tuhiwai. *Decolonizing Methodologies: Research and Indigenous Peoples*. New York: Zed Books; Dunedin, NZ: University of Otago Press, 1999.

Smoke Signals (Grand Ronde, OR). "Proposed Cowlitz Casino Receives Legal Setback." March 18, 2013.

———. "Tribal Leaders Express Dismay and Disappointment with Warm Springs' Casino Approach." May 15, 2002.

Soble, Ron. "Farmland Owners Claim Right to Build Casino." *Oregonian*, January 26, 2005.

Soderberg, William "Wink" J. Interview by the author. Grand Ronde, Oregon, August 10, 2010.

Spector, Joseph. "New York Voters OK Private Casinos." *USA Today*, November 6, 2013.

Spicer, Osker. "Community Helpers Builders Donate Camp Bridge." *Oregonian*, October 22, 2000.

———. "Community Helpers Clinic Gets Pacificare Grant." *Oregonian*, August 6, 2000.

Spilde, Katherine A. "Educating Local Non-Indian Communities about Indian Nation Governmental Gaming: Messages and Methods." In *Indian Gaming: Who Wins?* edited by Angela Mullis and David Kamper, 83–95. Los Angeles: UCLA Indian Studies Center. 2000.

———. "Rich Indian Racism: The Uses of Indian Imagery in the Political Process." Paper presented at the 11th International Conference on Gambling and Risk Taking, Las Vegas, Nevada, 2000.

Spilyay Tymoo (Warm Springs, OR). "Chairman Discusses Grand Ronde Plan." March 6, 2003.

———. "Gaming Discussion Enters Critical Phase." February 7, 2002.

———. "Governor Supports Casino Fee to Trust." August 4, 2005.

———. "Survey Supports Gorge Casino." April 4, 2002.

Spirit Mountain Community Fund. https://thecommunityfund.com/about-us.

Strickland, Rennard. *Tonto's Revenge: Reflections on American Indian Culture and Policy*. Calvin P. Horn Lectures in Western History and Culture. Albuquerque: University of New Mexico Press, 1997.

Stwyer, Aurolyn. Interview by the author. Warm Springs, Oregon March 4, 2014.

Sud, Veena, producer. *The Killing* (television series), AMC. Season 1, 2011.

Suppah, Ron. "Chairman Comments on Article." *Spilyay Tymoo*, February 1, 2007.

———. "House Committee Testimony of Tribal Council Chairman Ron Suppah." *Spilyay Tymoo*, November 24, 2005.

———. Interview by the author. Warm Springs, Oregon, March 11, 2008.

Taylor, Kevin. "Disenrollment Tragedy: Family of 1855 Treaty-Signer Getting Booted." *Indian Country Today*, December 9, 2013.

Taylor, Michael. "Casino Not Only Money-Maker." *Oregonian*, August 24, 2001.

Taylor, Siobhán. "Grand Ronde Continues Outreach to Warm Springs." *Smoke Signals* (Grand Ronde, OR), January 15, 2007.

———. Interview by the author. Grand Ronde, Oregon April 23, 2007, and Portland, Oregon, March 18, 2008.

Thompson, Courtenay. "Casino's High Profits Mean More Aid to Tribal Members." *Oregonian*, December 23, 2000.

———. "Indian Gaming Betting on Image." *Oregonian*, November 4, 1996.

———. "Indians Turn from Feds to State to Bolster Clout." *Oregonian*, January 24, 1997.

———. "Kitzhaber Signs Gaming Pact with Tribe." *Oregonian*, January 11, 1997.

———. "Museum Names New Center after Grand Ronde." *Oregonian*, June 30, 2000.

———. "Oregonians Rank as High-Rollers." *Oregonian*, May 7, 1999.

———. "PSU Native American Center Gets Boost." *Oregonian*, May 11, 1999.

———. "Tribe Gives Public a Piece of the Action." *Oregonian*, January 10, 1997.

———. "Tribes Turn to Casino in Madras." *Oregonian*, February 5, 2000.

———. "Tribes Won't Bet on Madras." *Oregonian*, May 25, 2000.

———. "Warm Springs Tribes Will Pause, Reassess New Casino Sites." *Oregonian*, November 6, 1999.

Thompson, Courtenay, and Jeanie Senior. "Decision on Casino Site Will Deal New Hand." *Oregonian*, October 24, 1999.

Thorsgard, Eirik. Interview by the author. Grand Ronde, Oregon, August 9, 2010.

Toensing, Gale Courey. "Bush-Era Commutable-Distance Gaming Rule Nixed." *Indian Country Today*, July 19, 2011.

———. "Feinstein Insists Carcieri Fix Address Her Opposition to Tribal Gaming." *Indian Country Today*, December 2, 2013.

Tom, Leon "Chips," and Kathleen Tom. Interview by the author. Grand Ronde, Oregon, July 10, 2007.

Tom, Robert "Bob" P. Interview by the author. Ashland, Oregon, April 30, 2007.

Toplin, Robert B. *Hollywood as Mirror: Changing Views of "Outsiders" and "Enemies" in American Movies*. Contributions to the Study of Popular Culture. Westport, CT: Greenwood Press, 1993.

"Treaty with the Kalapuya, etc., 1855." Oregon State Library Digital Collections. https://digital.osl.state.or.us/islandora/object/osl%3A33432

"Treaty with the Tribes of Middle Oregon, 1855." Oregon State Library Digital Collections. https://digital.osl.state.or.us/islandora/object/osl:33435.

Trimble, Charles E., Barbara W. Sommer, and Mary Kay Quinlan. *The American Indian Oral History Manual: Making Many Voices Heard*. Walnut Creek, CA: Left Coast Press, 2008.

Tsinhnahjinnie, Hulleah J., and Veronica Passalacqua. *Our People, Our Land, Our Images: International Indigenous Photographers*. Davis: C. N. Gorman Museum, University of California, Davis; Berkeley: Heyday Books, 2006.

Ulrich, Roberta. *American Indian Nations from Termination to Restoration, 1953–2006*. Lincoln: University of Nebraska Press, 2010.

———. *Empty Nets: Indians, Dams, and the Columbia River*. Culture and Environment in the Pacific West. Corvallis: Oregon State University Press, 1999.

———. "Gambling on Their Own." *Oregonian*, May 2, 1995.

———. "Grand Ronde Tribe Gets Go-Ahead on Gambling Hall." *Oregonian*, June 14, 1994.

———. "Indians Do Better Jobs than Feds." *Oregonian*, July 19, 1995.

———. "Most Agree, Tribal Casino Should Be a Good Gamble." *Oregonian*, September 28, 1993.

———. "Tribe First: Institutional Financing for Casino." *Oregonian*, March 23, 1995.

———. "Tribe May Try Hand at Casino Gambling." *Oregonian*, December 19, 1994.

Ulrich, Roberta, and Carmel Finley. "Siletz Plan Lincoln City Gaming Hall." *Oregonian*, November 16, 1994.

United Nations Declaration on the Rights of Indigenous Peoples. United Nations, 2008. www.un.org/esa/socdev/unpfii/documents/DRIPS_en.pdf

United States v. Oregon, 302, F. Supp. 899 (1969).

United States v. Washington, 384 F. Supp. 312 (1974).

US Congress, Committee on Interior and Insular Affairs. *Termination of Federal Supervision over Certain Tribes of Indians: Joint Hearing before the Subcommittees of the Committees on Interior and Insular Affairs*, pt. 3, *Western Oregon*. Washington, DC: Government Printing Office, 1954.

US Continental Congress. Ordinance for the Government of the Territory of the United States Northwest of the River Ohio. 1787. Library of Congress. https://www.loc.gov/item/90898154.

Vizenor, Gerald R. *Survivance: Narratives of Native Presence*. Lincoln: University of Nebraska Press, 2008.

Wahenika, Faye C. Interview by the author. Warm Springs, Oregon, March 14, 2008.

Walker, Polly O. "Decolonizing Conflict Resolution: Addressing the Ontological Violence of Westernization." *American Indian Quarterly* 28 (3–4): 527–49.

Waterson, Michael. "Sen. Lois Wolk Accuses Wappo Tribe of 'Reservation Shopping.'" *Napa Valley Register*, October 2, 2013.

Watson, Stu. "Odds Favor Alternative Plan for Gorge Casino." *Oregonian*, October 28, 2001.

———. "Tribe Revives Casino Plan." *Oregonian*, February 15, 2001.

Weaver, Jace, Craig S. Womack, and Robert Allen Warrior. *American Indian Literary Nationalism*. Albuquerque: University of New Mexico Press, 2006.

West, Wesley "Buddy". Interview by the author. Grand Ronde, Oregon, April 23, 2007.

Weston, Mary Ann. *Native Americans in the News: Images of Indians in the Twentieth Century Press*. Contributions to the Study of Mass Media and Communications. Westport, CT: Greenwood Press, 1996.

Whelan, Robert, and Carsten Jensen. *The Contributions of Indian Gaming to Oregon's Economy in 2011 and 2010: A Market and Economic Impact Analysis for the Oregon Tribal Gaming Alliance*. Portland, OR: ECONorthwest, 2012. www.otga.net/wp-content/uploads/2010 -2011-Final-OTGA-Report.pdf.

White, John, P. H. Hulton, and British Museum. *America, 1585: The Complete Drawings of John White*. Chapel Hill: University of North Carolina Press; London: British Museum Publications, 1984.

White, Richard. *The Roots of Dependency: Subsistence, Environment, and Social Change among the Choctaws, Pawnees, and Navajos*. Lincoln: University of Nebraska Press, 1983.

Wilkins, David E. *American Indian Politics and the American Political System*. 2nd ed. Spectrum Series, Race and Ethnicity in National and Global Politics. Lanham, MD: Rowman & Littlefield, 2007.

Wilkinson, Charles F. *The People Are Dancing Again: The History of the Siletz Tribe of Western Oregon*. Seattle: University of Washington Press, 2010.

Williams, Robert A. *Like a Loaded Weapon: The Rehnquist Court, Indian Rights, and the Legal History of Racism in America*. Indigenous Americas. Minneapolis: University of Minnesota Press, 2005.

Woodard, Stephanie. "Native Americans Expose the Adoption Era and Repair Its Devastation." *Indian Country Today*, December 6, 2011.

Wu, David. "Don't Detract from Our National Treasure." *Oregonian*, March 17, 2008.

Yazzie, Duane H., Clarence Chee, Steve A. Darden, Irving Gleason, and Jennifer Nez Denetdale. *The Impact of the Navajo-Hopi Land Settlement Act of 1974 P.L. 93-531 et al*. Public Hearing Report. Navajo Nation Human Rights Commission, 2012.

Zucker, Jeff, Kay Hummel, Bob, Faun Rae Hosey, and Jay Forest Penniman. *Oregon Indians: Culture, History and Current Affairs: An Atlas and Introduction*. Portland: Oregon Historical Society, 1983.

INDEX

Indigenous Confluences

Charlotte Coté and Coll Thrush
Series Editors

Indigenous Confluences publishes innovative works that use decolonizing perspectives and transnational approaches to explore the experiences of Indigenous peoples across North America, with a special emphasis on the Pacific Coast.